Advance Praise for *Web Visions*

"*Web Visions* cuts through the hype of the Internet craze and delivers the truth about marketing on the Web. Dr. Marlow's guide should be required reading for anyone interested in making money on the Internet or Intranet."

Bill Townsend, Vice President of Advertising
Lycos, Inc.

"I've got another title for Dr. Marlow's book: 'Wow!' *Web Visions* provides professional communicators and marketers with the most comprehensive examination yet of the business opportunities offered up by the Internet and WWW. While the full and complete story on the Internet has yet to be written, reading *Web Visions* is as close as you'll ever land."

Ron Solberg, President
EasyCom, Inc.

"This is great. The first case study of successes (and near successes) on the Internet. This book will be instructive for newbies on the Net and relative old-timers. The depth of coverage is very impressive."

Michael D. Donahue, Senior Vice President-Member Services
American Association of Advertising Agencies

"For the Internet to reach its full advertising potential, it must migrate from "new media" to mainstream. Every marketing and media person must be intimate with what the Web can, and can't, do. Knowledge will be the key to this transition and *Web Visions* plays a key role in filling this information void. Dr. Gene Marlow's breakdown of the Internet and Web will become a cornerstone of Internet marketing theory."

Edward R. Padin, Vice President–Marketing
SRDS

"Finally a straightforward, easy-to-read book about the Internet and Intranet with real statistics and solid case studies exemplifying effective uses of this new medium. This book is recommended reading for Webmasters, Web champions, marketers, and communications managers—whether you have your Web site up and running or if it's just on the drawing board."

John J. Sarsen, Jr., President and CEO
Association of National Advertisers, Inc.

"If you are benchmarking, these engrossing case studies can save you a lot of time and money. A detailed look at the three Intranet cases is of particular interest, recording the evolution of these early and effective models. There is nothing vague or theoretical here; rather, Dr. Marlow provides a ground-level view from where the action is."

Shel Holtz, Principal
Holtz Communication & Technology

WEB VISIONS

An Inside Look at Successful Business Strategies On the Net

EUGENE MARLOW, PH.D.

VAN NOSTRAND REINHOLD
I(T)P A Division of International Thomson Publishing Inc.

New York • Albany • Bonn • Boston • Detroit • London • Madrid • Melbourne
Mexico City • Paris • San Francisco • Singapore • Tokyo • Toronto

The ideas presented in this book are generic and strategic. Their specific application to a particular company must be the responsibility of the management of that company, based on management's understanding of their company's procedures, culture, resources, and competitive situation.

Printed in the United States of America

http://www.vnr.com   Visit us on the Web!

For more information contact:

Van Nostrand Reinhold   Chapman & Hall GmbH
115 Fifth Avenue   Pappalallee 3
New York, NY 10003   69469 Weinham
                                         Germany

Chapman & Hall   International Thomson Publishing Asia
2-6 Boundary Row   60 Albert Street #15-01
London SEI 8HN   Albert Complex
United Kingdom   Singapore 189969

Thomas Nelson Australia   International Thomson Publishing Japan
102 Dodds Street   Hirakawa-cho Kyowa Building, 3F
South Melbourne 3205   2-2-1 Hirakawa-cho, Chiyoda-ku
Victoria, Australia   Tokyo 102 Japan

Nelson Canada   International Thomson Editores
1120 Birchmount Road   Seneca, 53
Scarborough, Ontario   Colonia Polanco
M1K 5G4, Canada   11560 Mexico D.F. Mexico

1 2 3 4 5 6 7 8 9 10 QEBFF 01 00 99 98 97 96

Library of Congress Cataloging-in-Publication Data available upon request.

Marlow, Eugene.
    Webvisions : an inside look at successful business strategies on
the Net / by Eugene Marlow.
        p. cm.
    Includes bibliographical references and index.
    ISBN 0-442-02453-3
    1. Business enterprises–Computer networks. 2. World Wide Web
(Information retrieval system) 3. Internet marketing—Case studies.
4. Internet advertising–Case studies. 5. Intranets (Computer
networks)–Case studies. 6. World Wide Web servers—Management-
Case studies. 7. Executives—United States—Interviews.
I. Title.
HD30.37.M367 1996   96-41531
025.04–dc20   CIP

Production: Jo-Ann Campbell • mle design • 562 Milford Point Rd., Milford, CT 06460

CONTENTS

FOREWORD AND ACKNOWLEDGMENTS

---

*W*eb Visions: An Inside Look at Successful Business Strategies On the Net* describes and analyzes marketing, advertising, public relations, and internal organizational communications applications on the Net. It is about "what is" rather than what could be. The book's title is a reflection of not only the applications described and analyzed, but also a central theme: The Internet provides a heretofore unattainable ability to connect directly and strategically with customers and employees on a global basis, at any time.

Web Visions is intended to get behind the media headlines and unfold the underlying strategic objectives of the various Web sites described. During the preparation of this volume, I also learned a great deal about the virtually universal process organizations experience to develop their Web sites: the internal politics, initial top management involvement, the culture clashes, and the human resource consequences.

Many extant "how-to" Internet books have defined the Internet's use in terms of existing paradigms: "selling" products and services, traditional time and space advertising, getting a public relations message across, communicating top management policies "down" to employees. This perception of the cyberspace universe is what Marshall McLuhan used to describe as a "rearview mirror" content paradigm. For example, early television programs were really live audience radio programs and vaudeville. The first content in the early home video market was extant pornography and Hollywood movies. In all these instances, the "new" communications medium in time expressed its own unique characteristic, and demand grew based on this uniqueness.

The Internet is on the cusp of discovering itself. A central "message" of the Internet is that it continues the transcendent trend of electronic media in terms of eliminating barriers (physical or otherwise). One of the other significant characteristics of the Internet is that it enhances the ability for customers and employees to make decisions. This characteristic alone has major ramifications for every facet of an organization—whether internally or externally oriented. The experience of those interviewed in the various case studies attest to this view.

Web Visions delivers its content using as its primary source in-depth, in-person interviews with marketing, advertising, public relations, and internal organizational communications executives. This raw material is shaped into several application summary descriptions and eight case studies. This approach was chosen because it is rarely used in Internet books, and it inherently lends itself to a practical, hands-on narrative that readers can identify with and put to immediate use.

The case content is based primarily on in-depth interviews with various Internet/Intranet functionaries: so-called renegades (those internal to the organization who propose and launch a Web site), Webmasters (those responsible for the day-to-day technical aspects of the Web site), organizational "angels" (those high-level executives who godfathered the initial Web site project), and various executives administratively responsible for an organization's Web site.

Interviewees commented on the Web site's initial development (i.e., the process, initial funding, and ongoing maintenance), organization, strategic objectives, design, measurement, and results. Each case includes a profile of the company (for context) and a Web site description. A description of the backgrounds of those interviewed appears in the Appendix.

Bookstore shelves have exploded with Internet books—several hundred at last count. Many are technically oriented. Others are basic how-to-do-it or how-to-find-it guides that rely heavily on material available on the Internet itself. Out of these books, fewer than a dozen focus on marketing, advertising, public relations, or organizational communications uses of the Internet. Fewer still use detailed case studies to explain what works online. A few marketing books discuss online marketing, but these, too, are basic how-to books, emphasizing methods, with little detail about actual organizational experience.

Some books contain varying amounts of specific examples and business approaches to the Internet. But none provide a context for the Internet in the electronic media universe or explain its uniqueness in terms of the communications characteristics of more traditional electronic or print media; describe the use of the Internet for marketing, advertising, public relations, or organizational communications; provide a blueprint for developing an organizational Web site; offer guidelines for creating an effective Web site, deal with "measurement" issues; or present detailed case analysis material—all in one volume.

Web Visions: An Inside Look at Successful Business Strategies on the Net contains specific information about actual use of the Internet and is based heavily on the experience of those already successful on the Internet.

There are various professional audiences for *Web Visions*. It is intended for prospective organizational renegades, prospective and active Webmasters, high-level executives who have or intend to serve as Web site angels, and executives administratively responsible for an external or internal Web site. The book can also be used by marketing and advertising executives, public relations professionals working in PR agencies, and public relations managers working in for-profit and not-for-profit organizations, as well as consultants working in internal organizational communications.

A comment on the interviewees. Almost without exception, the people interviewed for this book were articulate, competent, and passionate. If there was any one visceral attitude that came across during the interviews, it was that the people involved in building their organization's Internet presence, while challenged and occasionally criticized, remained determined and motivated, and seemed to be having a lot of fun in the process.

Most of the interviews and the secondary research was conducted during May–July 1996. Since then it is highly probable that some of the statistics have changed, as well as some descriptions of the Web sites. It is hoped that the current volume, despite the inherent problem of the time lag between drafting and publication, contains pertinent, evergreen observations and perspectives.

I am grateful to the numerous executives at FEDEX, GE, HOTWIRED, IBM, USAID, Xerox, US WEST, and Sun Microsystems for their expert and frank testimony. Acknowledgment is due Neil Ruggles for use of descriptions of AT&T, Pathfinder, Chiat/Day, and Toyota Web sites, which he researched and analyzed, and portions of Chapter 6 which he authored. I also want to express my appreciation to Janice Sileo for her editorial contribution to Chapter 17 and to Eric Pinciss, who ably assisted in the overall research process.

My many thanks, too, to John Boyd, publisher at Van Nostrand Reinhold, Chris Bates, production manager, and Jacqueline Jeng, marketing manager, and their respective staffs, and the various reviewers for helping to shape this volume into a cohesive narrative.

EM
1996

CHAPTER 1

THE INTERNET: AN EVOLVING STRATEGIC COMMUNICATIONS MEDIUM

The Internet is in the process of becoming a ubiquitous strategic and tactical communications medium—for marketing, advertising, public relations, and internal organizational communications—on a global scale. It is acting true to a definition expressed by Marshall McLuhan:[1] "Once a new technology comes into a social milieu, it cannot cease to permeate that milieu until every institution is saturated." And, as one case study interviewee put it: "You would have to be living in a cave not to see that the Internet is impacting our lives."

In military terms, a strategy is the utilization, during both peace and war, of all a nation's forces, through large-scale, long-range planning and development, to ensure security or victory. Tactics deals with the use and deployment of troops in actual combat. While a military analogy may be anathema to some, the definition can be applied in this context: For an organization, a strategy is the utilization, during economic good times and bad, of all an organization's resources, through large-scale, long-range planning and development, to ensure survival, growth, market leadership, or domination. Tactics deals with the use and deployment of an organization's re-

1

sources in actual day-to-day interaction with internal and external audiences.

The Internet and the World Wide Web have the potential for reaching a multiplicity of audiences globally, 24 hours a day. From the experience of executives interviewed for this volume, what emerged is an organizational model defined by high levels of collaboration among disparate internal departments. An organizational Web site inherently creates a demand for large-scale, long-range planning. But the Internet is not a strategy in a vacuum. The larger strategy is the application of the Internet as the newest kid on the electronic media block. Similarly, an Internet presence, e.g., a Web site, is a tactical tool deployed on a day-to-day basis.

The ramifications of the Internet for organizational managers involved in strategic decision making and those middle managers involved in realizing those strategic visions have been and will be profound. Those organizational managers already experienced with the Net (as articulated in the eight cases in this volume) are well aware of the Internet's reorganizing characteristics and continue to make adjustments as the medium evolves. Those relatively new to the medium are entering a communications environment with both management challenges and rewards in store.

The Internet transcends time: It is a 24-hour-a-day, seven-day-a-week, 52-week-a-year technology. Day and night are transcended by the Net, as are time zones. The Internet also transcends and breaks down barriers: Geographic location, physical boundaries, political divisions, and differences in language, culture, national laws, gender, age, and religious persuasion are irrelevant to the Internet.

What is relevant is: Do you have access to the Internet? Do you have a modem? Do you have a computer? Do you have a telephone line? Do you have an Internet service provider? Can you get to the Net through an online service? Do you have telecommunications software? Will you make the time to learn some simple computer protocols?

Let's be clear at this point: We are not at the beginning stages of the Internet and the World Wide Web. This technology has its ancestry in the DARPAnet of 1968. And even the early Internet was a culmination of technologies. But worldwide "saturation" of the Internet and the World Wide Web into every institution is years away, particularly for Africa and Central and South America.

For those organizations with an Internet presence, however, all organizational communications activities are changing. This does not mean that all the strategic and tactical activities that marketing, advertising, public relations, and internal organizational communications managers have been engaged in until now will suddenly disappear. Many will remain. But the Internet will have an impact.

For example, marketing will be affected: The convenience of shopping via one's desktop could be as absorbing as playing Super Mario Brothers for hours on end. But, remember, when home shopping came along, some pundits decried the death of the shopping mall. Fact is the shopping mall appears to have enjoyed a renaissance in recent years. What the Internet will do—and the interviewees from FEDEX and GE corroborate this—is give customers an opportunity to get product and service information without having to deal with a salesperson or clerk and make purchasing decisions, or at least tentative purchasing decisions, before going to the car showroom or buying a refrigerator or deciding on a capital level expense. Salespeople and marketing departments will still be there. But their roles will change, as will those of 800-number operators and call-center clerks. The use of the Internet for marketing and selling can only increase. ActivMedia Inc. estimated that sales generated by the World Wide Web will reach $2.9 billion by the end of 1996. In 1997, sales are expected to reach $13 billion and, by 1998, over $45 billion.

With respect to advertising, more news and entertainment content will gravitate to the Net. There is already a multitude of "ezines" on the Net. In mid-1996 Microsoft and NBC launched a joint venture (MSNBC) to explore new technologies (such as the Net) for the dissemination of news. The online services have news sections. The Electronic Newsstand is the premiere Web site not only for disseminating news but also for hosting publications in a subscriber-building environment. And, just as cable television took a major bite out of the broadcast television primetime audience, so too will the Internet take a chunk of the television audience. There are only so many hours in the day. In how many more ways can we divide the television pie? A partial answer to this question is provided by FIND/SVP in a recent survey of adult Internet users. It was found that the Internet most displaces television viewing and phone use:

32% of respondents stated that their television viewing had decreased and 25% that their long-distance phone calling had dropped off. Respondents also experienced drops in watching videos, reading magazines, reading newspapers, and listening to the radio. In effect, every traditional advertising medium has been impacted.

Public relations practitioners will be affected. More and more journalists are gravitating to the online world, as are organizational public relations and corporate communications managers. Public relations firms have no choice but to follow. Some are leading. The definition of public relations is being stretched by the Internet: Does public relations still mean an event, a news release, a well-placed story, a relationship with the press? The Internet means that controlling the flow of information to the media so that the story comes out the way the organization wants it to is no longer viable. Remember the Intel Pentium chip flap? People on the Internet knew about the problem with the chip months before it was reported in *The New York Times* and *The Wall Street Journal*. But the reverse can also be true. When IBM made its move to acquire Lotus, the company made a strategic decision to use the Internet (through its Web site) to inform Lotus shareholders about its proposition. Lotus capitulated in a week!

Internal organizational communications will be affected. The Internet is the latest electronic communications tool in the 158-year history of electronic media. In the last 15 years or so electronic media—such as the computer, the telephone, satellites, teleconferencing, and videotape—have helped to flatten the organizational hierarchy. The Internet will continue this organizational megatrend. On the other hand, the Internet will also enhance business travel. Contrary to the wishes of some executives, high-tech technologies foster high-touch responses (so says John Naisbitt). However, as Jerry Neece at Sun Microsystems is quick to point out, if Internet technology can reduce the number of training trips for a sales force from four a year to three and if the company is of any size, there are tremendous savings to be realized.

The Internet will also have a major impact on the use of print as a communications medium. In the 1970s many organizational executives drooled over the prospect of eliminating a lot of paper as well as armies of clerks with the advent of the computer—which didn't happen. Today, the Internet can raise the efficiency level of internal communications with the elimination of paper forms and the creation of electronic forms. FEDEX is already proving that this is cost-effective with its external Web site. Goodbye, paper pallets; hello, forms by the byte.

MOVING TO CRITICAL MASS

A central strategic decision in the initiation, launch, and evolution of a Web site is timing. All the case study executives interviewed in *Web Visions* have had over two years' experience with the Internet. As strange as it sounds, these executives can now consider themselves Internet veterans; their cumulative knowledge base and commentary support the advantages of strategically applying the Internet for various communications purposes. These same executives also keep a close eye on the larger trends in the development of the Internet as a way of staying ahead of the curve and keeping their Web sites strategically competitive.

While the media headlines make it appear that everyone is on the Net, consumer adoption of online/Internet access is at less than 8% of U.S. homes. Nevertheless, it is growing quickly. The movement toward critical mass is accelerating.

Mary Meeker and Chris DePuy, global technology analysts at the investment firm of Morgan Stanley (the same firm that managed Netscape's initial public offering), in a comprehensive report aptly titled *The Internet Report*[2] point out:

> Due to technological advances in PC-based communications, a new medium—with the Internet, the World Wide Web, and TCP/IP at its core—is emerging rapidly. The market for Internet-related products and services appears to be growing more rapidly than the early emerging marketing for print publishing, telephony, film, radio, recorded music, television, and personal computers.

THE PC BASE

There are close to 150 million PC users worldwide who, in time, will become more active Internet users. Meeker and DePuy estimate 250 million PC users by the year 2000. Dataquest projects that, in the next few years, the number of PCs installed worldwide would grow from approximately 153 million in 1994 to over 328 million by 1999. Dataquest also estimated that those PCs with Internet[3] access would grow from 13.6 million in 1994 to 184.3 million in 1999. Thus, the compound growth rate of PCs with Internet access is likely to increase 68.4%, four times as fast as the overall installed base of PCs, in effect, steadily shrinking the gap between the installed base of PCs and those with Internet access. In short, there's lots of upside. For organizational executives, this can only mean increased demands on their extant Web sites and, probably, increased need for redesign.

E-MAIL

An almost universal feature of a Web site is an ability to communicate with an organization via e-mail. Meeker and DePuy project that e-mail should become pervasive.[4] This projection is corroborated by an April 1996 tally in *Webweek*: "By some counts, 75 percent of Fortune 500 companies have two or more e-mail systems." The *Webweek* article also projected that the 44 million e-mail boxes in use as of the end of 1995 will escalate to 216 million by the end of the year 2000.

THE GROWTH OF NETWORKS

Another gauge of the Internet's emerging pervasiveness is the number of networks. According to the Morgan Stanley analysis, the Internet now encompasses an estimated 70,000 networks worldwide, about half of which are in the United States. Users on the Internet are doubling annually, at a rate of about 0.19% per day. About 10 million computers (hosts) are attached to the Internet, plus at least that many portable and desktop systems only intermittently online.

WEB TRAFFIC

Other "infrastructure" evidence of the Internet's growing strategic importance can be observed by the growth of web traffic. According to the Internet Society, total megabytes x 10^{15} through 1995 was virtually flat. But in early 1996, this shifted dramatically and Web traffic by the end of 1997 is expected to reach 20 megabytes x 10^{15}. *Internet World* also recounts that 1995 was the year of the online push: America Online alone reached over 5 million subscribers.[5] As of this writing, it was over 6 million. Meeker and DePuy estimate AOL could reach 10 million subscribers in very short order.[6]

DOMAIN NAMES

The growth in number of domain names is further evidence of the Internet's emergence as a strategic communications medium. A domain name is a key component of an Internet address used for electronic mail and other data services on the global computer network. Internic, the organization with which you must register a Web site's domain name in order to make it official and unique, reported the following cumulative domain registration numbers in June 1996:

Commercial	394,865
Organizations	27,377
Networks	16,100
Educational	2,678
Government	448
United States	232
Other Country	175
Total	463,705

These numbers compare dramatically to those reported not even a year ago.[7] In September 1995, it was reported that more than 118,000 Internet domain names had been assigned to businesses, educational institutions, nonprofit organizations, and network service providers. Of these, about 102,000 were commercial domains, 8,990 nonprofit organizations, 5,694 network service providers, and the balance (2,030) education domains.

Clearly, what started as a quasi-government/educational network of four computers has grown into a significant business and organizational communications medium. This does not mean that there are 463,705 organizations on the Net. On the contrary, many organizations have applied for multiple names. Therefore, the actual number is lower. By contrast, according to Dun & Bradstreet, there are over 10,000,000 organizations in the United States. In effect, there is a substantial way to go before most organizations in the United States (let alone the world) sign on to the Internet.

THE ONLINE SERVICES

Another way to gauge the Internet's strategic potential is to look at the number of people subscribing to online services, such AOL (the largest), Compuserve (the oldest), and Prodigy (the most troubled). The investment firm of Goldman Sachs estimated that more than 14 million paying consumers will have access to the World Wide Web through the online services by the end of 1996 and 22–25 million by 1997.[8] However, these numbers contrast to the 97 million television households in the United States (the rest of the world notwithstanding). Comparisons to the growth curve of the Internet as a potential advertising, marketing, and public relations medium to the early days of cable television are obvious. It is not a matter of whether the Internet will become a significant venue for marketing, advertising, public relations, or internal organizational communications; it is a matter of when.

THE EMERGENCE OF PROFESSIONAL RESOURCES

Corollary evidence of the Internet's growing strategic importance is the proliferation of professional organizations that have sprung up in the last few years. They include the Association of Internet Professionals, the Electronic Frontier Foundation, the Institute for Global Communications, and the Internet Society. The establishment and growth of these and other organizations (such as the International Interactive Communications Society and the New York New Media Association) are underscored by an April 1996 report by Coopers & Lybrand for the Empire State Development Corporation that there are 4,300 start-up companies in New York City that develop and market Internet sites, as well as multimedia software, online entertainment, and other cyber-offerings.[9] The report states, "Not surprisingly, the field employs 71,500 people in the city alone—more workers than are employed in traditional media fields of broadcasting, book, newspaper, and magazine publishing."

A LONG-TERM TREND

As singer/comedian Eddie Cantor (1893–1964) once said: "It took me 25 years to become an overnight success." Something of the kind could be said of the Internet. The Internet phenomenon needs to be seen in the long-term context of developments in electronic media. The first electronic medium was commercially introduced in 1838, almost 160 years ago, by Samuel F. B. Morse with his demonstration of the telegraph. At that instant, the paradigm of communication by print means and all the attendant organizational structures that pervaded corporate life began a slow descent.

Between the introduction of the telegraph and today's Internet presence, we have seen the telephone, film, radio, television (both broadcast and cable), satellites, videotape, videodiscs, CD-ROMs, and computers (mainframes, miniframes, and PCs). While today the Internet and the World Wide Web are primarily text and graphics, audio and video via the Net (given improvements in modem speeds and bandwidth) are only a few years off. The Internet is moving us from the face-to-face communication of the tribal family around the campfire to the global village touted by Marshall McLuhan over 30 years ago.

The Internet and the World Wide Web represent the latest evidence of fundamental changes in our personal, educational, and professional lives. We have moved from the Industrial Revolution to the knowledge age, from teaching to learning, from organizations for learning to learning organizations, from pen and paper to computer tools, from subject-centered to action learning, from isolation to open learning, from the classroom to the World Wide Web, from instruction to construction, from low-order questions to high-order learning, from "hours open" to open all hours.

Meeker and DePuy corroborate what many of the executives interviewed in this volume perceive as the value of the Internet, whether an external or an Internet (Intranet) site—that using the Internet as an information distribution vehicle offers companies the ability to reduce distribution costs, support costs, and costs of goods sold—and, eventually, to target focused customer bases.[10]

On the flip side, lower costs and easier distribution open markets for new competitors in publishing, marketing and advertising, commerce, and software development. Dislocation of traditional companies in these areas is likely in time as new business models emerge based on free trials, subscribers, advertising, and transactions.

THE RAMIFICATIONS

Accordingly, there are several general conclusions that can be made regarding the evolution of the Internet and the World Wide Web with respect to its organizational use for marketing, advertising, public relations, and internal organizational communication:

Use of the Internet is expanding and will become a permanently significant factor in the conduct of commerce in general and electronic commerce specifically.

Yet the evolution of the Internet is still formative. There are few consistent models of who is on the Net. Transaction security is still very much an issue. Measurement of Internet use is in the early stages of development at best. Much of what is on the Internet is still experimental, although the learning curve for practitioners is not as steep as it was just a year ago.

The Internet is still in the early stages of its development. But, between 1994 and 1995, use of the Internet grew exponentially, and this curve will continue for a few more years. We are still in the early stages of adopting the Internet but, in the next year or two, a significant mass of users will make the Internet a primary focus for personal and commercial transactions.

As an electronic medium, the Internet will continue the "organizational flattening" that has been evolving since the commercial introduction of the telegraph in 1838 and will continue the breakdown of the modern organizational hierarchy that began sometime after the end of World War II.

In the last ten years or so, American corporations have been downsizing, rightsizing, and flattening. Much of this reduction, and the concomitant subversion of American corporate middle managers, is due in large measure to the advent of electrovisual media, such as videotape, teleconferencing, and computers and computer networks, including the Internet and the World Wide Web. In effect, these electrovisual media have contributed to the breakdown of hierarchy—the so-called traditional top-down, militaristic/bureaucratic, pyramid structure—in American corporations. What we are witnessing is the transition of the American firm from the militaristic/bureaucratic style typical of the 1950s manufacturing firm to a more dynamic and flexible organizational architecture.

Intranets (internal organizational Web sites) will provide employees with ways to increase their productivity and may, in the intermediate term, prove more important than external Web sites. In fact, Intranets are likely to expand to include suppliers (e.g., General Electric's Trading Process Network to manage supplier bids for GE product requirements).

It has long been a dream of organizational managements to have employees understand the so-called corporate "big picture," receive training in the shortest period of time for the least amount of dollars, and spend the vast majority of their time on the job doing productive and profitable work. Further, it has always been a problem for organizational managements that employees receive news about the company from outside the company before management can communicate it to the employee force.

For many years, organizations have used a variety of face-to-face, group, print, and electronic means to convey organizational goals to employees in the hopes that employees would appreciate the so-called "corporate context" and, therefore, fit with the organization's objectives. For just as many years, organizations have provided employees with on-the-job training, off-site training, audiocassettes, videocassettes, distance learning (teleconferencing), and manuals to help increase employee productivity. Managers have always had to make sure that employees were doing work rather than using organizational resources (such as the telephone and the office copier) for personal reasons.

An organizational Intranet is in various ways nirvana with respect to all these managerial wishes. An Intranet can provide an employee at any time with information about the company. In effect, by accessing a corporate internal Web site, an employee can find out what's going on almost immediately. At some companies, employees can modify their benefits packages at will. By accessing an internal Web site, employees can begin to form a mosaic picture of the organization, leading to a concept of the organization that is whole rather than piecemeal.

Training is also a potentially major content item on an Intranet. With audio and video capability on the horizon, an Intranet can provide employee training on demand at highly reduced cost.

Through an internal Web site, organizations can make their employees more productive, by making information and knowledge more accessible to employees without any direct intermediary, i.e., a supervisor or manager.

In addition to helping to further "flatten" organizations (by requiring fewer middle managers as messengers), the Internet, and especially, Intranets, will break down barriers among departments and divisions.

Communication among the various parts of the organization is also enhanced. Employees can communicate with each other at will.

In keeping with the breakdown of hierarchy, and the erosion of barriers among organizational departments and divisions, the Internet will also help break down barriers between an organization and its customers.

In effect, the Internet, as an external Web site, will allow customers to do business with an organization at the Web site. If the Web site is not conceived strategically as a place for business, if the external Web site is not set up as an extension of an organization's business, the company is wasting its resources. An external Web site is a place where a customer or prospect can get information about an organization's products or services and then make a purchase decision based on the content found at the Web site. In a potentially significant way, the external Web site can become the initial sales contact with the customer. While it is unlikely that external Web sites will eliminate the need for a marketing and sales force, it is likely that the role of the salesperson will change: Rather than serving as the opener for a sales call, the human salesperson will close sales or, at least, move the sales process toward a close.

Advertising on the Internet—e.g., in electronic magazines, such as *HotWired*, or on search engines, such as Lycos and Yahoo—is different from traditional print and electronic advertising.

Advertising on the Internet is not just an electronic version of a print or radio or television advertisement. The Internet represents an opportunity for advertisers to interact with potential buyers. It is clear that the rules for advertising on the Internet are highly formative: They are being defined by a small number of savvy young agencies with little background in, or commitment to, traditional media.

It is also clear that traditionally oriented advertising agencies need to create interactive departments to handle the Internet. Further, those agencies with direct marketing or direct response departments or associated companies will fare better than those without these specialties. The reasons: The Internet is direct response personified. The parallels between advertising on the Internet and direct marketing are numerous, not the least of which is that for some time now, the trend has been toward one-on-one marketing.

There are also parallels between the Internet as an advertising and marketing medium and cable television. In the early 1980s, when cable television was just beginning to reach critical mass, advertising agency media buying departments and independent media buying companies considered a cable buy (whether network or local) to be a very small consideration, almost an afterthought. Today, cable television, with its many narrowly targeted audiences, is a major element in an advertising agency media plan, despite the extra media buying complexity. Advertising on the Internet is in the same place in 1996 that cable television was in the 1980s. It makes up a trivial portion of most advertising budgets and is only an important source of revenue for companies specializing in interactive marketing. It consists of many small niche audiences and affords many media buying opportunities with no clear buying guidelines. The similarities between the Internet's niche audiences and those of cable television suggest that, within five years, the Internet will be a major factor in media planning. As we shall see in Chapter 4, advertising revenue (according to Webtrack) is growing, as is the number of online publishers and advertisers.

External Web sites, with their cross-audience appeal, are a public relations vehicle. Whether the strategic vision of the external Web site is marketing, customer service, or information—and whether or not there is a media relations section on the site an external Web site must be viewed as a public relations environment.

Public relations is a natural application on the Internet. As Chapter 8 will detail, in the last year or so, it has become increasingly evident that journalists are using online services to get their work done. Organizations and their public relations agencies have no choice but to follow suit and communicate more with their media brethren via the Net or via e-mail.

BEYOND THE HOME PAGE: TOWARD TRANSACTIONAL COMMUNICATION

The Internet is no fad. The Internet and the World Wide Web are now at a stage similar to that of the cable television industry just prior to 1980. At that time, there were few channels, and low penetration, cable advertising was minuscule, media buyers considered cable a nuisance, and prime time broadcast television was still king. But cable was growing.

The Internet was born in the late 1960s as part of a Department of Defense project. In the early 1980s, the personal computer came along which, in turn, tied into the growing global telecommunications network and, suddenly, we had a phenom called the Internet. It will only continue to expand. And as Marshall McLuhan was fond of pointing out, when a new medium comes along, it does not stop until it permeates every milieu. Microsoft's Bill Gates believes this, too. He is banking on it.

A Web site is another step in the chain of electronic media that began with the introduction of the telegraph in 1838 and includes, among numerous electronic media, the telephone and the computer. In the last 15 years or so, many organizations have reduced their management layers. This is no mere coincidence. A Web site, whether external or internal, will have a similar organizing effect: A Web site has the potential for reducing the layers of personnel between customers and the organization. In effect, a Web site allows a customer, or an employee, for that matter, to have direct access to an organization's database. FEDEX, for example, is saving huge dollars because customers are filling out shipping documents on the Net, thus reducing reliance on its 800-number. General Electric is looking forward to raising the level of sales effectiveness through its Web site. US WEST expects to move aggressively into the new competitive market it finds itself in. Xerox expects a stronger community of employees. Sun Microsystems has moved to use its Intranet ingeniously for training. Training via a Web site has far-reaching ramifications. Imagine a day when employees and customers can use a Web site to self-train at an individual pace. Imagine the potential cost savings; imagine the training efficiency and effectiveness.

Time and time again, the case study interviewees and other subject experts contacted during the course of researching and drafting this book used the word *transactions* to express their perception of the strategic value of the Internet and the World Wide Web. Their collective view is that, with time, the Internet will evolve into a highly transactional communications medium: People will communicate there, do business there, learn there, and share there. As audio and video technologies are adapted to meet the web, these transactions will only become more personal and intimate. In effect, contrary to those who view media as dehumanizing and separating, the effect will be the opposite. The Internet could literally create a world community.

A stampede to the Internet is not encouraged. Rather, it should be approached with common sense, analysis, and intelligence. It should also be approached with a strategically oriented open mind.

When videotape first came onto the scene commercially in 1956, most people thought it was a medium to help with broadcast time-zone delay problems. Instead, it spawned the home video industry and, the corporate video business and gave commercial television producers great flexibility. Videotape also helped lead to the development of the videodisc, in turn the CD-ROM. There are some who presume to know what the Internet will evolve into. Take your own guess. At the very least, the medium is fast becoming a viable and primary strategic communication tool.

NOTES

1. M. McLuhan, *Understanding Media: The Extensions of Man*, 1964, p. 177.

2. M. Meeker and C. DePuy, *The Internet Report*, HarperBusiness, New York, 1996.

3. Dataquest chart, "Worldwide Installed Base of Personal Computers Vs. Users with Internet Access," *New York Times*, March 26, 1996.

4. E. Booker, "The Tower of (E-Mail) Babel," *Webweek*, April 29, 1996, p. 4.

5. C. Wilder, "The Net on the Edge," *Internet World*, April 29, 1996, p. 36.

6. Meeker and DePuy, op. cit.

7. P. H. Lewis, "Prime Internet Address Will Now Cost $50 a Year," *The New York Times*, Sept. 14, 1995, pp. D1, D6.

8. E. S. Philo, Michael K. Prekh, and Storm Boswick, "CyberPublishing: A New Front in Content Liquidity," *CyberCommerce*; On-Line and Internet Services, Goldman Sachs, July 26, 1995, p. 2.

9. K. Scott, editor, "Where It's @ in New Media," *Information World*, April 22, 1996, p. 12.

10. Meeker and DePuy, op. cit.

CHAPTER 2

MEASURING WHO'S REALLY ON THE NET

The lack of consistent and standardized information about Internet user demographics is a major obstacle prohibiting the Internet from moving from trial activities to mainstream business applications.

That's the usual story—but is it true? In 1995, most advertising on the Internet was sold with little concern for audience demographics. Why? Because the companies buying such advertising considered the entire Internet a perfect audience, based on a "general" understanding of who was on the Internet. Ostensibly, organizations constructing Web sites did so more for the experience of doing it and the image of being "hip" than to gain measurable results from their Internet presence.

From another perspective, demographics is a nonissue. The online services know who is online at any time and what they are doing although they do not make individual details available to advertisers. Businesses that assign customer or account numbers to customers have a built-in way to track site usage. And the accelerating number of Intranets is independent of demographics because organizations have knowledge of employee use of the Intranet by means of conventional network password controls.

In 1996, however, as more organizations become interested in the Internet and as companies that rushed online in 1995 begin to measure their results, knowing the audience is becoming strategically more important. Why? The answer is a traditional one: so that advertisers, online publishers, traditional and interactive advertising agencies, Internet Webmasters and designers, and Intranet Webmasters, designers, and steering committees can not only design effective Web sites from the outset but can also refine existing Web sites so that they better serve the people who visit there.

If there is any lesson to be learned from the several dozen executives interviewed for the case studies in this volume, it is that Web site design is critical to optimizing strategic value. To move a Web site toward a realization of an organization's strategic vision, having an understanding of who's really visiting the Web site is critical to success.

Measurement of who's on the Net can be accomplished on two levels: in the aggregate and Web site by Web site. Both approaches are valuable. By reviewing and comparing aggregate surveys that take a broad look at Internet usage, an organization can contextualize its own Web site and strategic vision for it. Second, by gauging an organization's specific Web site traffic, the organization can also determine the specific effectiveness of the site.

AGGREGATE SURVEYS

Everyone asks, "What is the size of the Internet and who's there?" Unfortunately, no one source provides a definitive answer. A way of gauging who's on the Net and what they are doing there is to look at the growing number of domestic and international surveys that are being conducted on and off the Net courtesy of Internet consulting company NUA (web@nua.ie and www.nua.ie/surveys/surveylinks), following are summaries of some of the recent methodical looks at the web with respect to electronic commerce, PC use, number of users, and demographics.

NUMBER OF USERS

The usual first question is "How many?" Several studies have been conducted and published in recent months and, while the results certainly vary, the collective order of magnitude provides an overview of how many people are on the Net and where the trends are.

FIND/SVP ■ In January 1996 FIND/SVP published the "American Internet User Survey," which states, "Some 9.5 million Americans now use the Internet, including 8.4 million adults and 1.1 million children under 18, who tap into it from the workplace, school and homes ... 7.5 million total users access the Worldwide Web; 7.3 million home users, including adults and children, use the Internet (for any application) from home; 5.8 million adults use the Internet for business activities, vs. 6.0 million adults who use the Internet for personal activities. Sixty percent of adults use it for both."

Gartner Group Internet Strategies Section ■ In January 1996, the Gartner Group forecast that there will be over 150 million Internet users by 1998. Some of the "dominant trends" Gartner isolated include: "The Internet is going through adolescence in 1996: experiencing tremendous growth spurts, shedding some of the insouciance of youth, acquiring some of the maturity, disciplines and responsibilities of adulthood. The promise and appeal of universal connectivity and access to people and information is overwhelmingly compelling, and will continue to drive Internet growth in a rapid upward trend (despite the Internet's flaws), accompanied by interim corrections."

Project 2000 ■ A study published in April 1996, entitled: "Internet Use in the United States: 1995 Baseline Estimates and Preliminary Market Segments," estimates that "28.8 million people in the United States 16 and over have potential or actual access to the Internet, 16.4 million people use the Internet, 11.5 million people use the Web, and 1.51 million people have used the Web to purchase something."

Odyssey Ventures Inc. ■ An American study, based on telephone interviews conducted in January 1996 with 2000 randomly selected households, found that, in the previous six months the number of web users in America had doubled. It further stated that, in July

1995, only 45% of households surveyed had heard of the Internet but, by January 1996, that figure had risen to 73%.

PC USE

The growing number of Internet users is directly tied to PC use. Two surveys supported the contention that the growing adoption of PCs was leading to increased Internet usage.

Computer Intelligence InfoCorp's "Home PC Study," published in May 1996, states, "Home PC use in the U.S. increased to 38.5 percent of households at year-end 1995, an increase of 5 percentage points from the previous year." The study found that children are an important factor in the decision to purchase a PC.

Odyssey Ventures Inc. found that more than half of computer users who access the Internet from home do so through a commercial online service, such as America Online; 35% of American households now have computers.

DEMOGRAPHICS

After the "How many" question comes "Who are these people?" Several surveys have gleaned answers to this question with some consistent results.

GVU Web User Surveys ■ In the "Fifth User Survey," (conducted from April 10 to May 10, 1996), and published in June 1996, findings include: "Average age has risen again slightly to 33.0 years old. The gender ratio continues to become more balanced with 31.5% reporting being female, compared to 29.3% for the Fourth Survey. Estimated average household income has dropped slightly, but remains high in general at $59,000 US dollars. US respondents represented 73.4% of total respondents; Europe was the next largest category with 10.8%. More than half of the respondents access the Web primarily from home and are paying for their own access. Over 80% of respondents access the Web on a daily basis, and most use it simply for browsing and entertainment purposes. More than a third (36%) surf the Web instead of watching TV at least once a day."

Jupiter Communications, April 1996 ■ A comprehensive survey carried out in conjunction with Yahoo found: "Home-based accounts were the primary access method to the World Wide Web for 55 percent of respondents; the profile of the survey respondent is a single American male between the ages of 25 to 34 in a professional managerial career with an income between $35,000 to $49,999 and at least a college degree."

Nielsen Media Research ■ Main findings of a comprehensive Nielsen/CommerceNet survey, published in late 1995, estimated that there were 23 million on the Internet in the United States and Canada, and that "Males represent 66% of Internet users and account for 77% of Internet usage; on average, WWW users are upscale (25% have incomes over $80K), professional (50% are professional or managerial), and educated (64% have at least college degrees). Approximately 14% (2.5 million) of WWW users have purchased products or services over the Internet."

ELECTRONIC COMMERCE

The Internet is obviously eyed as a potentially profitable marketing and advertising venue. While it is certainly useful to know "How many?" and "Who are these people?" a vital question is "Are people spending money on the Internet?" Several surveys have attempted to answer this question.

ActivMedia ■ Findings from "The Real Numbers Behind Net Profits," a study published in June 1996 by Internet market research firm ActivMedia, include: "The top 10% of Web sites with products or services for sale now average more than $30,000 per month in sales, compared with only $4,800 in external maintenance expenditures. In a brief six months, the Asian/Pacific share has increased from 3.5% to 5.4% of the 1,104 web marketers responding to ActivMedia's study. ActivMedia predicts that the Asian/Pacific region will nearly double its share of sites by the end of 1997." A study released in January 1996, entitled "Trends in the World Wide Web Marketplace," found, among other things, that "Seventy-one percent of businesses with Web sites in the travel industry had some sales during the previous month, which is far higher than any other sector."

CIC Research ■ The monthly "Net Traveler Survey" is designed "to poll and track the travel decisions, choices and preferences of travelers who use the Internet." A May 1995 survey—with 900 respondents—found that 79% saw the Internet as an important part of their travel planning, with 92% interested in using it to book their travel.

I/PRO (Internet Profiles Corporation) ■ An I/PRO study published in April 1996 found that advertising response rates on the Web varied between 2.4% and 17.9%; the majority of Web users were male (72%), ages 25 through 54 (73%), and well off (58% sport a household income in excess of $50,000).

Manning, Selvage & Lee ■ MS&L's Corporate Cyber-Cash Survey found that, while many companies have their own Web sites, company communicators are not using the Web very much yet. Findings include: Of 500 corporate communicators questioned in the United States and Europe 66% had access to the Internet. However, 80% did not consider it an important communications tool. On the bright side, respondents felt that, by the year 2000, there would be a four-fold or higher increase in the importance of the Internet for reaching target audiences. The survey also found that e-mail is very popular, with company communicators spending an average of 1.19 hours a day using it.

INTERNATIONAL SURVEYS

There have also been several studies conducted in Europe with respect to use of the Internet. The strategic importance of these kinds of aggregate surveys to American organizations is simply that a Web site has a potential worldwide reach. While an organization may not have an international audience as a target objective, the "globalization" of the Internet experience is a growing reality. For some companies, like IBM, FEDEX, and GE, the global marketplace is indeed a desired target. Having an overview of the international visitors to a Web site can be strategically valuable. Moreover, having these kinds of surveys at hand can help executives design and refine a Web site to accommodate cultural differences. Overall, the international surveys support the contention that the United States is the lead country with respect to Internet penetration and usage, followed by the Europe countries. Also, in Europe there are considerably more men on the Net than women, compared to the two-thirds, one-third split in the United States.

Killen & Associates' "Internet: Global Penetration and Forecast 2000" survey published in May 1996 estimates that, at the beginning of 1996, there were 30 million Internet users worldwide. The survey states, "In early 1996, 170 countries were connected to the Internet. By 2000, as many as 250 million people worldwide will have access to the Internet, through almost 96 million host computers."

International Internet Marketing conducted a survey of European usage of the Internet based on analysis of previous GVU Web surveys. The results from the analysis of the May 1996 GVU survey include such findings as: "The average age of European Web users decreased slightly during the last 6 months from 29.7 to 28.8; Europe is still behind the U.S. as far as ending the male domination of the Internet. Whereas women make up 34.4 percent of the U.S. Web community, the percentage is only 15.2 in Europe. The strongest growth in a European region can be found in UK/Ireland, where female participation has grown to 22 percent from 15 percent 6 months ago."

NUA Limited: In August 1995, NUA Limited, in conjunction with the Dublin Media Centre, carried out the first major survey of attitudes to, and usage of, the Internet and multimedia among Ireland's 250 largest companies. Main findings: 44% of those responding had an Internet connection; 17% of Internet users felt that it was "very important" to their company, while 54% believed that its importance would increase "substantially" over the next twelve months; 31% of companies who have an Internet connection have their own Web site; 63% of respondents who do not currently have an Internet connection intend to get one over the next twelve months; 77% of respondents felt that the Internet was something they felt they needed to be better informed on.

RIS, Slovenia: In a major survey of Internet usage in Slovenia, in Eastern Europe, preliminary findings (as of June 1996) include the fact that between 17% and 25% of Internet users in that country are female.

MEASURING WEB SITE EFFECTIVENESS

The flip side of aggregate Net demographics is the issue of measuring the effectiveness of a specific Web site by determining who visits there, when, why, and from where. This is not an issue specific just to the online advertising world. Across the board, the measurement issue is raised time and time again—by advertising industry executives, those in marketing and public relations, even Webmasters and organizational communications managers.

MEASURING MARKETING AND PUBLIC RELATIONS WEB SITES

USAID (U.S. Agency for International Development) is conducting several kinds of measurements. According to Joan M. Matejceck, Acting Director, Office of Information Resources Management, "I get statistics every month that show who and where that site is being hit. Legislative and Public Affairs (LPA) gets those as well, as does the Executive Secretariat. We have a lot of anecdotal kinds of information, but I don't know that we've got a lot of statistical kinds of information."

Because of the inherent nature of USAID's work, its external Web site gets a lot of international visitors. According to Webmaster Jim Russo, "We have a WebStat package, and we track everything, but we focus on the domains of people coming in. We get approximately 25,000 people coming into our site a month. That's people, not hits. Frankly, that's modest. There are sites out there that have that kind of load a day or an hour. But, again, you have to think about our constituency. Most of our clients are overseas and, oftentimes, most of the people who care about what we do are in developing countries that don't have access to the Internet. So I suspect that, as developing countries come online, our statistics will go up."

At General Electric, according to Al Blanco, President of META4 Design, the firm GE hired to serve as its external Webmaster: "The standard measurement is just getting people to the site. For us, it implies getting them to do things. In other words, we started with the premise of not only wanting them to come to the site but wanting them to interact with things and get specific information or request specific things to be done." Thus, GE is measuring not only how many visitors there are or how often they come but also how often they use the set of tools that GE is providing.

According to Blanco, "Because the user is defining his point of interest, he creates a profile that we use, not to identify that particular individual but to create some demographic information about the people visiting our site. And that's then routed to specific GE companies whose customer profile fits that individual.

"To me clicking means nothing. It doesn't tell us much about the user. Our point of view is that all this interactive stuff is not broadcasting, it's not even narrowcasting. It's down to the individual. It's a market of one, basically. "

According to Ed Costello, Webmaster at IBM: "There was a tool called Get Stats written almost two years ago, and we've been using that for a while, but we've written a new tool in-house that we call Bean Counter. It's not a product. We can get stats on one site and that tells us how much traffic that site gets. The goal is to have it running on all 85 Web sites. Right now, I think we have it running on 10 or 15.

"What happens is that it runs and produces a statistics report for that site for a given week, and then we have another program that runs off one of our auxiliary systems that runs around to all the Web sites running Bean Counter and fetches that report. The report is done in such a way that we can merge it into other reports and basically get a Web wide view of our statistics, of our traffic. It measures raw hits—a hit being anything from a graphic to a sound clip to an HTML file, as well as specific URLs—how many people actually hit your home page, and what countries they came from. IBM has a marketing geography concept, so we attempt to break down what traffic comes from which marketing geographies because the marketing organizations might be able to use that and, if the information is available, we also try to track where people came from using the referring URL."

The results? "For the IBM home page, we still use Get Stats. We look at raw hits because that gives us an indication of how the server's performing. We look at the raw number of hits just to gauge how the server's performing, we look at some specific URLs, like how many actual hits are on the home page itself and how many are on specific URLs and the products and services area or the search area, to give us an idea of how many people are actually hitting the system a day."

MEASURING ADVERTISING WEB SITES

The advertising side of the Internet house is a different matter although there are more similarities than contrasts to marketing, public relations, and Intranet sites. Internet media buying is complicated for several reasons. First, it is hard to get any real information about who the audience is at any Web site unless the site registers visitors, assigning them a password. Online services and private bulletin board systems assign passwords to their users and can track them in great detail. Also, businesses that have customers with account numbers have the potential to track them as they use a Web site. Sites that register visitors can also track their audiences.

Second, the sheer number of Web sites and the variety of advertising opportunities are a media buyer's nightmare. It is much worse than buying in the spot market for cable television advertising or in the radio market. If a program on a cable channel is comparable to a content area on a Web site, imagine a market of literally tens of thousands of programs, with no directory to quickly categorize the opportunities. SRDS (Standard Rate and Data Service) is about to release a print directory to help identify interactive media opportunities. In addition, the online site, The Traffic Resource is attempting to do the same thing online. The Traffic Resource has signed up 25 advertisers and has rate information on literally hundreds of Web sites around the Internet.

Last, there is the issue of traffic monitoring, or measurement: How many people are actually visiting any given Web site "page," how long are they staying there, and where are they going next? From the advertisers' perspective, which links are pulling the most visits and, ultimately, which visits are leading to sales or other results? The measurement business, as it is emerging on the Net, is looking at the "clickstream," or sequence of clicks that a visitor makes with a mouse on various parts of a screen image as the key source of information.

There is some progress on the horizon, however. On June 3, 1996, worldwide circulation-auditing leader BPA International announced it had completed the first independent third-party audit of an Internet site. According to the announcement, the audit report for The Economist Group's d.Comm (www.d-comm.com) includes not only verification of the number of registered users but also key demographic and traffic patterns that advertisers can evaluate when buying interactive ads.

d.comm reports news and information targeted to information technology professionals. The BPA International audit of d.comm is for three months' activity, January 1 through March 31, 1996. BPA confirmed that, as of March 31, d.comm had 12,021 registered users. Among the significant verified traffic patterns and user demographics are the following:

Of all registered users, 19% work in the information technology industry, 10% in communications, and 10% in education; 8% said they were in the banking/finance industry.

More than 65% of d.comm registered users are between the ages of 26 and 50; 14% are 19 to 25, and only 9% are over 50.

Of the site's registered users, 47% are from the United States; 17% are in the United Kingdom, with 12% in continental Europe.

The most popular day of the week among d.comm's registered users is Tuesday, based on average daily page requests over the three-month period. The most popular hour of the day for accessing d.comm is 11 a.m. EST.

In conducting the d.comm audit, BPA required access to the complete logfile and entire database as opposed to a sample. In verifying data from the logfile, BPA employed methodology and multiple software analysis developed during a beta-test phase in late 1995. An auditor conducted random checks via e-mail and confirmed registered activity along with demographics elicited by d.Comm when users registered to access the site.

It is possible that the BPA-style independent audit will provide the kind of objective audience measurement advertisers are looking for in order to become increasingly convinced that a Web site is worth the advertising expenditure. It is also likely that online publishers, as well as organizations with marketing, public relations, and Intranet-oriented Web sites, will want to have their own software tools to measure the traffic at a site independent of any "outside" auditor.

MEASURING INTRANET USAGE

Many Intranet Webmasters are using basic software tools, such as WebStats, to gauge the volume of visitors. Several organizations have developed their own software tools. Many reported that anecdotal feedback was a sure gauge of usage. But it is clear from the case study interviewees who were questioned directly for this book that the measurement issue (whether internal or external visitors) is still formative and has not achieved standardization.

For example, evaluation of the Intranet is an evolving consideration at US WEST and is an aspect of Intranet management consistent with virtually all organizations interviewed for this volume. Said Sherman Woo: "We watch how people use it, and we have accounts. Basically, the server lets us know that the thing is really going. We also have quite a few user testimonials on how this has helped employees literally take time out of their projects and has increased their flexibility and ability to communicate with large teams."

US WEST Webmaster Mullison described the Intranet measurement activity from her position: "We have a WebStat tracking tool that our technical person dragged down from the Internet. And then we are able to tell how many times each site is hit. The main thing that we use at this point, from WebStat, is to find out approximately a total number of users. I think that, at some point in the future, we'll have to get a better grip on exactly who we have as clients and who we don't, so that we can move forward and get those clients that we don't have online. But, at this point, because ours was a ground up group and chaotic like the Internet, we don't have that."

At Sun Microsystems, a group is developing measurement tools using some existing shareware. Webmaster Debra Winters pointed out that they have been seriously impacted by cache servers because "Once you implement a cache server, you lose visibility as to who is actually hitting your server if they go through cache to get your page. And that's a big problem." Winters elaborated: "We have a program that goes out and collects data from all of the different cache servers. Let's say your server is called doctor.com. You can go in and do a search and it brings all of your logs back." But, Winters added, we "... have work to do there, too."

A FINAL WORD

A study by SRI International reminds us that, despite all the press and the growing number of surveys, most of the world has yet to gain access to the Net. SRI's analysis of Web user trends during 1995 concluded that the gender gap indeed, is narrowing (66% male, 34% female), age (30ish), income levels ($40,000 plus average) are lowering slightly but that education levels (college degree average) remained relatively stable.

But SRI's "Exploring the World Wide Web Population's Other Half" special survey paints a picture of two Web audiences. The traditional technoliterate Web users, SRI claims, represent 50% of present Web users and 10% of the American population, SRI concluded that "their behaviors and characteristics are of limited usefulness in understanding the future Web." The second Web audience, however, comprises a diverse set of groups that SRI calls the Web's "other half." SRI points out that understanding their attitudes and needs is vital for the future growth and success of the Internet. In effect, even though a significant portion of the U.S. population has yet to sign on to the Net, understanding and measuring the attitudes and needs of those who are already on the Net remains a formidable task.

CHAPTER 3

MARKETING ON
THE INTERNET

ADDING STRATEGIC VALUE

When a new technology or communications medium comes along, there are always those who predict that the new medium will replace everything that has come before. If this were so, we would have stopped talking, reading, listening to the radio, and watching television sometime ago. Fact is: When a new technology or communications medium comes along, it builds on the previous media, allowing people to do things that were not possible before.

If we were to look at a cross section of the Grand Canyon, we would see several strata, each one built on another. The communications technology strata structure is the same: On the bottom we have oral communication, then print, then electronic. The usual scenario is that the new medium causes shifts or adjustments in the media landscape but the older media do not vanish: Their role may be diminished or become evolved, or their share of the communication marketplace may shrink or take on new functions. In any event, the new medium may become more dominant but, in the early stages, it acts as an addition to the media environment rather than a replacement. Also, the new communication medium can incorporate all the previous media but the reverse is impossible.

All of the above are true for the Internet. The Internet allows access to marketing, advertising, public relations, and internal organization communication information on a 24-hour basis, on a global scale, at the speed of light. And it provides an informational platform that reaches out to a multiplicity of audiences. The Internet offers organizations of all kinds strategic communication value not heretofore available. This is especially true for organizations marketing products or services.

The Internet has strategic value for marketing and selling products and services because of its ability to provide transactional communication: accessing product or service information, evaluating that information, making preliminary or final purchase decisions, getting closer to the sale—in other words, electronic commerce.

Product and service information is available on the Internet at any hour of any day from anywhere in the world. In the case of FEDEX, for example, access to their Web site is not just about providing customers with information; it is about actual transactions. The Internet is especially suitable for delivering services that might be needed at any time. Yet, while many view the Internet as just another advertising, marketing, public relations, and internal corporate communications medium, it is actually a leap forward in communications. It is better seen as a platform for delivering products and services directly to the customer—for example, travel advice or reservations, customer account status, package location, or repair instructions, in fact, any kind of information with value to an existing or potential customer, supplier, government official, media person, and so forth. Another message of the Internet is that it is not just a one-audience medium: It cuts across many audiences.

REDUCING BARRIERS: HIGHER-ORDER DIALOGUE

The Internet is also about reducing the barriers between buyers and sellers. The reduction in the number of barriers between customers (consumers or business-to-business) and organizations (whether profit on nonprofit) has major ramifications in human resources terms. If it is indeed correct that the Internet, through the World Wide Web, reduces the number of people required to market products, then another round of layoffs could be in the offing. Perhaps.

Executives at FEDEX and General Electric addressed this issue. The thoughtful response was that, while a reduction in the number of ordering clerks might occur, what is more likely in the intermediate term is that 800-number clerks will be answering higher-order questions from customers. In effect, the Web site can serve as a communications vehicle for answering 80% of customers' basic questions so that, when the customer gets to the salesperson or the 800 answering clerk, the questions are of a higher order and closer to a sales context. It is likely that the salesperson function will continue to exist, but the conversation, the dialogue between customer and salesperson, could be on a higher level.

DATABASE MANAGEMENT

An Internet Web site raises database management issues. As Rich Costello at General Electric points out, it's one thing for an expert 800-number clerk to access the corporate database when dealing with a customer; it's quite another for that database to be made directly accessible to a customer via a Web site. Frank Scudder, formerly with US WEST, pointed to the problems of enabling legacy systems to talk to each other so that information "buried" in the older system can be accessed by salespeople. Internal organizations have a major task in taking existing databases and massaging them into viable vehicles for use at a Web site. But the payoff can be enormous.

ORGANIZATIONAL COOPERATION

When external barriers between an organization and its customers come down, a similar effect is felt internally. For those organizations that have begun to use the Internet, almost universally there has been a higher level of cooperation among disparate departments, a level not heretofore recorded in the annals of organizational success stories. Because the Internet characteristically provides in-depth information to a multiplicity of audiences 24 hours a day, management information systems people are now talking more frequently with people in marketing and sales who are, in turn, talking more often with public relations and corporate communications people. The Internet provides a communications environment in which isolated departments now see the strategic value of talking to each other.

SECURITY

Marketing products and services on the Net raises security issues. Securing credit card transactions on the Internet is still a major concern, although IBM and Sun Microsystems have introduced software packages that claim to obviate this problem. Many still remain to be convinced, although this issue may fade away with time as more and more consumers begin to use the Internet for purchases. Still, though, the Internet is primarily about accessing information, not purchasing product and services. For the near future, the security issue will not stall the growth of the Internet, but it may temporarily stall the growth of financial transactions on the Net.

CONDUCTING BUSINESS ON THE INTERNET

Commercial use of the Internet today is largely a big business phenomenon. Perhaps we should not be surprised. When videotape first became commercially available in 1956 (introduced at a Chicago trade show in April of that year), it was large corporations and organizations in the Midwest (such as Ford and Buick) that first glommed onto the new communications medium. But it was not until the introduction in the United States of the ¾-inch U-Matic videocassette in 1972 and the VHS format a few years later that medium-sized and, ultimately, small organizations started to use the medium. What made the difference is that the cassette was standardized, portable, and relatively inexpensive. In the last two years, it has been the large companies, with their deep pockets and internal resources, that have experimented on the Net. As time moves forward though, and as the Internet becomes more commonplace, medium-sized and even smaller companies will gravitate to the Net in larger numbers.

The other message is that already successful companies will continue to be successful in the Internet communication medium. For example, while Time-Warner's Pathfinder Web site attempts to convert its popular site (30 million hits per week, $800,000 in ad fees) to a for-pay site, a host of organizations are setting up Web sites to reach out for customers, such as American Express Company's Internet travel site (www.americanexpress.com/travel), and NASDAQ's www.nasdaq.com, designed to create an online trading community. Meanwhile, the innovative DealerNet now boasts 700 dealers signed on, with 500 online and with hits creeping up to the 7 million a month mark.[1]

The counter argument to this scenario is that the Internet levels the playing field: Small organizations can compete with much larger organizations in the world of electronic commerce. The argument doesn't hold up in the real world. The truth is probably somewhere in between. Let us not forget that it was the commercial availability of satellite transponders that allowed a small outdoor advertising company run by a precocious and visionary Ted Turner, who bought long-term leases on several transponders, to create one of the most successful cable companies in the world. Yes, the Internet can level the playing field but only for those with the vision to take advantage of the formative nature of the medium, along with the talent and tenacity to stay ahead of the rising tide.

Overall, there are two parts to the electronic commerce experience: marketing to consumers, and business-to-business marketing. First, a look at the former.

RETAILING IN THE ELECTRONIC COMMERCE ENVIRONMENT

One indication of the rise of electronic shopping, or one-on-one direct marketing, is the growth of the electronic home shopping market. According to Kevin D. Thomson, writing in *Your Company*, the magazine for small business owners, more and more women in the 35- to 54-year-old age range are doing a chunk of their shopping from the comfort of their living rooms.[2] With phone and credit cards close by, they're looking for convenience and unique new products. The volume of sales indicates that electronic home shopping is in vogue. By 1994, industrywide sales had grown to $2.8 billion, up from $2.5 billion in 1993. Sales are expected to reach $100 billion by the year 2000.

Steven Kernkraut, John Balaskas, and Mark Picard, retail securities analysts at Bear, Stearns & Company, express an optimistic perspective on the Internet as a viable complement to, but not a replacement for, existing retail channels.[3] They look for home shopping as a retail industry subsection to attract much attention over the next few years as the Internet and interactive services become more of a reality. In their view, the Internet is developing faster than its detractors want to believe. Many in the 18- to 25-year-old age group use the Internet daily, and the Bear, Stearns analysts see a rapid transition as content becomes more interesting and less data-based. They also state that more catalogs should transition from the printed page to the interactive. They say this $60 billion industry will become more reliant on the interactive world, which will enable it to lower marketing and circulation expenses and, finally, to adjust prices on the fly, much as a retail store currently marks down goods. Under the present format, catalog retailers need to mail out sale books in order to lower prices.

Kernkraut, together with Pamela Abramowitz, in an earlier analysis of home shopping on the Internet,[4] make an even stronger statement: "For retailers, we believe developing a site on the Internet's World Wide Web will become a strategic imperative." They explain that as the baby boom generation moves beyond its prime spending years, retailers are looking toward the next generation (the so-called Generation X) to enter its thirties. This group is more technologically savvy than its predecessor and spends much more time on the computer. Kernkraut and Abramowitz argue that retailers who are to remain competitive over the long run will need to develop exciting, interactive Web sites to tap into this market. Moreover, it is relatively inexpensive to create a Web site, opening the door to significant cost savings that could be passed on to value-conscious consumers.

The Bear, Stearns analysts further point out that PC-based shopping has a number of advantages over traditional forms of home shopping. Chief among these is its ability to be directed by the consumer. Among the criticisms of cable-based television shopping is its linear format, which requires consumers to watch a program until they see something they want to buy or tune in at specific times for scheduled programming on particular products. Interactive computer technologies, they point out, put consumers in charge, giving them the ability to search for specific items, to browse through specific categories or merchandise areas, or to sort the data by any specification they choose.[5]

In addition to pointing to the primary motivation that online shopping can be more profitable for retailers, the Bear, Stearns analysts underscore the concept that the Internet reduces barriers between customer and organization. "Because the Internet is an amorphous and unregulated entity," they state, "there is no gatekeeper. Therefore, retailers do not have to negotiate deals with, or share profits with, a third party." The authors again argue that the relatively inexpensive costs of creating a Web site should encourage retailers.

CHALLENGES TO THE PACKAGE GOODS COMPANIES

On December 20, 1995, the 2nd annual Tenagra Awards for Internet Marketing Excellence were awarded to the Federal Express Corporation, Yahoo!, NetPOST, Software.Net, Virtual Vineyards, and RAGU. The Tenagra Awards for Internet Marketing Excellence are announced each December to recognize innovative and significant successes in the Internet marketing industry. Award nominations are made and discussed by a diverse panel of internationally recognized Internet marketing experts, and final awardees are selected by the Tenagra Corporation.

RAGU Spaghetti Sauce (http://www.eat.com/) was selected because of the company's online marketing and brand awareness campaign, which is both useful and entertaining. Their online presence has effectively allowed them to gather customer opinions and collect valuable information about market trends. The apparent success of RAGU's external Web site must be seen in the context of the package goods industry's use of the Internet. The Internet is a one-on-one, electronic medium not seemingly à propos for the marketing of package goods to a mass audience. On the contrary, the Internet (likewise the World Wide Web) is more appropriate for business-to-business marketing.

Nonetheless, package goods companies such as RAGU have begun to explore the Internet for its marketing value. For example, more than a year after Ed Artzt warned marketers to wake up to the potential of new media, Procter & Gamble is finally showing it intends to practice what its former chief executive preached. Procter & Gamble has asked its brand managers to present ideas for setting up individual sites on the World Wide Web for about a dozen of the company's packaged goods. In what amounts to an internal review, the company is expected to select five brands and construct Web site venues for each.

Artzt, now chairman of the executive committee of P&G's board, sounded his clarion call in a speech last year at the annual meeting of the American Association of Advertising Agencies. Since then, the company has revealed little about its new media plans. Thus far, P&G has produced but one Web site, an online art cafe for its new men's fragrance, Hugo, created by Grey Interactive, which handles the company's Giorgio Beverly Hills fragrance business and is P&G's lead agency for interactive media. The site, launched in October, taps into the popularity of poetry competitions, although it does carry some product information.

The Web project may be only one of many interactive moves the Procter & Gamble company will make public in 1996. It is believed that P&G's silence on new media masks much behind-the-scenes activity and expect the firm to announce, by early next year, at least one new media alliance, perhaps with a Hollywood studio. Even if such a deal is signed, P&G will find itself in the unaccustomed role of playing catch-up. The Bristol-Myers Squibb site, devoted to women's concerns and integrated with product information, is the sort of new media initiative observers expect from P&G.

Unilever has created one Web site, the well-received venue for RAGU spaghetti sauce, and Colgate-Palmolive has not yet entered the fray, though it is expected to launch a site targeted to kids.[6]

The RAGU Web site, together with those of P&G, Colgate-Palmolive, and others, is symbolic of the overall need of the retail industry to take itself out of the doldrums. On February 14, 1996, for example, Wal-Mart announced that it intended to create a Web site to sell products over the Internet. On January 11, 1996, retailers as diverse as 13-store Petrini Markets on the West Coast and 150-store

Pathmark Stores in the East are finding common ground in a new Web site called the Supermarket Connection, which serves as a conduit to various retailer and brand manufacturer home pages. In addition to Pathmark (Woodbridge, NJ) and Petrini (San Rafael, CA), other retailer participants in the project include Shaw's Supermarkets (East Bridgewater, MA), Byerly's (Edina, MN), Scolari's Food & Drug (Sparks, NV), and Cub Foods (Lithia Springs, GA).

The Supermarket Connection Web site (http://www.shopat.com/) contains links to RAGU's home page, as well as those of Coca-Cola, Nabisco, Frito-Lay, Hershey, Perrier, and Snapple. A hot link to a site developed by Ben & Jerry's is also included. Retailer Web sites linked to the Supermarket Connection also contain a broad array of retailer-specific information, including store locations, company history, and weekly specials.[7]

The strategic problem for package goods companies is this: How do you sell toothpaste on the Net? The answer is: You don't. You sell the company, you sell the image, you sell information, you sell interaction with the consumer, you sell purchasing decisions. For larger, more expensive items, such as a refrigerator or a car, the strategic decision is the same: You sell the company, you sell the image, you sell information, you sell interaction with the consumer, you sell purchasing decisions.

SELLING HARD GOODS

The Toyota USA Web site is a good example of an online marketing strategy that sells not only information about its product (cars) but also a relationship with the prospective customer. The Toyota USA Web site started in December 1994 with a request for proposal (RFP) sent out by Toyota's advertising agency, Saatchi & Saatchi. The RFP described a Web site that was really nothing more than an electronic brochure for Toyota USA but also asked for ways to include some kind of material that would keep people coming back.

Novo Media Group, one of three firms invited to respond to the RFP, suggested that Toyota use its Web site not as the electronic brochure described in the RFP but, instead, as a tool to develop a relationship with customers and prospective buyers. To do this, Novo Media proposed using two distinct content areas—Toyota car and truck information, managed by Saatchi, and a lifestyle section, managed by Novo Media. The proposed lifestyle section included six "destinations" designed to appeal to the demographic and psychographic groups for key Toyota brands.

Arno Harris, President, Novo Media Group also suggested keeping "a very large boundary between [the lifestyle information] and the advertising and product promotion that was on the site," allowing the Web site to "present these things as independently published magazines that Toyota was sponsoring." A final and key element of Novo Media's pitch was its custom Web site traffic-monitoring software. That software tracks everything a visitor does while at the Toyota Web site and can even track repeat visits by the same person.

Toyota has found that 56% of its owners have access to a PC and that some 80% of luxury-car owners use a PC.[8] Most of the car and truck information, for example, is aimed at Toyota owners or people considering a Toyota car purchase, but the Car Culture section aims more broadly at people who want to learn how cars work. The other six lifestyle sections have been designed to appeal to "a target audience very similar to the demographic and psychographic groups that Toyota establishes for each of its models."

The IBM and GE Web sites (see case studies) are also representative of a successful use of the Internet. The IBM Web site, while full of computer product information, is nonetheless highly public relations in orientation and tone. The GE Web site seeks to combine a variety of objectives. Clearly a purveyor of hardgoods—from window fans to jet engines—the Web site is designed to accommodate the needs of consumers, businesses, and so-called others: the press, students, even prospective employees.

Collectively, all these sites offer access to information so that a visitor to the web site can make a tentative or firm purchase decision. In one sense, the purchase decision is about an individual product; in another sense, the Web sites help a visitor to make an emotional purchase decision about the company that perhaps, in the longer term, will result in sale.

BUSINESS-TO-BUSINESS MARKETING

While some Web sites, such as those of RAGU, Toyota, and Colgate-Palmolive, are designed specifically for consumer visitors, some sites, such as those of GE and IBM, are designed for both consumers and business-to-business customers. Others, though, are designed specifically for business-to-business customers, such as CHIAT/Day and FEDEX.

The TBWA CHIAT/Day Idea Factory Web site launched in February 1995. It includes press releases, white papers, and examples of agency creative output. It provides a showcase for client projects and is a tool for conducting online surveys and online focus groups. The Web site was originally conceived as a way to demonstrate CHIAT/ Day's creativity, establish the agency's credibility in new media, provoke the visitor's interest, and attract talent. Least important was the site's potential to generate qualified new business leads. The CHIAT/Day Web site was supposed to show clients what could be done with new media. Now that the site has demonstrated that it can generate sales leads, however, prospecting has become a significant objective for the Web site.

CHIAT/Day's own employees are another key audience for the Web site. Jay Chiat was quoted in the May 22, 1995, issue of *Interactive Age* as saying, "The biggest issue is that this agency should be comfortable in this world [the Internet]—everyone from creative [staffers] to our accounting department. We want everyone to become conversant with Internet technology." A survey section targets more specific audiences by asking respondents to identify themselves as a journalist, advertising professional, or surfer.

The FEDEX Web site (see case study) is not only a marketing site, it is also, according to company executives, the place where they want customers and prospective customers to do business. One of the company's strategic goals is to see its Web site become the place where most, if not all, of its customer transactions take place.

It is a toss-up whether consumer-oriented Web sites or business-to-business Web sites dominate the Internet scene. In the intermediate term, it is probable that business-to-business will prevail for two reasons: (1) The rapid expansion of internal organizational Web sites (so-called Intranets) will foster increased organization-to-organization transactions; (2) the commercial portion of the Internet in terms of domain names is the largest, a reflection of the strategic value of interorganizational communication via the Internet. In the longer term, as more consumers gravitate to the Internet through either online services or directly through an Internet service provider, and as electronic commerce security issues are solved (at least, perceptually), consumer-oriented Web sites will catch up with the electronic commerce trend.

WEB SITE COSTS

A caution here. In a December 1995 Forrester Research study, John Bernoff and Andrew Ott reported the cost of a promotional site at $304,000 for a year, $1.3 million for a content site, and $3.4 million for a transaction site. The Forrester Research report also concluded that future site costs would increase between 52% and 231% over the next two years, depending on site type. Bernoff and Ott explain that "The demand for skilled site staff, new security and interactive features, marketing efforts, and increased server capacity and bandwidth will drive these increases."[9]

The various executives interviewed in the case studies in this volume tend to agree with these figures. On one end of the scale, most companies initially spent between $100,000 and $300,000 on a Web site, while General Electric, at the other end, claims to have spent over $2.5 million on redesigning its external Web site. Of course, in various media nooks and crannies, one can find a Web site designer to create a simple Web site for less than $100, while other vendors will charge between $500 to $1000 to set up a site.

It is believed that Procter & Gamble will spend heavily to produce and promote its Web sites. Each venue will have a production budget of about $300,000. By comparison, some prominent commercial sites, such as one for Saturn, have been launched for as little as $20,000. Procter & Gamble is said to have budgeted as much as $8 million to promote its sites. With the many advertising banner opportunities available in new media, it is likely that some funds will go to creating links throughout the Web to Procter & Gamble venues.

The cost of creating a Web site is much like the cost of buying a car: You can spend somewhat less than $5,000, or you can spend $250,000 and more. *The New York Times* reported last year that the average start-up Web site for a mid-sized company was $2,500, including two to three home pages and an ordering form.[10] It depends on what an organization wants and what it needs. But you always get what you pay for. Critical, though, to any marketing Web site is that, whatever it is or whomever it belongs to, it must have a clear, strategic vision.

NOTES

1. Business Research Publications, *Report on Electronic Commerce*, April 16, 1996 pp. 4-12.

2. K.D. Thomson, "Cashing In on the TV Home Shopping Boom," *Your Company*, Feb./March 1996, pp. 19–25.

3. S. Kernkraut, J. Balaskas, and M. Picard, *Retail Quarterly Equity Research*, Bear, Stearns & Company, April 12, 1996, p. 35.

4. S. Kernkraut and P. S. Abramowitz, *Home Shopping: Make Way for the Internet*, Bear, Stearns & Company, Sept. 8, 1995, p. 3.

5. Ibid, p.4.

6. C. Taylor, "P&G's Slow Journey from Soap Box to Web Brand," *Adweek*, Dec. 12, 1995.

7. *Supermarket News*, Jan. 1, Jan. 11, 1996.

8. B. Johnson, Crain Communications Inc., 1995, Oct. 16, 1995.

9. J. Bernoff, A. Ott, "People and Technology Executive Summary: What Web Sites Cost," Dec. 1995.

10. L. Saslow, "For Business, Internet Can Open Marketing Doors," *The New York Times*, June 25, 1995.

CHAPTER 4

FEDERAL EXPRESS

fedex.com
2005 Corporate Avenue
Memphis, Tennessee 38119

Our ultimate goal? To have 100% of our transactions come through some online media ... the Web obviously is that very powerful tool to make that happen.

—Winn R. Stevenson, Vice President
Network Computing

We now know that more than 60% of the people who track packages on this Web site would have called customer service had there not been this resource available to them.

—Robert G. Hamilton, Manager
Electronic Commerce Marketing Group

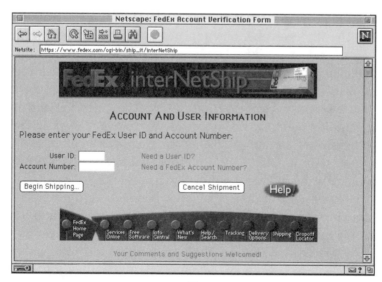

INTERVIEWEES

The Technology Executive: Winn R. Stevenson,
  Vice President-Network Computing

The Marketing Renegade: Robert G. Hamilton,
  Manager, Electronic Commerce Marketing Group

The Technology Renegade/Webmaster: Susan Goldener,
  Internet Technology Manager

THE STRATEGIC VISION

Winn Stevenson, Vice President-Network Computing, elaborated on the company's strategic vision of its Web site: "What's our ultimate goal? It would be to have 100% of our Federal Express transactions come through some online media, so all transactions are done electronically and the Web obviously is that very powerful tool to make that happen. For one thing, it's got a worldwide reach, so anything we do, any minor change we make, a new feature or function, is almost instantly made available worldwide. For another, it allows us to have a presence on desktops, in parts of corporations that we never had access to before."

INTERNET FOCUS AT THE SENIOR LEVEL

Stevenson pointed out that, given the technology tradition at FEDEX, the Internet phenomenon not only continues to infiltrate the FEDEX hierarchy but also receives strong attention from top management. According to Stevenson: "The Internet is an incredibly intense focus at Federal Express. We've got departments with titles like Internet Technology and Internet Engineering and we've got a standing meeting of senior executives every week where we discuss the Internet and electronic commerce as a common opportunity. At that meeting are the CIO, Sales and Marketing and Customer Automation and a division called LECC—Logistics, Electronic Commerce and Catalogs—their business is to provide logistics functions and to help catalog market growth and create electronic commerce. They're all represented at this meeting, and we talk about strategies and directions. There are somewhere between 25 and 30 people in the room. Hardly anybody has a title lower than director."

THE INVESTMENT

According to Robert Hamilton, Manager, Electronic Commerce Marketing Group, the investment to launch the Web site was surprisingly little, compared to what a lot of other companies face, because FEDEX had a lot of the resources internally and the IT infrastructure already existed from years of doing Power Ship: "It was really sort of a next step for us rather than a first step and, by best reckoning, it took us less than $100,000 to get this Web site up and operational.

"There's a line item for my marketing department and the network computing department that has people dedicated to this resource now. But a good many of the things that are features on the Web site were initially developed for other platforms as well or will be generalized to other platforms so, frankly, the development occurs out of different buckets and we kind of repurposed it as needed for the Web site."

FEDEX: A TRADITION OF FIRSTS

Federal Express Corporation began operations in April 1973 and, on the first night of operation, a fleet of 14 Falcon jets took off with 186 packages. Ten years after start-up, Federal Express reached $1 billion in revenues, becoming the first U.S. business to achieve that status without mergers or acquisitions. Federal Express was among the first express transportation companies to realize the benefits of technology. As early as 1978, the company pioneered the first automated customer service center. To provide real-time package tracking for each shipment, FEDEX uses one of the world's largest computer and telecommunications networks. The company's couriers operate SuperTracker, hand-held computers, to record the transit of shipments through the FEDEX integrated network. Its use of technology is further differentiated by a focus on the customer rather than merely all possible locations along the delivery route on-site through the use of either Power Ship terminals or FEDEX tracking software.

Today, FEDEX is the largest express transportation company in the world, handling millions of packages and documents every night. FEDEX aircraft, which constitute the world's largest all-cargo fleet, have a combined lift capacity of more than 15.3 million pounds daily. In a 24-hour period, FEDEX planes travel nearly 500,000 miles. FEDEX couriers log 2.5 million miles a day, the equivalent of 100 trips around the earth. In fiscal year 1995, revenues totaled US$9.4 billion. Total employees were approximately 120,000 worldwide, serving 210 countries.

www.fedex.com

The FEDEX Web site launched in late 1994. Self-described zealot Robert Hamilton, inside the Marketing Department, and another zealot inside the Network Computing Department at FEDEX, Susan Goldener, Manager of Network Computing, were the two primary individuals who originated the site as a standalone Web site. An online presence already existed on America Online. The evolution of a standalone Web site grew out of FEDEX's development and rollout of its FEDEX Ship software. According to Hamilton, one of the things the company did initially as a distribution mechanism was to start evaluating the online services. But, to their surprise, Hamilton's group found that FEDEX's technical group already had a FEDEX Web site up with some basic facts and figures about the company and some boilerplate PR and a great big "under construction" sign. Hamilton recounted: "We're talking about September, October, of 1994. Frankly, the issue of getting an Internet address and owning the domain and those kinds of things had already been taken care of."

The original function of the FEDEX Web site was typical of what many organizations started out doing: using it as a site primarily for experimentation and for outreach to their counterparts in other companies within FEDEX to understand the implications of browsers and TCP/IP stacks. Hamilton added: "We hit the ground running and, in essence, agreed on some basic things we could do to repurpose some existing code for access via the Web site. We were able to hit the ground running probably in December 1994 with this tracking application."

The current FEDEX Web site opens up with a simple home page, where the surfer has to scroll down simply to arrive at the options available. For a period preceding the Olympic Summer Games, which were held in Atlanta, there was a banner entitled Atlanta Summer Info. Several options are listed, including: Services Online, Free Software, Info Central, What's New, Help/Search, Tracking, Delivery Options and, last, Your Comments and Suggestions.

Atlanta Summer Info. This banner was clearly a temporary addition created for the enormous amount of traffic that would be going through Atlanta in the summer of 1996 for the Olympic Games combined with information about FEDEX's involvement as a sponsor of the American team. Atlanta Summer Info offered FEDEX's Atlanta shipping centers sorted by location, information about U.S. customs regulations, an opportunity to sign up for service, a map showing FEDEX-staffed shipping and drop-off locations, general shipping information covering FEDEX's efforts to provide a level of consistent service despite traffic problems during the games. Additionally, there was e-mail registration regarding business operations during the Olympic events between July 19 and August 4, 1996.

Services Online. In this section, a visitor may choose from a variety of options, including: "Track your FEDEX package wherever it originated, and wherever it is headed. If it has been delivered, you may find out who signed for it. If it is still in transit, you may find out its current status in the FEDEX system." The second choice on this site explores FEDEX delivery options and explains the full range of FEDEX services available, with emphasis on the company's service commitments. Last, there is free downloadable software that can be used to prepare time-definite packages, verify them online, print bar-coded shipping documents on your own printer–no airbills need to be completed manually anymore. This could offer customers more convenience as they will no longer need actually to contact the Web site, which could also decrease traffic.

Info Central. This is actually the main home page and includes important sites such as: Who is FEDEX? with a description and background of FEDEX, Customer Service Information, a help desk where representatives can be e-mailed, press releases that offer up-to-date articles regarding FEDEX Corporation, interesting FEDEX fun facts, and FEDEX services.

FEDEX Learning Lab. The FEDEX Learning Lab is dedicated to helping companies maximize strategic distribution. The goal of the Learning Lab is to provide a registered customer with a rich learning experience, allowing visitors to move around the site, increasing their knowledge base and satisfying their need to know. The Learning Lab offers the following helpful tools:

Case Studies. ■ Short, problem/solution-formatted, customer-benefit focused reports demonstrate how distribution solutions can affect real customers in real situations.

Glossary of Logistics Terms. ■ Provided by *The Management of Business Logistics* by Coyle, Bardi, and Langley, this resource keeps the customer up-to-date with all current buzzwords, theories, and concepts. This area can be considered a personal information agent, ready to serve the user 24 hours a day, seven days a week.

Value Analysis. ■ This feature examines how distribution can affect a business and its customers' businesses by looking at success metrics familiar to the user.

WEB SITE PROMOTION

Winn Stevenson pointed out that the FEDEX Web site practically promotes itself: "One thing about the Internet that has fascinated us is that we put the home page up and we put the tracking application on the home page and we never advertised it. In fact, to this day, we really have not advertised that capability. And, before we could even turn around, we were exceeding a million hits per month on the home page and exceeding 15,000 tracks and traces a day. Without saying anything, just by putting up a dynamite home page, we were getting a lot of transactions that would have come through 800 numbers and would have come through other customer service means. They're now coming to the Internet, and we never said boo about it."

THE ECONOMIC RAMIFICATIONS

There are numerous actual and potential economic ramifications from FEDEX's Web site strategy. The first actual ramification is that a significant portion (although still a definite minority) of customers use the Web site to conduct business with FEDEX rather than using the company's 800 number. If this practice could be pushed to the limit, the Web site could save FEDEX millions of dollars annually. Further, if the FEDEX Web site does not convert all its customers to working on the Web site, at the very least, those customers who choose the 800 number as a way of doing business may talk to a live clerk who can respond to higher-order questions. The GE Web site described in this volume has a parallel strategic objective.

According to Hamilton, "We can't find the dip yet in the customer service call volume only because the orders of magnitude are different. Customers now track about 20,000 packages a day at the FEDEX Web site. The customer service organization across the nation takes 300,000 calls a day. We just finished some research and we now know that more than 60% of the people who track packages on this Web site would have called customer service had there not been this resource available to them. That's quite a new finding. It's really exceeded our assumptions." The research was conducted for a week online and then corroborated with offline, telephone-based research to the audience of people who were tracking on the Web site.

There are potential staffing impacts. If FEDEX can reduce customer reliance on the 800 number and increase use of the Web site for transactional communication with customers, this could eventually lead to a reduction in the need for 800-number operators and shipping clerks—to what degree is uncertain. We need to remind ourselves that, in the 1970s, many organizations were drooling over the prospect of reducing their administrative staffs as a result of purchasing mainframe and miniframe computers. Of course, this didn't happen. As *Megatrends* author John Naisbitt has pointed out, the most common job in America today is "clerk." At one time, it was laborer; previously, it was farmer. It is also a fact that, while many mid- to large-sized organizations have downsized in the last 10 years or so, employment in America has never been higher. As Patricia O'Connor Wilson and I iterate in *The Breakdown of Hierarchy: Communication in the Evolving Workplace* (Butterworth-Heinemann, 1997), the jobs of tomorrow will require higher-order skills and expertise, and people with only a high school diploma may want for even a labor-intensive job—if, indeed, there are any. The question then becomes: Is the FEDEX and General Electric Web site experience leading the way to reducing reliance on 800-number clerks while Web site staffs grow internally to handle the increased traffic and business that is transacted on the Web site? The perspectives offered by the Web site leaders at FEDEX tend to underscore this scenario.

Hamilton perceives that the Web site has had, and will have, several impacts, including higher levels of customer service and the development of more electronic tools: "I think that the audiences who find this technology useful and who are able to use it will continue to grow and, at some point, I would expect that we could find in the trends and our customer service call centers the impact that this Web site is having. I think it will get that big over the next couple or three years.

"I think it's a win-win as far as customer service is concerned, because, obviously FEDEX's business overall is growing, and so the last thing we're about to do is to outsource any people. I mean, we're not going to lay off anybody as a result of this, but it lets the customer service people focus on the higher-leverage interactions with customers. If customers are willing to use this tool for doing the routine status queries about their package and eventually even the shipping of the packages, then, when they do call customer service, they've got something that needs some attention and some human interaction, and that frees up the agents from taking tracking calls. So I expect we'll maintain high service levels for a long time, with the agents focusing on this dimension."

Stevenson pointed out that FEDEX expects its Web site to contribute earnings in several ways: "Electronic transactions are cheaper than human transactions. So, we see that anytime we can reduce the calls to customer service or reduce humans doing business, just like banks do with ATMs—anytime we can reduce that interaction, we've improved our bottom line. The next thing that's going to happen, we think, is that the Internet is going to encourage electronic commerce. Electronic commerce is good for Federal Express because that means packages moving from a supplier to a customer and we certainly would like to take advantage of that opportunity. The growth of the Internet theoretically implies a growth of electronic commerce, which implies growth of packages moving, literally, around the world, which is another positive business growth opportunity for us."

Another ramification of the FEDEX Web site is the enormous opportunity not only for saving expense dollars but also for reducing reliance on paper for transactions. This tree-saving measure is also a potential reality for companies with Intranets: for doing away with all those forms, forms, forms!

DISSEMINATING CONTACT THROUGHOUT THE CORPORATION

As a direct result of its technology-driven tradition, FEDEX has provided hardware and software to customers to enable them to do business with FEDEX, to create the labels, and to provide the tracking and tracing. About 65 to 70% of FEDEX's volume is processed through these devices. By having an Internet presence to do shipping and other activities, every desktop in a corporation theoretically has access to it electronically. Says Stevenson: "So I don't have to (a) provide hardware or even software, and (b) I've got a presence throughout a whole corporation basically, assuming they are already on their own Intranets. The Internet allows everybody to have a reason to interact with Federal Express and the electronic means to do that, be it inquiring about a package status, sending us an information request, and even shipping with us. So they do not have to go to a physical place somewhere else in the corporation to do that. They can now do that at their desktops."

FEDEX doesn't have a hard and fast penetration timetable, but Stevenson says that if, by the year 2000, 90+% of transactions are done through electronic means, it would consider that a very successful long-term Web site strategy implementation.

THE EVOLVED STRATEGIC VISION: ELECTRONIC COMMERCE

The FEDEX Web site now has three basic functions: first, as a resource for customers who are ready to do business with FEDEX utilizing the online presence; second, as a showcase for talking about, showing, and making available FEDEX electronic commerce tools for other people who are doing their own electronic commerce applications; and, third, as a communications vehicle about new services, new enhancements, and changes to service for customers and prospects.

Electronic Commerce Tools. According to Hamilton ,"As for the overall site, I think, for the next 18 months or so, the site's objectives as a resource will continue to be where you see the majority of activity. There's so much of what we consider to be low hanging fruit inside the company in terms of applications and functions that we could accomplish from the Web site. We've got quite a set of activities going on to put things on the site that are truly useful and interactive. Eighteen months from now and from then out for another couple of years, you'll probably see the showcasing of FEDEX electronic commerce tools as the most active dimension of the site because, as more and more companies find value in being on the network or as more and more companies develop Intranets for their own use to stitch together not just their own employees but their own suppliers, their own vendors, their own customers, then the use for some of these applications, resident on an Intranet for some customer, is going to be immensely important."

The Intranet Impact. Hamilton continues; "Not a lot of companies are deeply connected inside their enterprise to the public Internet. Issues of security or just not having gotten around to it, or whatever it might be, right? There tends to be a core of people, usually those involved in their own Internet activities that can get to the Internet from their desktop at the office and beyond a point there's not a deep set of connectivity. Consequently, a lot of employees in those companies—we're talking fairly large companies now—a lot of those employees who would be able to get closure on what the status of that shipment is can't because they don't have a way to get to the Internet.

"If we had our tracking application sitting resident on an Intranet of that company, well, then, all employees can get to their own Intranet or will be able to soon. There are no security issues at all. They're inside the firewall. So, that's a way to extend applications to the enterprise as a whole in one fell swoop. And I'm not just talking about tracking, which doesn't produce revenue for FEDEX. It just delivers better customer service. Think for a moment about the ability of an entire enterprise to ship FEDEX packages by interacting with the browser and a set of forms and our server rather than having to find airbills and having to understand what the rules are for filling those out and all that kind of stuff. So, suddenly you've got an immense use of the tool with immense research that takes FEDEX all the way to the mind of the person who put the contents in the box. If you think about this from the marketing point of view, it's one thing to be able to streamline the activities of a shipping dock manager who has lots of packages to ship that day. It's quite a different matter to get to the person who put the contents in the box where the issues of FEDEX and reliability and brand and global and all these other attributes of our company come into play directly in their choice of who they'd like to ship it by. This is a tool with tremendous reach and a resource to help those people who are now doing airbills."

INTERNATIONAL REGIONAL SERVERS

FEDEX is clearly a global company, with a very strong presence in the United States and, obviously, internationally. But how does it deal with the issue of somebody shipping from Saudi Arabia to the United States? How does it deal with the differences in culture and language? Says Hamilton: "I guess we have to go a generation at a time in terms of features for our Internet Ship application. At the moment, again, just to get something out there and begin to get some customer learning on it, the features that it has are U.S. domestic features only. In its next generation, it will have U.S. export capabilities, and it will have intra-Canadian shipping available through it. And, from there, we, in effect, chart a course to one tier at a time, adding functions to it that will enable it to be a global tool for the various regions, so it's probably a generation or so out from there that we would be able to have anyone ship from any point to any other point that we serve and have all those issues coordinated by the application itself."

Does FEDEX see the potential for having, in effect, regional servers in the Middle East, in Europe, and in Central and South America? Hamilton answered: "Very much so in conceptual terms.

At the moment, it's still the primary advantage in terms of maintenance, and additional development and so forth call for having the
server here in the headquarters where the critical mass of talent is
for that. But, as this medium becomes more and more important for
customers all over the place, then scaling this up and having sub-
ordinate servers in the regions is still on the drawing board."

THE EVOLVING WEB SITE

Stevenson comments: "One of our goals would be, in essence, to
make available information that our customers need concerning
the business relationship, be it billing information, shipping information, any other information that's important between two corporations, and to make that information accessible to our customers
through the Internet. Then customers can access the information
through their computers in their own time frames—obviously with
a security blanket around it so it's available only to them."

Is FEDEX going to have a closer, one-to-one relationship with its
customers? According to Stevenson, "Absolutely, that would be the
goal. The closer we get—we can apply the term AT&T uses—the
more we can "entangle" our customers. That's the Federal Express
story: information—that's the cornerstone of our product. The
information aspect of our business has always been as important
as, if not more important than, the actual service we provide. We've
hammered that home from Day One and we've created a very sophisticated infrastructure of technology to support our products."

THE INTERNET AS A COMPETITIVE TOOL

FEDEX believes that their Web site has put them light-years ahead
of their competitors in terms of using the Internet as a competitive
tool. Says Stevenson, "I would say that we're in another galaxy. One
of the reasons is that, three years ago, we went to a client/server
technology on some of our customer automation PowerShip systems with a product called PowerShip 3, which is your classic
client/server and, doing that, going through that exercise—even
though we didn't realize it at the time—positioned us to make this
bold move on the Internet. With all that client/server infrastructure

already in place, putting this home page up was like a two-week job, including hooking up the tracking routines. I think our competitors are still struggling with the infrastructure problem."

Stevenson pointed out that one of the payoffs of extending FEDEX's Web site will be reaching their customer's customer, with a win-win result: "Because our customers are using the Internet, we are helping our customers be more successful with their customers. We hope we're going one or two steps further down the food chain here and enabling more things to happen because of our Web site."

CHAPTER 5

GENERAL ELECTRIC

ge.com
320 Great Oaks Office Park
Albany, New York 12203-5965

It's the equivalent, at a more sophisticated level, of an ATM machine, where customers spend their time and energy finding the answer to the question themselves rather than having our people do it. Of course, we've got to have the right database.

—Richard A. Costello, Manager
Corporate Marketing Communications

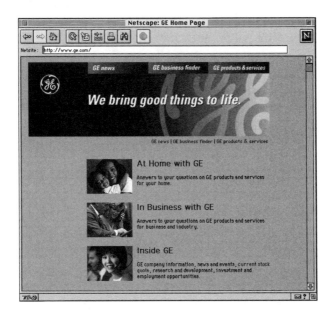

INTERVIEWEES

The Renegade: D. Richard Pocock,
General Manager, Marketing Communications, GE Plastics

The Executive: Richard A. Costello,
Manager, Corporate Marketing Communications

The Internet Program Manager: Susan Moyer

The Webmaster/Designer: Alberto Blanco,
President and Founder, META4 Design

Author's note: Susan Moyer and Alberto Blanco were interviewed prior to the re-design and relaunch of GE's external Web site on April 15, 1996. Richard Costello and Richard Pocock were interviewed following the relaunch. The Moyer interview was conducted by Neil Ruggles.

BACKGROUND

Based on year-end 1995 data, General Electric generated revenues of $70 billion and net earnings of $6.753 billion ($3.90 per share). The market value of GE stock (at $78 per share) was $132 billion, the largest in the world. Exports from the United States totaled $9.2 billion; international revenues were $26.9 billion (38% of consolidated revenues). GE's total assets were $228.035 billion. Today GE is a diversified technology, manufacturing, and services company with a commitment to achieving worldwide leadership in each of its 12 major businesses. General Electric operates in more than 100 countries around the world, including 250 manufacturing plants in 26 different nations; it employs 222,000 people worldwide, including 150,000 in the United States.

THE ORIGINAL GE WEB SITE

It is probable that GE's experience with the Internet is senior to most companies in the United States. According to Richard Costello: "The original GE Web site really was a cross-routes thing that happened out of a combination of our plastics business and our corporate R&D center. Our corporate R&D center has been on the Internet for many years because it uses their research organization and a government contracting research organization. Corporate R&D was involved in the Internet back in the very early days when it was a defense mechanism."

IN THE BEGINNING: DEFINING MEANINGFUL COMMUNICATIONS CHARACTERISTICS

In more recent times, the father of the GE Web site is D. Richard Pocock, General Manager, Marketing Communications, GE Plastics. According to Pocock, in late 1993 and early 1994, there was a growing feeling that the rate of change of communications technology was phenomenal and yet GE Plastics was continuing to communicate with customers in very traditional ways and with media that they had used for decades. Pocock recalls: "We began scratching our heads here, saying, 'There's got to be something better.' The first temptation was to go out and talk to customers and ask them to look at an array of media and find out which ones they favored. What we did is speak to more than a dozen customers face to face and ask them not what media they preferred but what were the characteristics of communications that were most important to them. And when we said communications, we were talking essentially about how they capture information."

THE RELATIONSHIP BETWEEN PRODUCT AND INFORMATION

Pocock elaborated on the nature of the GE Plastics product line and the importance of information to customers: "GE makes quite a portfolio of what's called engineering thermoplastics, and that term applies to those polymer families that tend to be higher-performing materials. In the spectrum of plastic materials, it ranges from commodities that are relatively low-performance, low-price materials up to some exceptionally high-end materials. We tend more toward the higher end. The reason I think that's important is that higher performance brings along with it higher price. It's critically important that an engineer designing a component select the right material. There's no point in overengineering and paying more for the performance of the material than you really need. So it becomes a fairly technical, information-enriched process. People need a lot of technical data when they go to select engineering plastics and obviously when they design a part and process that part."

THE THREE CENTRAL COMMUNICATIONS CHARACTERISTICS DEFINED

Speed. From the customer research process, Pocock's group identified three central communications characteristics that customers wanted: "They said speed was important. They didn't want to have to wait long. We've always prided ourselves on how our inquiry fulfillment center and our product support team always Fedexed information out, and we always felt pretty good that information always went within a day and arrived within a day after that, so that the longest a customer ever waited for printed information was two days. Yet, to our surprise, a number of people said two days can seem like an awfully long time—so speed was important.

Accurate Information. "The second thing that they pushed for was the accuracy of the information. They wanted to make sure it was current data because we have a fairly dynamic product and, if you pull a catalog off a shelf that's been there for three years, in all probability there could be products that are no longer made and a host of new products that aren't reflected. So they wanted to make sure they were viewing the most current database.

On Their Terms. "And they wanted it on their terms regardless of their time zone or wherever they might be around the world or what time of day or day of the week it was. They wanted to be able to get it.

"Those were the three characteristics that came back to us time and time again. They were pretty self-evident. I mean having asked the question and gotten the answers, it certainly made sense, and I can't say there were any great surprises. But, at least, it focused us in on looking at what media could deliver to those three characteristics and, to us that meant the World Wide Web."

LEADING THE CHARGE

At this juncture, Pocock's group took a proactive stance and decided to take things a step further: "We took an informal poll and found out that very few of our customers were actually able to access the Internet, but it just seemed to us to make so much sense that we took a bit of a leap of faith and said, 'If this medium can deliver the capability that we think it can, it's just a matter of time before people migrate to it.' We also thought we'd rather lead the charge than follow, so we made a commitment in August 1994 and to my amazement, two months later in October 1994, we held a press conference in New York City and announced that our site was being made public on that day. We started off with about 1500 pages of technical information." At this point, the GE Web site was 95% GE Plastics content; the balance was other corporate content.

THE INITIAL RESOURCE COMMITMENTS

At the outset, GE Plastics had several pluses going for it in terms of the resources needed to mount this Web site effort. Pocock recounted that GE Plastics was fortunate to be a part of a company that's rich in resources. There was some internal expertise at the corporate R&D facility in Schnectady. In Princeton, New Jersey, computer hardware and software were available through an internal MIS group. And the cost was very little. The major expenditure was contracting and paying a content provider to take some of the digitized files and many printed pieces of literature, convert them into electronic documents, and embed the HTML code. Pocock also indicated that Joyce Rupport from Marketing Communications and GE Plastic's ad agency of record, RT Blass, of Old Chatham, New York, also worked on the original Web site. In turn, the agency introduced GE Plastics to One World Interactive in Steventown, New York, which also worked on the Web site. Pocock estimated that GE Plastics went from start-up through the first year of the project for less than $100,000.

INITIAL EXPECTATIONS AND CONCERNS

While the Web site presence made a lot of sense to Pocock's group, there was concern about how quickly the target plastics industry would gravitate to the Internet: "We toyed long and hard with the idea of what we would do. Did we want to just put up a bulletin board? Did we want to jump straight to a CD-ROM and live with the pros and cons of that medium? We really had no way of knowing how quickly the Internet, the World Wide Web, was going to be adopted, and it was kind of funny. At the press conference, we were asked by a couple of reporters and editors, 'You seem to have a very strong edge on your competition. We assume you don't look forward to the day when all your competitors have done the same thing.' Our response was that we'd wished they would and we wished they'd do it right then. We felt that the more legitimate this medium was seen to be by our customer community, the higher their interest in moving to it would be and, clearly, if all the other thermoplastic resin producers followed suit, there would be a pretty compelling proposition for our customers.

Rapid Adoption. "In hindsight, the thing that has surprised me is that, by all appearances, customers have migrated to the Internet at an amazing rate. We looked at some data from a publishing company, which had surveyed design engineers who specify a material of some kind—not necessarily a plastic, maybe an aluminum, but that was the population that was sampled, and this goes back to about August 1995. That survey said that 11% of the respondents had regular access to the Internet. In March 1996, we made a survey of engineers among our customer population, and 68% said that they were on the Internet regularly. That seemed to us to be pretty impressive."

THE ORIGINATORS' STRATEGIC VISION: THEN AND NOW

Not untypically of most companies that launch a Web site, Pocock observed that GE Plastics' initial strategic vision of the Web site was narrower then than it is today: "I think we've learned some things along the way. We looked at it very, very narrowly. Initially, we said, and we still do say, that we're on the Web for a very specific purpose. We're not there to appeal to the world. Our content is directed to appeal specifically to people who have a vested interest in the utilization of engineered thermoplastics. That hasn't changed. But, back then, we saw a Web site primarily as a service to our customers to make technical information easily available to them, and I think, over time, what we've learned is that it can fulfill that purpose very handily, but that the power is much greater than that.

Interaction and Dialogue. "We can make the Web site far more interactive than we originally dreamed and, in doing so, make it a more powerful marketing tool. We've done things to try to attract people to the site for the sake of beginning some dialogue with them. For example, we originally had about 1500 pages of technical information. The total number of Web pages now is approximately 3000 but the site is made up of not just technical data. We have added things like some elementary polymer education.

Training Content. "It's our intent in 1996 to add much more sophisticated education and training material, the kind of thing that would be incorporated into a vocational technology curriculum, and the reason we want to do this is that our customers have told us, time and time again, that one of the greatest constraints on their growth is finding the entry level manufacturing talent that it takes to run a plastics part manufacturing facility.

Virtual Reality Tour. "We have put up a virtual reality tour of our living environment's concept house, which we built in Pittsfield about six years ago at considerable cost, many millions of dollars. That is a facility that is meant to demonstrate the credibility of using plastics in many nontraditional building and construction home environment applications. People tend to think of this as the all-plastics house, and that's the last thing it is. Where we like the aesthetics of wood, we use wood; where wallboard makes sense, we use wallboard, so it's not an all-plastics house, but we're proving the viability of a lot of design concepts in this house, and it's a stimulating structure. It's visually exciting. It's kind of a dream house in many ways, so now what we've done is we've made it possible for people to tour that house and to witness the applications of our materials via the Web.

Showcasing Leadership. "We're featuring the house because it's a way of showcasing our leadership within the plastics industry—

it's a way to continue to pioneer and innovate and break new ground. We will be doing the same thing for the automobile. That is work in progress right now," Pocock stated.

THE EVOLVING STRATEGIC VISION

As with many Web sites that start with a narrow focus, and sometimes no focus at all, the GE Web site very quickly evolved into a much broader application with a specific strategic vision. Richard A. Costello, Manager, Corporate Marketing Communications, reviewed the evolution of the strategic vision of the GE Web site from the time of its initial launch in October 1994, particularly with respect to the relative decentralization of the effort: "In late 1994 and early 1995, we were suddenly beginning to see first GE Plastics and then a number of other businesses primarily driven by our technological capability to be on the Web. Different businesses were acting as somewhat independent agents with really no coherent overall strategy. One business was using it for selling, another for a tour through its application center, which was really just a demonstration of what could be done on the Web without any kind of driving, strategic marketing focus."

Technology and Marketing Talk to Each Other. The process through which the GE Web site began to evolve is also typical: At some point, a content group and a technical group gravitate toward one another in the realization that they must work together to make an Internet Web site succeed. Costello observed: "We started seeing a lot of activity ad hoc, bottoms up and driven from a variety of different operating businesses, with a variety of different objectives. At that time, our technology people who run our telephones and who actually own the technology of the site and the service came to me and said, 'This thing is beginning to get out of control from our perspective. It's difficult for us to manage. We're not in the business of marketing and yet we've certainly got this thing here that is beginning to look and smell more like a marketing tool than it is a telephone line or a computer site.'

"So I took a look at it. At the same time, our plastics division, the people there who were using it probably more strategically than anyone else, and who perceived it as a customer, communications, and relationship-building tool, said, "Look, that's what we're trying to do, but we don't see anyone else doing it. Are we out of sync or are these other businesses missing an opportunity?"

The Coordination Begins. "At that point we regrouped and got together a number of players and said, 'O.K., what do we want to do?' Out of that discussion and a quick look around at best practices—although there weren't very many at that point in time, we're now talking early '95—the consensus was that there clearly was an emerging technology here that could be both a marketing top-line growth tool if we used it right and a tool for providing service to existing customers, and information particularly to existing customers, that would improve our productivity in serving them.

A Marketing *and* a Customer Service Tool. The managers at GE also realized that the Web site could appeal to a multiplicity of audiences: "Those two underlying concepts started us down the path of developing the site. The other thing we did was to look at the way customers deal with us through other communications mechanisms, particularly our telephone call centers and to ask ourselves, 'What are they looking for and what do they request?' What we found when we looked at the data, at the GE answer center in Louisville, Kentucky, and our GE business information center in Albany, New York we asked them, 'Who comes to us, why do they come to us, and what do they ask?'

Customer Perceptions. "Out of that, we learned that the first and foremost thing customers want when they're dealing with a huge company like GE is one single source. The customer coming into General Electric from the outside doesn't perceive it as this division and that division, one located here, one located there. It's all just GE.

"The way we designed our telephone centers is to preserve that perception. Behind the scenes we are integrating lots of data and resources. To the customer we are putting on one face and one number and one person who, at least in theory, can get access to whatever resources the customer is seeking."

Integrating the Databases. Costello added: "We've got 12 operating divisions and somewhere between 50 and 70 businesses clustered within those 12 divisions. So, within them, there's a huge amount of human and technical resources that we can serve a customer with. Part of the problem is that the customer may come in and say, 'I want a replacement motor,' and he has a model number and that's all he knows. Well, it takes some knowledge of our organization to know who can help him to provide that replacement motor and, in fact, depending on what size it is and what the application is, there are probably five or six different service places in the organization that we could send that person to. So, we try to do all that research ahead of time. We have a relational database supporting our customer center in Albany that essentially has much of the data in there that we've collected over the years, and so, when that customer comes in, the agent on the phone can say, 'Okay, give me that number and where you reside and what the application is. Then the database tells the agent what questions to ask, and it can give them the answer. Oh, yes, send them to such and such a place and talk to Charlie. We have that sort of intelligence that we've built up inside the company."

Migrating the Database to the Net. "So we said, well, if people are phoning and that's what we do for them, that certainly seems to us a beginning point for what they might want on the Net. And, if we can get them to answer their own question interfacing with the Net, and if it has that level of data, we get rid of a phone call and we get rid, ultimately, of human resources involved in managing that call. The process is automated. It's the equivalent, at a more sophisticated level, of an ATM machine, where customers spend their time and energy finding the answers to the questions themselves rather than having our people do it. Of course, we've got to have the right database."

THE PERCEIVED PRELAUNCH STRATEGIC ADVANTAGES

Prior to the relaunch of the GE external Web site, Susan Moyer, Internet Program Manager, General Electric Global Marketing Communications Network, elaborated on the perceived strategic advantages of the Web site: "The whole world is beginning to realize that the Internet is becoming critical, and we looked at it as really the first new medium to emerge since the '40s. When you take a look at the penetration rate of both television and the telephone over the course of the first 30 years and extrapolate the Internet over its initial existence over the same 30 years, it actually can grow to reach a larger base.

Cost Reduction. "But we also look at it as having several basic advantages—one obviously is cost: delivering material, literature, printing, distribution, and storage in a different way and not spend a lot of money. Second, there is the timeliness and the ability to change things very easily and quickly.

"Also, we're looking at it as a cost reduction in the area of our telecommunications and customer service centers. We're thinking that the type of information we want to provide is the type people would call into our customer service centers for. That was the basic strategy for the skeleton of the site.

Relationship Advantages. "We're working with the businesses to develop added value applications like order tracking, dealer locators, and distributor and customer support packages and, then eventually, when we figure out how to get this whole commerce thing straightened out, that hopefully will become a reality.

www.ge.com

On the GE home page, the user has numerous elaborate options available, starting with a banner that graces the top and offers: GE news, GE business finder, or GE products and services. Underneath it is an option entitled At Home, where one is able to send questions to GE representatives about products and services that GE offers for the home. Second, there is In Business with GE, a place where visitors can learn how to make a profit with GE, locate GE distributors in the area, ask about training and education services, or get help from a GE Customer Service expert. Third, there is Inside GE, which offers company information, news and events, current stock quotes, research and development investment, and employment opportunities.

GE News. In GE news, there is a list of news releases going back a year and updated to the present day, all of which can be accessed immediately with a click of the mouse. Most of the news comes in the form of short, concise articles about any issue relating to the corporation.

Business Finder. In the GE business finder, located next to a skyscraper graphic, one may access any of the many GE subsidiaries, including GE Aircraft Engines, GE Appliances, GE Capital Services, GE Corporate Research and Development, GE Electrical Distribution and Control, GE Information Services, GE Lighting, GE Medical Systems, GE Plastics, GE Power Systems, GE Supply, GE Transportation Systems, and NBC. NBC.com is, not surprisingly, a huge site by itself.

At each of these locations, it is almost like entering a totally new and separate Web site. There is the same banner as the original home page with the original three options of news, business finder, and products and services, and then a list offering the choices: Who We Are, A History of Innovation, Continuing the Tradition, and GE Brand Name.

At the bottom of the page is a list of GE's most successful products/appliances: GE Monogram, GE Profile, GE Appliances, RCA, and Hotpoint, all of which can be explored in depth. Additionally, there are Consumer Services, Global Activity, and Contact Option.

Who We Are offers a brief description of each subsidiary and what services they offer to the consumer. A History of Innovation lists chronologically GE innovations and product discoveries. Continuing the Tradition is a current look at new GE development and products, emphasizing the technological and other advantages of GE products. GE Brand Name offers a glimpse at what the GE name means and how consumers perceive that name.

GE Products and Services. In GE Products and Services, there is a product finder for the consumer called GE Answer Center and, to answer other inquiries, there is the GE Business Information Center. At both locations, one may purchase a service contract, schedule a service call, or order parts and accessories from GE.

In conjunction with GE Products and Services is At Home, where one can select any GE product, see a full listing of GE products, and find out where to buy these products. Also, one can save money with rebates and special offers, read about warranties and service contracts, access product literature, research financing and credit options, and watch NBC httv.

Inside GE. In Inside GE, one can participate in the GE Trading Process Network for suppliers, discover corporate research and development, find out about the GE Fund, locate a GE employee, and obtain information on the GE Fund grants. Additionally, one can explore GE's corporate identity standards and locate information about GE retirees.

Much can be accomplished on the GE Web site, and it should be no mystery to anyone who has visited the site why GE is one of the standard setters in the relatively new Intranet communications medium. For the consumer, business, and employee alike, this site accommodates many needs and offers information that previously would often have been unattainable or, at the very least, difficult to obtain. It is apparent that GE must also be saving money through this site and that it will gain new customers in the process, regardless of location and demographics because these factors will not be issues on the Web, once it becomes fully integrated.

Further, although GE is in the hard goods business and FEDEX is in the transportation of packages business, both companies' Web sites have similar strategic objectives: to encourage customers to do business at the Web site and make higher-order buying decisions there. While General Electric is slightly over 100 years old and FEDEX is a relative newcomer to the billion dollar company list, both companies have evolved a strong management system and a clear strategic vision for their respective Web sites. In GE's case, the strategic objective long term is to raise the level of customer decision making, whether at the consumer buyer, or business-to-business level. The clear-thinking managers at GE understand that many customer questions can be answered by a well designed Web site, so that, when the 800-number customer service call is made, the customer is closer to a buy than not. Again, there are human resources ramifications. But GE is reluctant to say that a Web site can reduce its call-center staff. Nonetheless, from the interviews, one comes away with a strong sense that CEO Jack Welch's reputation for effective, strategic decision making is well deserved. Throughout, GE looked before it leaped into the Internet in a corporate strategic way through its Plastics division. And even though the results were not especially scientific and in-depth, GE Plastics took a leap of faith into Internet technology based on the belief that it was going to provide a strategic advantage on a broad range of competitive objectives.

RESULTS: HIGH-QUALITY QUESTIONS; CLOSER TO TRANSACTION QUESTIONS

On April 15, 1996 GE relaunched its Web site.

Costello described the initial results from the newly configured Web site. One significant response is that the quality of calls to the phone centers has risen: "We have some very preliminary data from the phone centers as to two things: the number of questions coming in—we've seen a slight uptick—and the quality of the questions, which has improved substantially. It appears that the data we've been able to put onto the network is absorbing a lot of what we would consider lower-level, lower-value questions. So the site has been able to provide answers to the basic level of questioning that people have. People calling the phone centers are asking higher-level questions, and closer to transaction completion questions."

PROMOTION

GE's experience with promoting its newly redesigned, relaunched site is similar to FEDEX's—in effect, both companies did not do much promotion or advertising. Nevertheless, people are finding the sites and using them. Costello reported: "There was an initial surge, and it's dropped back to a somewhat higher level than before. But we also haven't been promoting it heavily. We basically just slid this thing onto the Net, took the other one off, and sent out a press release.

Featuring the URL. "What we're beginning to do is get our advertising and other promotional materials to start featuring the URL, and that will either be the overall URL or an individual business' URL. It depends on what communication we're doing and with whom, but that has really only just begun. In fact, I'd say it really hasn't started even now, and television commercials don't have it on yet, but we wanted to have this thing up, and we wanted to get it operating effectively before we really started doing more active promotion of it, so I would anticipate that we are going to start seeing a steady increase in traffic over the next six to twelve months, an increase that's faster than the growth rate of the Net.

THE FUTURE OF THE GE WEB SITE: MORE TRANSACTIONAL

What kinds of results is GE expecting to go forward in the next six to eighteen months with this current Web site?

Toward More Transactions. According to Costello: "I think the first thing is that we're going to make it more transactional. I think one of the things we're looking for—this is the very, very beginning—on the top line gross side, is to find ways to make it transactional. I think this is going to come initially from our business-to-business businesses as much as it will come from our consumer businesses.

The Intranet Factor. "The reason I say that is what we're observing is that many of the businesses we're dealing with are quickly shifting themselves to their own Intranets for internal communications. Once you do that, you also get access to the external Net, and so you're getting very high levels of penetration. To give you an example, *Design News* did a study of plastics and design engineers about the third quarter of 1995, and they were reporting about a 15% penetration of the Net among engineers. They did a similar study in the first quarter of 1996, and the penetration rate was up to 60%. I did a check of my own function's penetration, in other words, the people who do the marketing communications inside GE. A year ago this month, there was less than 10% penetration of access. I checked last week and we had about 80% to 85% penetration.

"Because of Intranets, businesses are something that you can penetrate at relatively high levels, and I think we're seeing that in certain segments. I think Intranets are going to be very, very rapidly disseminated, so that suddenly a medium that was penetrating at 10%, 15% now has 80%, 90% access to your customer groups, at which point it becomes a very, very viable alternative distribution mechanism to paper, telephone calls, catalogs, telemarketing, and the other things that we're using other than traditional distribution systems.

"I know there are a number of our businesses that are exploring moving to a much more a transactional mode, often with an access code at the beginning. It won't be open to the public. It will be open only to approved customers, but that, I think, is going to occur quite rapidly, both in our traditional manufacturing businesses and in probably some of our service-oriented businesses at GE Capital."

POTENTIAL IMPEDIMENTS TO GROWTH

Bandwidth and Behavior. Despite the sanguine scenario, Costello also pointed to two of the common misgivings about the Internet: "On the business side, I think it's two things. Speed is a real problem. It's what you can get down, and how quickly it loads down. The other problem, which I think is more profound, is behavior. I've got this thing sitting on my desk, and it was really neat the first few weeks that I had it. And now I'm not going in there very often. And so, one thing I'm skeptical about is whether people are really going to change behavior and become more reliant on the Net.

The Quality of Content. "I think it's going to be completely dependent on the quality of the data involved, and my suspicion is it's not going to be clever promotion stuff. I think it's going to be real nuts and bolts transactional value. For example, which I'm picking out of the air ... let's say I'm in the traditional advertising business, I'm buying air time, if there was an electronic marketplace out there for buying air time, I think that would be very appealing for people who are in that game, but just seeing promotional literature from NBC or even being able to access CBS's schedule electronically is vaguely interesting. But if I knew that today's availability of air time, pricing, and actual transactions could take place real-time, then I think I'd use it. I think that's an analogy to what's happening with the brokerage houses, you know, there are a number of electronic brokerage houses out there. From what I hear, they're doing pretty good business, and I think what they're doing is they're offering a lot of transactional costs and immediate availability and letting the customer do much of the transaction themselves.

"You know there are a bunch of retired guys down in Florida playing with these things now, and hurting Schwab and Fidelity and all of the lower-cost guys who are now having to get on there and compete and undercut their own pricing through their more traditional low-cost mechanisms. That's one example of that. I suspect that is going to be a big deal. There ain't going to be more of that kind of glitzy, home page stuff. It's going to be much more nuts and bolts, real added-value. I think, unless there is real value on there, content value, and it isn't cute stuff, in fact, the page could look grungy for all I care. If it really was useful, I might be persuaded to get up there and get on it."

REDUCING LAYERS BETWEEN COMPANY AND CUSTOMER

Costello also commented on the Internet's impact on allowing a customer to access content directly, as opposed to working through the usual layers of salespeople and clerks: "I think that, in the best possible scenario, it gives a customer access to information direct and it gets rid of salesmen and transaction clerks, and it cleans up the whole process. Now, whether the business that is selling will allow that to happen is one issue, and whether there are robust enough and user-friendly enough systems to handle that is another issue. Sometimes the interface of a salesman or a telemarketing clerk was there out of necessity, which also created a nice buffer, so you could kind of edit and manage the information fed back to the customer. When it's unfiltered, your ability to ration availability becomes a little more difficult to execute. Suddenly, it becomes first come, first serve, and the guy who's good at manipulating the computer wins, whereas that customer may or may not be your most profitable or most desirable customer.

The Problem with Creating a Web Database. "With a database, it may be fairly primitive or difficult to operate. When you suddenly say, why don't we make that available to the end user, you have to make that incredibly simple and easy to operate and easy to understand and written in English and, in many cases, it means you have to redo the database, and that requires investment and both design and doing the front interface and all that stuff, and that effort requires money. I know a number of our organizations are not ready to do that. And they've got stuff that an expert can handle, but it's not designed in any way for a regular customer to get at."

ELECTRONIC COMMERCE: A SHRINKING DISTRIBUTION CHANNEL?

Susan Moyer also described how some of GE's businesses are looking forward to conducting electronic commerce through the Web site: "There are a couple of businesses that would like to be doing commerce on the Internet. One of our GE Capital businesses is creating what the client refers to as a consumer shopping network. One of our businesses is talking about selling parts eventually over the Internet. But one of the issues that we have is that when you've got a lot of sales channels and you know a lot of distributors, there are all kinds of marketing issues at middle layer within the sales process."

Moyer addressed the potential of the Web site to reduce the number of layers between the customer and the company: "I don't even think we've really begun to address these issues. But, for example, in the appliance businesses, we've got all kinds of appliance dealers. I don't even think I'd really want to say, or even insinuate, that we would be eliminating that—because I'm not in the appliance business obviously, and I'm not intimately involved with the business—but I know that when we talked with dealers initially, they said the real concern was that they have a very strong dealer network and what their real goal at this point was not just to start to sell stuff but to start to provide more dealer support, provide more product information, and help customers get a lot more information before they actually go to make their purchase. But I don't even think we've begun to address all those issues at this point."

CHAPTER 6
ADVERTISING ON THE INTERNET

AGGREGATE ADVERTISING SPENDING

Robert J. Coen, Senior Vice President, Director of Forecasting, at McCann-Erickson (speaking at a June 18, 1996 seminar sponsored by McCann, a unit of the Interpublic Group of Companies) projected that advertising spending in 1996 is expected to total $172.8 billion, an increase of 7.4% over Coen's final figure for 1995 spending of $160.9 billion.

Coen projected that the Summer Olympics and the elections should increase ad sales by about $1 billion. Coen's 1996 total breaks out to $101.7 billion in national advertising and $71.1 billion in local advertising. He also expected worldwide advertising spending in 1996 to reach $385.9 billion, a gain of 7.2% over 1995.[1]

INTERNET ADVERTISING SPENDING

Advertising expenditures on the Internet in the United States, on the other hand, are paltry compared to projected "billion dollar" advertising expenditures. Total World Wide Web ad revenue for the first half of 1996, according to New York-based Jupiter Communications (www.jup.com), was an estimated $71.7 million. Revenue for the second quarter of 1996 totalled $46.4 million, a relatively robust 83 percent increase from the previous quarter.

According to the AdSpend report, Internet advertising is on pace to total more than $312 million this year. Peter Storck, a senior analyst at Jupiter Communications and editor of the monthly AdSpend report, says, "Revenues for advertising are on track to reach Jupiter's projection of $5 billion a year by 2000."

The AdSpend report added that while some 600 sites offered ad space, the top ten collected 66 percent of all ad revenue. Twelve publishers drew more than $1 million in the second quarter of 1996.

Netscape led all Web sites in ad revenue for the quarter, taking in $7.7 million. Eighty-one percent of Netscape's revenue came from the five search engines now paying $5 million apiece for a year of featured buttons. Second to Netscape in ad sales were four of those five search engines: InfoSeek, Yahoo, Lycos, and Excite. Four content companies (producers of mainly information and/or entertainment) made the top ten, including c|Net, ZDNet, Newspage, and ESPNet SportsZone.

Most of the ad spending continued to come from a relatively small number of advertisers, the top ten accounting for 31 percent. The number one advertiser was Microsoft. Netscape, Microsoft's arch rival in the battle for browser market share and a major reason for its high ad spending, ran fifth among banner buyers in the second quarter, though a closer second for the first two quarters combined.

A solid half of the top ten Web advertisers in the second quarter were the five major search engines, largely because of their major buys on Netscape. Although tech related ads still dominate cyberspace, non-computer related consumer product advertisers accounted for 14 percent of spending in the second quarter.

Table 6-1 Top Ten Online Advertisers (as of end of June 1996)

Rank	Company	1st Half Spending
1	Microsoft	$2,905,742
2	InfoSeek	1,772,652
3	Excite	1,850,173
4	McKinley Group	1,468,040

Table 6-1 (continued)

Rank	Company	1st Half Spending
5	Netscape	2,172,901
6	Yahoo	1,339,998
7	Lycos	1,294,848
8	AT&T	1,735,668
9	c l Net	1,554,708
10	NYNEX	1,548,985

Table 6-2 Top Ten Online Publishers (as of end of June 1996)

Rank	Site Name	1st Half Revenue
1	Netscape	$9,664,490
2	InfoSeek	5,785,432
3	Yahoo	5,689,105
4	Lycos	4,123,229
5	Excite	3,641,044
6	c l Net	3,176,312
7	ZD Net	3,183,088
8	NewsPage	2,145,137
9	ESPNET Sports Zone	2,443,311
10	WebCrawler	2,160,000

A comparison between Jupiter Communications' latest report and an earlier report from late 1995 is significant. It identified spending by advertisers on Web banners and links of a mere $12.4 million in the fourth quarter of 1995. The company researched over 175 commercial Web sites that solicit paid advertising and identified over 250 active Web advertisers with media budgets for electronic ads ranging from $5,000 to over $500,000. There are now over 500 advertiser hyperlinks on the Internet. These advertisers include organizations in the following areas: apparel, business and financial, drugs and toiletries, foods and beverages, general and retail, home and building, and transportation, and agriculture.

Rich LeFurgy, Director of Advertising at Starwave (operators of the ESPNET SportZone site), believes that "1996 promises to be a watershed year as advertisers start to think more strategically about their Web sites and dedicate specific funds to ensuring broad exposure." Brian Gardenhire, Group Media Director of American Airlines, emphasizes his company's commitment to the Web but echoes the measurement concerns expressed in Chapter 2, namely, "In order for advertisers to be fully satisfied with the Web as an advertising medium, they will need to know far more about Web users and their habits."

Advertising via the Internet and, therefore, shopping for certain products and services via the Internet are natural next steps in the evolution of electronic home shopping. The state of advertising and shopping on the Internet is very similar to the state of advertising and shopping on cable television in the early 1980s. According to the National Cable Television Association, combined local/spot and cable network advertising revenue was $58 million in 1980, at a time when the number of cable television households was slightly under 20% of all television households in the United States. By the end of 1995, cable advertising revenue was $5.342 billion, and cable television households numbered slightly under 63 million compared to approximately 96 million television households in the United States. When we talk of large advertising revenues from the Internet, it is a matter of *when*, not *if*.

NET ADVERTISING: SOME OBSERVATIONS

According to a consensus of comments from several dozen interviewees in the advertising industry (online publishers, advertisers, traditional advertising agencies, interactive advertising agencies, measurement companies, association executives, and journalists), several broad conclusions that can be drawn with respect to the use of the Internet for advertising, as follows:

1. There are several Internet advertising tiers, in order of audience size: (1) the online services, especially

America Online; (2) the browser vendors, such as Netscape and Microsoft; (3) the search engines, such Infoseek, Excite, Lycos, and Yahoo; (4) the general interest content sites, such as Pathfinder, HotWired, and ESPN; and (5) niche-oriented content sites, such as Condé Nast Traveller.

2. The role of the advertising agency is being transformed by interactive media, and this transformation is accelerating because of the Internet. Successful agencies provide their clients with strategic planning advice, interpret Internet Web site traffic patterns for clients, and often act much like business partners of their clients. Agencies find themselves competing for clients with management consultants, planning consultants, information systems consultants, and even investment bankers.

3. While the Internet is about global access to products and services, Web sites are becoming increasingly localized—by language, presentation, and offers—within broad brand and corporate identity standards. International advertising agencies are well positioned to help clients deal with these localization issues and to help formerly regional brands use the Internet to enter global markets.

4. The Internet provides audience and traffic measurement potentials that do not exist in any other medium. The Internet is, in many ways, an extension of direct-response marketing. The experience direct marketers and direct-response vendors have constructing experiments and analyzing results provides them with a significant advantage in Internet marketing.

5. Internet audience measurement, however, is still volatile and requires a new set of parameters for measuring advertising effectiveness. Factors like search "robots" and page "caching" complicate the counting process, while the "stateless" nature of the World Wide Web makes it hard to link successive page views

with individuals visiting the site. Traditional players in the audience measurement business may not be able to adapt to the new information environment.

6. The development of advertising on the Internet parallels the development of the cable television industry in the United States in the early 1980s: Then, the media department allocated very small sums to the new television medium and was skeptical of its success. Today, a major broadcaster (like CBS, NBC, ABC, and Fox) is just another cable channel on the box, and advertising revenue is distributed across the entire cable channel spectrum. Similarly, the Internet is at less than 10% penetration in the United States. Advertising expenditures are minuscule compared to advertising dollars in broadcast, cable, magazines, and newspapers.

7. In 1995, Internet "ads" were most often paid for out of public relations budgets and, occasionally, from experimental or research and development lines of advertising budgets. In 1996, many advertising budgets explicitly include money for online advertising.

8. Internet advertising will not suddenly do away with traditional advertising, marketing, and public relations. The traditional advertising and interactive advertising worlds will coexist for some time. The best values from Internet advertising will be realized by combining Internet advertising with traditional marketing.

9. Traditional advertising agency creative and media departments rarely get involved with new media. Fierce competition for accounts has made agencies nervous about tinkering with any aspect of their successful teams. Therefore, existing account teams tend to stay focused on the media that have worked in the past for the client. Agencies must develop new media expertise either through acquisition (DMB&B, Einstein & Sandom), strategic partnerships (Messner Vetere, Free Range Media), or by building a separate

internal new media team (Ogilvy & Mather, Poppe Tyson).

10. At this time, the Internet advertising market is incestuous. The top Internet advertisers fall into several groups, all with a clear vested interest in the Internet. These groups are: (1) technology suppliers, such as AT&T, MCI, Microsoft, Netscape, and Sun Microsystems; (2) companies existing only online, such as HotWired and the Internet Shopping Network; and (3) companies extending their franchise to the Internet, such as c|net and Mastercard. These firms all profit from any growth of the Internet as a marketplace.

11. Like other direct-response media, Internet Web sites benefit from testing and feedback. In fact, analysis of Web site traffic patterns and use of this feedback to redesign the site will be more important to long-term success on the Internet than initial Web site design. This will be true for sites that provide ongoing business services to customers. The success factors for short-term Web sites, such as one created to follow the Super Bowl, will mirror the success factors for special events.

Other conclusions that can be drawn from the experience of advertising executives working on the Internet are that:

1. Print advertising is not effective for promoting online Web sites. Companies will back into traditional print media outlets for brand recognition purposes as time goes on, but not now.

2. Commercial Web sites do not use advertising agencies for placements of ads; so far, the traditional advertising agency does not have a place in this industry.

3. Commercial advertisers (Internet Shopping Network, SportsLine) occasionally use an advertising agency to help design an ad, but usually advertising for the Internet is created in-house.

4. The Internet directories (like Lycos, Yahoo, Infoseek) and the browser home pages (like Netscape) appear to be the most effective sites.
5. Call-for-action banner ads seem to be the most effective advertising approaches.
6. Web sites are using various ways of measuring advertising effectiveness: hits, page views vs. clicks, serving an ad from their own server, and so forth.
7. Companies are spending $100,000 to $150,000 a month on advertising but are asking to test a potential advertising Web site before signing on.

ADVERTISING FORMS

There are different kinds of advertising opportunities on the Internet—banners or billboards, keyword-linked ads, miniature Web sites within Web sites, sponsored messages—and any Web site can host an advertisement of some kind. Clearly, though, not all of these sites have similar value. They fall into several broad categories:

ONLINE SERVICES: AMERICA ONLINE, COMPUSERVE, PRODIGY

Unlike most Web sites, the online services have subscribers. That means that they can closely track everything a subscriber does while connected to the service and can share that information with advertisers and content partners. Today, each of the three leading services—America Online, CompuServe, and Prodigy—has connected itself to the Internet and World Wide Web. America Online is the most aggressive in making the Internet accessible to its subscribers. It is also the largest online service, with over 6 million subscribers, and it has recently agreed to allow independent auditing of its traffic statistics.

BROWSER VENDORS: NETSCAPE, MICROSOFT, AMERICA ONLINE

All browsers link to a "home" site on the World Wide Web when they start up. Unless the user takes other action, the browser first links to its manufacturer's own Web site. Because most people do not change their browser settings, these Web sites therefore get "hits" every time anyone anywhere starts using that browser. However, many of these people either stop the browser before the complete home page downloads or immediately specify a new location. The demographics of these companies generally mirrors the demographics of the Net (except AOL) because the browsers appeal to all Net users. The best these sites can do is count and offer eyeballs to the advertiser.

SEARCH TOOLS AND GENERAL DIRECTORIES: YAHOO, MCKINLEY, ALTA VISTA, EXCITE, LYCOS

Because people have no way of knowing in advance what they can access on the Web unless they have taken a Web address from some source, most people go places by using a directory or search tool as a starting point. Some of these tools know who is using them, and some don't. They all get used by the whole Internet audience, so that their demographics mirror the Net. However, all search tools know what is being searched for. That means that they can let an advertiser display an ad to someone who has demonstrated an interest in a given subject—an industry, product, business, or even a competitor.

GENERAL-INTEREST CONTENT SITES: PATHFINDER, HOTWIRED, ESPN

These Web sites aim to appeal to the entire Internet audience and may or may not require audience registration. They often do surveys of some kind to find out who is visiting the site, and this provides audience information. These sites are much like an online service in both content, organization, and the way production is organized but lack the audience tracking capability of the online services.

SPECIAL-INTEREST CONTENT WEB SITES: CONDÉ NAST TRAVELLER

These Web sites are much like special-interest magazines in their appeal to specific audiences. These sites are a natural place to offer services to specific audiences, but the Web site owner may easily emerge as a competitor to the advertiser placing ads on the sites. The Web site owner could also become a business partner to the advertiser by offering not just links to the advertiser's Web site but actual transaction capabilities within the Web site. An example of this is the Condé Nast Traveller Web site. This site is built around magazine content. However, the interactive nature of the Internet allowed the magazine to easily create a kind of online travel agency to advise visitors what they might enjoy. This site might also make hotel and travel reservations. In fact, it is a natural extension of the site to do so rather than making a visitor traverse a link to another site to make the reservation.

When evaluating niche-oriented Web sites, advertisers should carefully consider the Web site owner's potential to compete with the advertiser for business. In some cases, it might be wiser for an advertiser to buy an interest in the Web site, become a sole sponsor, or develop its own competing Web site.

THE BLUR BETWEEN ONLINE EDITORIAL AND ADVERTISING

In late 1993, colleague Dr. Eugene Secunda, a highly experienced and knowledgeable media practitioner and consultant, expressed concern in an *Advertising Age* editorial[2] that the arms-length separation between editorial and advertising in the traditional media world had begun to blur in recent years. At HotWired, the first online publishing venue to offer banner advertising, the blur has become a focus. There is a deliberate attempt to meld advertiser goals with editorial content. Whether this melding ruffles the feathers of traditional journalists (or advertisers, for that matter) remains to be seen, if it matters at all. The HotWired mission is clearly not to imitate its print counterpart in the online world, although there are parallels in tone. It is probable that, over time, HotWired (along with the universe of other online ezines) will evolve a new journalism with new opportunities for editorial expression, as well as new opportunities for mercantile transactions piggybacking on this content. But seeing how it will evolve is difficult. It is far easier to see that the Internet publishing medium is following in the footsteps of every other medium that has preceded it. When print came on the scene, its first content was what people said. But, over time, the print medium evolved its own inherent communications characteristics, structures, and rules. Jumping forward to this century and the advent of talking movies, the print headlines read "Radio with Pictures." In other words, we tend to define new media in terms of the older, more established ones.

HotWired is one example of online publishing and advertising that will probably help define the new rules of journalism and advertising in cyberspace. For example, in the next few years, the ability to use the Internet and the World Wide Web for audio communication and then video communications will become commonplace as the Internet becomes ubiquitous and the technologies are improved and integrated. HotWired, with its leading-edge editorial and strategic bent, will surely be one of the first Web sites to employ these technologies. But we are still in the early stages, and it will be several years before the Internet reveals its full publishing and advertising personality.

NOTES

1. S. Elliot, "Forecast of Growth in Ad Spending Is Cut for a 2d Time," *The New York Times*, June 19, 1996, p. D7.

2. E. Secunda, "Ad-Editorial Wall Crumbling," *Advertising Age*, Oct. 4, 1993.

CHAPTER 7

HOTWIRED

hotwired.com
660 Third Street
San Francisco, California 94107

We want to own the MTV of the Web, the CNN of the Web.
—Andrew Anker, CEO
HotWired

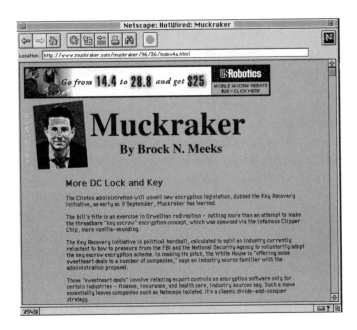

INTERVIEWEES

The Co-Founder: Andrew Anker, CEO
The Advertising Director: Rick Boyce, Vice President
The Senior Designer: Jonathan Louie

THE STRATEGIC VISION: LEVERAGING SUCCESS

HotWired's vision is to combine the leading-edge savvy, design, and editorial style of its sister publication, *Wired* magazine, with the multimedia, hyperlinked, interactive resources of the Web.

HotWired was co-founded by CEO Andrew Anker and Louis Ros-setto who, along with his partner, Jane Metcalfe, founded *Wired* magazine. Rossetto also serves as HotWired's Director of Programming.

Given the context at the time and the leading-edge, contemporary editorial content and style of *Wired* magazine, it seems almost a natural that *Wired* looked at the media horizon and said "Let's create an online publication." The decision, according to CEO Andrew Anker, "… to create another media product" was an economically strategic one. Based on a media smorgasbord analysis, online looked like the best combination of media outlets and development paths and the place where *Wired* could leverage its small resources into a much bigger presence.

The start date of the HotWired development project was April 1, 1994. The physical launch date of HotWired was October 27, 1994, about seven months later. The objective at the outset: "To become a dominant media brand in a new media space." Anker—who also holds the title of Vice President, Interactive, at *Wired*—was hired to map out HotWired's construction. To help finance its development, in late August 1995, HotWired sold 15% of the company to a number of large investors, such as WPP, which represents Ogilvy & Mather, J. Walter Thompson, and Hill & Knowlton.

Two years after its 1994 launch, HotWired membership had grown to over 430,000 registered members as of 31 August 1996, and it boasted a staff of over 125 reporters, editors, designers, and ad sales personnel.

BREAKING DOWN THE EDITORIAL VS. ADVERTISING BARRIERS

HotWired claims bragging rights as the premiere advertising site on the World Wide Web. According to Anker, it innovated the web banner ad format. In various ways, HotWired is the flagship of the Internet generation in terms of its daily battering of the politically correct. Its editorial tone smacks of anarchy. It is not in the mainstream in terms of traditional media, but it could very well be in the mainstream in terms of where the Internet is going journalistically with respect to the relationship between editorial style and content and advertising.

HotWired is an *ezine*—short for electronic magazine. Today, there are at least 750 ezines on the Net (according to the ezine database maintained by Otis Gospodnetic at www.dominis.com/Zines/, as of mid-July 1996), all of them advocating freedom of "the press." HotWired, though, with its advertising underpinning, is pushing the breakdown of the separation between the editorial side of journalism and the advertising sales function (see Chapter 4, "Advertising on the Net").

While Jonathan Louie, Senior Designer, is not directly involved in designing a client's ad, he is involved with ad placement, the size and dimensions of ads, and configuring relationships between the advertisers and HotWired's content. While it is gospel in traditional media that editorial content and advertising remain separate, at HotWired, this journalistic commandment appears to be dissolving. According to Louie: "HotWired pioneered the ad banner and it seems to have worked for us. But we're finding there is too much of a schism between the advertising and the concept, although there are times when it's helpful to have that schism, for instance, when you want to avoid a conflict of interest. But there could possibly be more of a partnership between advertisers and the content area of HotWired. It would have to be very judiciously worked out so that there is no conflict of interest and so that we have the reader's benefit in mind from both points of view. We haven't quite worked this out. But that's what we're questioning right now."

Louie elaborated on this issue: "For instance, in a traditional print magazine, the message of the advertiser doesn't always bene-

fit the reader. It doesn't bring anything to the content of the magazine. We're trying to resolve that so that the ads are more integral to
the site itself as we learn more about our readers, as we find out
what they're interested in."

In this context Louie pointed out that HotWired had just
launched the HotBot search engine. It works like this: Someone puts
in a query about skiing, for example. HotWired, when it returns the
results of the search, knows that that reader is interested in skiing
and can serve up a recreational equipment advertisement to go
with it. It's still using the ad banner model, but it's a more responsive, interactive use of knowledge about who the readers are. Louie
added: "We can also do that if we know they are coming to a section,
say, on medicine, when they come to "Ask Dr. Weil." We know what
it is they're looking for. We position the advertising but it's not
simply putting on a banner from, say, Squibb. We try to find a partnership with someone. Perhaps it's Squibb, perhaps it's the Envi-
ronmental Protection Agency—as long as there's a relationship that
benefits our reader and it's what we believe is in his best interest."

www.hotwired.com

Sustaining HotWired editorially has been a major hurdle. CEO
Anker compared the rigors of the online publication world to traditional print media: "It's very typical in things like magazines, where
issue 1 gets out great and issue 2 is dead. You get six months to sell
issue 1 and one month to sell issue 2. In HotWired's case, because
we're daily, we had six months to do issue 1 and a day to do issue 2.
So, the next step was not so much how do we build an initial product, but can we build an initial process that could then take us
through on a regular basis, adding more advertisers, adding more
content, and adding more subscribers?"

As a result of this strategic analysis, HotWired's editorial content
has evolved to reflect its executives' editorial and advertising vision. The HotWired home page opens with a great many choices to
click on, beginning with HotWired, Guide, Packet, Webmonkey, Netizen, Pop, Wired, Cocktail, Rough Guide, Talk, and Ask Dr. Weil, all
of which at first glance, seem foreign to the first-time visitor. After

some exploration, the content feels very contemporary, with an antiestablishment veneer:

HotWired. This section describes and lists the different departments and top executives at HotWired. The departments or central services include: editorial, design, production, audio, talk, engineering, administration, and advertising. Additionally, there is a list of those involved in the creation and general upkeep of the previously mentioned sites. Via e-mail, visitors can develop a direct interaction with the staff.

Guide. On this page, if you're a member, you have the opportunity to log on; if not, you may become a member free at this point. In this section you can choose from numerous sites dealing with issues regarding the Internet, a description of what HotWired is, other analytic news articles, Q&As, live chat, movies, music, a gallery, an index, and polls.

Packet. On Packet, the choices include Tools of the Trade, Net Surf, Market Forces, Muckraker, Fetish, and NetSoup. Tools of the Trade links the user to the AT&T Business Network which, in turn, can link the user to over 1,000 free business bookmarks. In the Flux category, there is the largest unnavigable archive site on the Web. Net Surf–Surf Central is a searchable collection of Web site reviews. It includes all the Net Surf reviews that have been published. A new site is added to Net Surf Central every weekday, and the collection is constantly monitored to make sure that everything served is worth surfing. If a site gets stale, or if its server goes down, the site is taken out and put in the graveyard, where old and tired sites are put to rest. As far as surfing goes, one may choose by keyword, adjective, genre, date, or title.

Netizen. In Netizen, or Impolitic, journalistic columns are updated every weekday. Plus, there are other columns that may be of interest to the politically inclined.

Pop. In Pop, the different sections include music, movies, gallery, books, multimedia. In each section, there are articles on the latest developments in each of these categories, for example, a review of a current movie or album, plus the option of reviewing older ones.

Wired. In Wired, there are more opinion articles to read and a banner ad for the Guggenheim Museum.

Cocktail. Yet more articles, this time about alcoholic beverages.

HOTWIRED'S ADVERTISERS

AT&T Consumer Products Division was HotWired's first advertiser, signing on in April 1994. Rick Boyce, Director of Advertising, recounts: "They were at the time, and continue to be, one of the biggest advertisers in *Wired*. We went to them and said, 'Here's the basic architecture of HotWired, and what we're going to do. You can have your pick of all these content areas. Which would you like?'"

In its first year of online publishing, more than 40 different advertisers have made use of the HotWired site, from Fortune 500 corporations like IBM and General Motors to emerging technology leaders like Xircom and Personal Library Software.

Automotive: Chrysler Corporation, Ford Motor Company, Nissan Motor Corp. USA, Pontiac, Saturn, Toyota Motor Company, and Volvo

Travel: American Airlines, Cathay Pacific Airways, Club Med

Financial: Wells Fargo Bank

Internet Services: Individual NewsPage, BBN (Internet service provider), Netscape Navigator, Netscape Server Solution

Technology: Adaptec, Adobe, Apple Web Servers, Hewlett-Packard, IBM Corporate, IBM OS/2 Warp, Metricom, Microsoft, Motorola Modems, Personal Library Software Time Warner (The Palace), Xircom

Telecommunications: AT&T Calling Card, AT&T Consumer Products Division, AT&T Business Services, MCI Developer's Lab, Network MCI, 1-800-COLLECT, Sprint Business, Sprint Corporate

Entertainment: RAI/SACIS (Italian public television), Sony Pictures (*Johnny Mnemonic*, *The Net*), 20th Century Fox (*Strange Days*), Ticketmaster

Beverages: Stolichnaya, Zima

Consumer Electronics: JBL Speakers, Toshiba TIMM

Online Retailers: eShop Plaza, Internet Shopping Network, Marketplace MCI

The ads found on the HotWired Web site also reflect the ezine's strategic vision:

Huntington Banks on the Web. The Bank has a banner that graces the top right side of the home page, next to two other advertisements, Kodak and Pointcast. When you enter this site, your choices include Huntington, Services, Huntington Web Bank, Tools, and Feedback. Each of these sections describe Huntington's services. Under Tools, there are ways in which you can calculate your net worth and create a retirement savings plan. In Huntington, they include the bank's mission statement and a description of the company. Plus, under Huntington Web Bank, you can set up an account and accomplish all banking business over the Internet.

Kodak. On Kodak's advertisement, at the top of the page, there is a graphic with a man holding a camera. It is called Scott's World. Underneath there are two choices, either DC20 Products or Shockwave Graphic. Then, there is a section called Welcome to My World, as Scotti introduces the visitor to the Kodak Webpage and the products. Additionally, at the bottom of the page, there are choices ranging from the Latest Episode, Past Episode, Scott Shows You How, Where to Buy, Win a DC20, and Picture Postcard S/W.

DC Product Info. At this site, the Kodak Digital Science DC20 Camera is marketed. After you look at the advertisement, if you want to locate the nearest Kodak dealer, there is an online search tool. Additionally, in regard to this product, there are more choices, which include Camera Specifications, Digital Camera Drivers, Frequently Asked Questions, Picture Postcards from NECC, Intro, plus press releases, which include how digital cameras give people a way to share pictures on computers.

Pointcast. On Pointcast, there are four choices: Download PCN, Products, Support, and About Pointcast. On About Pointcast, there is a company backgrounder. Founded in 1992, Pointcast broadcasts personalized news and information to anyone on the Internet. The Pointcast Network broadcasts

personalized news, stock quotes, weather, and more, directly
to your computer screen. The service is free. In Products,
there is more information about Pointcast, with opportunities
to download Pointcast, to find out about advertising, and to
see press releases.

SELLING AD CYBERSPACE

Anker described the ad cyberspace selling part of the equation,
with an emphasis on the differences and similarities between traditional media ad selling and cyberspace ad sales: "Our rate card is
$15,000 a month. In the print business, you gauge it with an eight-
page, four-page, half-page, quarter-page spread, but how do you
gauge it in terms of cyberspace? I think what advertisers are looking
for are really two things. And this is no different than any other
medium. They're wondering: How many people are going to see my
ad? And what's the quality of those people? What's the demographic, who are they, are they the right people for my ad? We've
designed around 15 advertising places where they're being seen by
a comparable amount of all the different advertising buys, and by a
representative sample across all the areas."

ADVERTISER VOLUME

Anker expects the advertising volume in 1996 to be at least double
that of 1995: "If we're at 15 advertisers now, I would certainly hope
we're at 30 advertisers, if not more, by the end of 1996 in terms of
gross numbers. We're doing a significant ramp up of the content of
HotWired. We're going to add a number of different channels, a
number of different places to advertise. Obviously, it depends on
audience growth, too. But, with the Web, you never know if it's going to be 100% or 1000% growth. So, it's a function of both of those
things. If we're getting 5,000 people today, and it's still only 5,000 a
year from now, then we're not going to add. But I would certainly expect it to at least double.

"We're not about a mass market audience, so I think I'm much
more likely to get a higher percentage of the current Web audience,
which is the early adopter, the opinion leader, than I am to get the

AOL people who are coming in. Now, having said that, I think there's a good chunk of the AOL people who are demographically similar. So I expect that the subscriber we have today is not going to be it, and we'll get some of the new AOLs. We've certainly seen a lot of hits from AOL, Prodigy, and CompuServe."

ADVERTISING REVENUES

According to Rick Boyce, Director of Advertising, "Our ad model is the driving revenue stream for HotWired, so we're interested in other potential ways to generate revenues. At this point in time ads remain the principal vehicle for us to make money, about 95% of our revenue. We do a little bit of retailing. For example, we sell *Wired* subscriptions, and *Wired* pays us a little bit of money for those. We sell some other things, like HotWired mouse pads and T-shirts and what not. It's not a big deal, but we're doing some retailing."

THE BANNER ADVERTISING FORM

Generally, HotWired's advertisers are using what has become known as the banner ad. Boyce described the rationale behind the approach: "I think that, right now, at this stage in this medium, the prevailing strategy is 'I want to drive traffic to my web site, so let me set up those gateways, so the people can easily click through it and arrive there.' I wonder sometimes if that's going to remain the strategy forever and, in fact, I doubt that it will. I think that advertisers will begin creating smaller, much more targeted pieces of communication that will reside within sites like HotWired, and the objective won't always be, let's drive traffic to my home page."

EVOLVING ADVERTISER STRATEGIES

According to Boyce, when HotWired first started, a lot of advertisers didn't have Web sites, or they had Web sites that had been created by the engineers, but marketing hadn't had a chance to put their thumbprint on it yet. Said Boyce: "Out the gate with HotWired in October 1994, we had a lot of advertisers that had, in most cases, messages designed just for HotWired. As 1995 picked up speed, all of those advertisers, plus thousands of others, built their own home pages and their own sites and, at that point the strategy shifted from 'Let's create a nifty little piece of communication to talk to the HotWired audience' to 'Let's try to get traffic to our site.' But I think the former strategy is going to come back because I think, if people are real honest with themselves, they've got to wonder there's an awful lot to see on the Web, why are people going to be seeking these sites necessarily? I think that all the people we're working with right now have a straight link to their site."

THE AD SALES OPERATION

As of early 1996, there were eight people dedicated to HotWired advertising. A traffic manager makes sure that the right ads appear at the right place on the site at the right time, which according to Boyce "… is a pretty big job, when you think about the resources that television and radio stations dedicate to traffic; it's a big deal, making sure that things happen as promised." The production manager physically makes sure ads are integrated within the site, that the links work, and that they're engineered correctly. If there are any problems with production, he'll tweak them and/or adjust them as necessary to make sure that the ad functions as well as possible. If HotWired is also housing pages for an advertiser, he makes sure that works and is functional. A one-person promotions department works with clients that are interested in doing promotions, whether sweepstakes or cross-promotions with other advertisers or giveaways, helps pull those together, and makes sure that they get executed. HotWired has five people—two in New York—dedicated to sales.

THE AD SALES PROCESS

Boyce elaborated on the ad sales function and its viability and pointed to the variance of client ad buying on the Web as opposed to traditional media ad buying: "About 90% of the buys come through agencies, about 10% come direct. And when they come direct, either the client doesn't have an agency or it has one but hasn't assigned it Internet responsibilities. Within the agencies, there's a whole spectrum of possibilities. Sometimes it's someone from the media department, sometimes it's someone from the research department, sometimes it's someone from account management, and sometimes it's somebody from a newly formed interactive group.

"The knowledge levels are drastically different. So we tailor our approach to the buyers. The dialogue we have with the most forward-thinking and the furthest along agencies just wouldn't be appropriate with some of the other companies that we call on. So we tailor to the audience—for some, we're doing a hell of a lot of education. And we're willing to do that. I think that, at this stage in the medium, our attitude is one of intense collaboration, if that's necessary."

Sales Reps Who Share the Vision. HotWired's sales representatives are paid a base salary plus commission on sales: "… when we look for people at HotWired, whether it's ad sales or elsewhere, we're looking for people who share the vision of our company. And so our sales force tends to be not typical, not motivated by dollars only. Our salespeople understand the medium and they understand the possibilities of this company, and they understand the potential for their growth with the company. So, I think they're more motivated by the idea than they are by the money."

HotWired offers frequency discounts and combination deals. Accordingly, everything is 15% commissionable. HotWired also has an electronic rate card. Boyce explains: "We're building that right now, and we have an e-mail kit. We haven't put our whole media kit up on the site, but we're going to. But, at this point in time, we have people send us information when they want information, so that we can control the communication early. It's really hard to sell HotWired to Steve at Netcom. He's a competitor—who knows? So, we do want to put the entire kit up there, we just haven't so far. We try to get face to face as quickly as possible."

Partly because HotWired is an electronic publication, ad copy deadlines are defined somewhat differently from those of traditional media. Says Boyce: "There's a lot of flexibility in this medium. If we get materials shipped to us that follow our spec, we can literally get them integrated into the site in about two minutes. We generally post new copy every Monday, and we generally review copy by Wednesday of the week before. But we can take it as late as late Friday."

Speedy response to a client's need can occur in a different way, such as with a specific promotion or contest of some sort: "We've gotten calls. We had a call on a Wednesday from a technology company that wanted to buy all the available inventory we had for the following week. We sold him everything we had.

"I think the company was pleased with, one, our ability to accommodate them and, two, the speed with which we responded to their immediate needs. It was a launch, and it was done all in one week. They wanted as many hits as they could get in one week. It was pretty awesome. It was pretty good presence for them."

ADVERTISING COPY SPECS

"We've got a detailed spec, and we want to get the stuff plug and play so we can just put it in and go. That, of course, doesn't always happen. But we try our best and, in the spirit of working closely with our advertisers and collaborating, we'll do whatever we have to. If we get something and it's not engineered right, we'll reengineer it at our cost. If we get something, and it doesn't look right, we can change the colors. We can resize it, we can resize the elements."

MAINTAINING LEADERSHIP

Boyce expressed HotWired's strategic need to remain in the forefront with respect to its advertising: "We feel that the market feels we are the leader and, as the leader, we have a responsibility to see that the advertising on our site looks right, functions right, and is as effective as possible. We'll do whatever we can to help make that happen, and we're not looking to use that as an opportunity to make more money. We're looking at it as a way to make our advertisers more effective, and to make them happier. I think what's going to happen is that whatever problems exist in the area of production in this medium right now won't exist for very much longer because the people who are doing the production and the creation, those companies are maturing at a very rapid rate, and I think people are getting it all figured out."

ADVERTISING GUIDELINES

HotWired won't take tobacco, but they will take alcohol. Says Boyce: "We take a real hard look at pornographic stuff. We haven't carried any thus far and we really aren't interested in it, and those policies are shared by *Wired* and HotWired. We've never been approached by a tobacco company or an agency representing a tobacco company."

EVALUATING THE BANNER ADS

"What's interesting is how radically different the performance is between banner ads. Some do much better than others. We have found it to be a pretty slippery slope. I mean if someone asks us, and they frequently do, 'Honest opinion, what do you think?' We'll give them the honest, straight scoop. If they don't ask, we usually don't volunteer a criticism or even a constructive criticism, so it's tough, and I've experimented with that, and I found that if we're not asked our point of view, it has not been welcome. I think part of what's happening is that, as this thing's taking shape, a lot of different players are trying to demonstrate their expertise."

SITE PROMOTION

HotWired is using a combination of traditional media and online to promote the site: magazine advertisements in *Wired*, trade shows, and events. For example, HotWired sponsored the New York Music Festival. How does it relate? CEO Anker observed: "It relates in the same way that we're about being a cool place, we're about being a hot sort of happening. And so, when we sponsor an event, it's going to be the New York Music Festival kind of event. We know what our brand's about. It's about being on the cutting edge. It's about being very technologically savvy. The New York Music Festival was a festival that, among those things, had a full video hookup from every single club where it was taking place, which was then being shot out over the Web. So, we're going to do those types of events when we go into real spaces.

Using the Web to Promote. "The Web is about links—it's about providing links, providing data when you want it—and so we have a number of people whose only job is to go out and find interesting Web resources on the Net that HotWired content could fit in with in terms of linking and stuff, and say, 'Hey, you've got a home page on John Waters. We just wrote a story on John Waters. Why don't you link to us? Your home page readers would love to know about us and the story we did. We've got people who post to Usenet groups.'"

AUDIENCE AND MEASUREMENT

According to HotWired's reported demographics, HotWired members are well-educated, affluent, young, and Net-savvy consumers with a wide array of backgrounds and interests. Nearly one third (28%) report visiting HotWired "... to view product information and/or advertising." HotWired states that 36% report bookmarking an advertiser's home page, and 11% report purchasing a product that HotWired recommended. As for education, 72% of members are college graduates or have completed postgraduate studies. The average member earns $50,000, and is a 32-year-old male who has used the Web for less than six months. Questioned about their preferences on the site, 83% responded that they visit HotWired for news and information, 80% for entertainment, 50% to read something of interest in HotFlash, 57% to discover other Web sites, and 28% to view product information or advertising.

One of the key factors in HotWired's success has been the audience it has attracted. According to Anker, when HotWired launched, it was very clearly an early-adopter demographic—that was HotWired's audience, as it was generally on the Web. Anker perceives that HotWired is now getting to the point where the Web is maturing in terms of the diversity of its audience, and the Web is starting to get other people besides the early fanatics: "'Mainstream Culture for the 21st Century' is one of our tag lines. It's about the people who are the advanced consumers, who are not just experimenting for the first time in the Web, but have been around for a while. It's a dedicated audience that sees this not as just a place and gee, isn't technology neat, whiz bang, but this is a very viable, valid new media space where you do things you can't do anyplace else, such as interact and sample lots of different types of media and get video and audio at the same time as you're getting text."

Not surprisingly, Anker is positive about the initial response to HotWired: "It's been exactly what we want. It's lots of good, some bad, but everybody's talking. We don't pretend that we do everything right. We're just trying to make it up as we go along and provide a good space where people can interact with us and with other people. And so we get data from them, we get messages from them that tell us what we're doing right and wrong, and we adjust accordingly. It's also a consistent response. I think there are always going to be people who just don't like what we're doing, and there are people who do like what we're doing, and I think it's always been a vast majority who do. That hasn't really changed."

Page View. For the three months ending August 31, 1996, the HotWired Network had an average of over 24,000 visitors per weekday (over 106,000 including HotBot), and it had approximately 9.7 million page views (42.8 million including HotBot) during that period.

The Mercurial Measurement Issue. HotWired provides advertisers with weekly data with the page views experienced by their banner, which are usually on a whole series of pages. They provide the raw number and the percentage of people who have viewed the banner and clicked through it and gone on deeper into the message. But do they know what kinds of people they are? According to Boyce "We're not there yet, but that will be next." Are they exploring a way of doing that? "Yes, we are." Is it something HotWired is going to roll out anytime soon? Says Boyce: "It's something we'd like to begin testing. I would define the idea broadly as smart messaging, being able to put the right messages, the smart messages in front of the right people based on either their demographics or their product.

"We're going to be working with I/Pro, an auditing company. We send weekly reports to our advertisers every Tuesday. But we will begin adding a third-party audit so that advertisers will not only get our report but will once a month get an audit that will look at the previous four periods and verify that the numbers we gave them are true and accurate. But no one has questioned what we've sent out either. My sense is that no one wants a third-party audit. Everyone recognizes though that there are a lot of different technologies vying for the lead. No one's certain who's going to win, and no one's certain that any of those players have developed the right model yet, so I think what we're providing is pretty widely accepted."

MEASURING STRATEGIC SUCCESS

Short-Term Goals: Pioneering Web Advertising. In terms of shorter-term goals, HotWired has had a few. One was launching successfully with a number of advertisers. When they launched, advertising on the Web hadn't been done yet. Says Anker, "Just the fact of being able to set out with a mission of selling the Web as an advertising vehicle and being able to launch a fully sold-out plate of advertisers, and that was very clearly the first hurdle, we passed with flying colors."

Long-Term Goals. Anker differentiates between HotWired's long-term and short-range goals: "I think our long-term goal and our long-term success will be measured by developing dominant media franchises. Our point of view on what the Web is right now, what the Internet is in general, is that it is an entirely new media space that's opening up in the same way television did, like cable did, magazines at an earlier time, and radio, and there's a very clear path, very clear development."

Anker sees an advantage to HotWired and the Internet as a new media development compared to what has become traditional media and to the leaders in traditional media: "As all these new media happen, the people who are leaders in the old media aren't able to transition into the new media. We see that we're able, in this media space, to capture the sports brand or the entertainment brand and to be as good as any of our larger New York media cousins. We want to own the MTV of the Web, the CNN of the Web.

"Our goal is to start a number of very vertically defined channel content spaces and to have some percentage of them to be the MTVs, the CNNs, the ESPNs. It's probably five years before we're at a point when the shakeouts, the backlashes, the regroups, and the fifteen stages that we need to go through happen."

HOTWIRED'S FUTURE: AUDIO, THEN VIDEO

Anker's perception of the HotWired site goes beyond the current view and reaches forward to where some see the Internet going: "HotWired on the Internet is interactive television the right way. It's not taking a few hundred million dollars and dumping it into an Orlando system that works for 4,000 people maybe. Interactive television the right way is a bottom-up approach that takes using technology and continues to take it incremental steps and sometimes larger than incremental steps until it does things that look like video.

"Right now, the Web is, to some extent, still at the magazine with buttons stage. It's still more about text and pictures than anything else. With technologies like RealAudio and StreamWorks, you're going to get into the radio with buttons stage real fast. We've hired audio people to build audio content. I think the next step—and it's just a question of better software, and better bandwidth to the desktop—will be video with buttons, and that's interactive television.

"The Internet is a whole set of protocols and technologies and functionalities, and it's about people who are very able to just keep taking steps and adding on, and filling in and growing, until it's a wholly different beast, but it should be a lot of fun. This is the thing that surprised everybody who is trying to make 200 million dollar bets on this technology. It's a great technology, it's an international technology, and it's just a lot of fun to play with."

FUTURE ADVERTISING PROSPECTS

A number of sources show total industry ad revenue estimates for 1995 somewhere in the $30–$40 million range. For Anker: "I see no reason why it won't at least double if not triple in 1996. Forrester Research is saying that it will be a $2.7 billion industry by the year 2000. That's in paid links, not Web development. Someone estimated that it was going to be a bigger market than spot radio in the year 2000 in terms of ad revenue. It's impossible to project in this medium, but that's certainly exciting and, even if it's only a fraction of $2.7 billion or even if it's only a fraction of the total radio ad revenues, it's certainly a huge market that's come out of nowhere really fast.

"I think for what our mission is—the leading Web publisher—our advertisers expect us to have the best ideas first."

CHAPTER 8

PUBLIC RELATIONS
ON THE NET

TELLING THE STORIES OF THE TRIBE

"The Internet is coming! The Internet is coming! Print journalism as we know it is dead."

"Television and radio news will never survive the onslaught of news on the Net."

It is amazing how quickly people unfamiliar with electronic media specifically and communications technology in general jump to the naive conclusion that when a new and seemingly glamorous technology comes along, all else before it will cease to exist. In part, the general misinterpretation of Marshall McLuhan's media theories (mainly the "when a new technology comes along, it obsolesces older technologies" theory) has contributed to this false view of the media landscape. The ubiquity of television around the world also tends to give the impression that nobody reads anymore or even listens to the radio. And, now, here comes the Internet. You would think from all the "press" the Internet gets that everyone is on the

Net and everyone has stopped doing everything else they were doing before 1993. The facts, however, tell quite a different story. To
paraphrase Mark Twain, reports of the demise of public relations
and journalism as a result of the Internet are greatly exaggerated.

In the 1970s, the rate of growth for journalist jobs was in solid
double digits, and it seemed that the sky was the limit. Enrollments
at schools of journalism soared. Everybody wanted to be the next
Walter Cronkite or a Pulitzer prize–winning columnist for *The New
York Times*, *The Washington Post*, or *The Wall Street Journal*. In the
1980s however, technological and economic shifts changed the out-
look for journalists and the job market appeared to shrink. True, in
some sectors of the journalism profession, there was shrinkage,
notably in broadcast network television news bureaus and at local
newspapers. More recently though, *The New York Times* reported
that journalism graduates with good writing skills and knowledge
of, and experience in, cyberspace can draw down significantly
higher starting salaries than graduates without cyberskills.[1]

These instances, however, are only a part of what constitutes the
journalism marketplace. Despite all the headlines, there are still
11,500 or so newspapers in the United States, 11,710 magazines,
11,708 radio stations playing to 500 million radios, 1,145 commercial television stations, and more than 11,000 cable systems reaching 95 million television households. News—"telling the stories of
the tribe"—is an important content element for these media outlets.

How people get the news and product and service information
has certainly changed from prehistoric days when the old men sat
around the campfire telling the stories of the tribe. Today, it is media people telling the stories of the tribe through a multiplicity of
distribution channels, including television, the so-called electronic
fireplace. But it should be noted that there are more books in print
today than ever, despite the apparent hue and cry that nobody
reads anymore. In the United States, more than 75,000 book publishers, large and small, publish books on all manner of subjects.
Forty thousand new book titles are published every year in the
United States; 300,000 are published worldwide.

What has really happened is this: Because we don't all read the
same books, there is a perception that no one reads anymore. The

mass market has become the vertical information market. Each year, according to Arnie Semsky, Media Director at the advertising agency BBDO, close to 500 new magazines come onto the market. Of course, many do not survive. But new technology has put the potential to publish a magazine into anyone's hands. And magazines are converting themselves into CD-ROM products and Internet sites.

Media crossover is everywhere. For example, Bloomberg Financial Services, a leading purveyor of worldwide financial information via a worldwide network of leased computer terminals, also packages its content into a radio channel, a newsletter, and a direct broadcast satellite transmission.

Cable television is a major growth area for news and public relations material. News 1/New York, the innovative local all-news 24-hour cable television channel, is one of half a dozen such operations in the country. Within five to eight years, most major television markets in the United States will have such a cable news operation. News operations in the electronic media are growth areas primarily because they are relatively inexpensive to produce. The programming is repackageable on a daily basis. Technology has made it possible for a few people to produce this kind of programming which, just 10 years ago, would have required many people. The ratio is about four to one.

As communications technologies of various kinds become even more pervasive, and they will, and as print media become even more widely produced and distributed on a global scale, there will be an increasing need for people who can "tell the story of the tribe"—in newspapers, in magazines, on the radio, on television, and in other forms of electronic media, including the Internet—people who can find information, gather it, analyze it, organize it, and communicate it in context and with meaning. The paradigm of virtual instant access to information in a virtual environment on a global basis is yet another milestone in the process of the democratization of information nurtured by the Greeks around 700 B.C. when their culture evolved what we call the alphabet, a series of standardized, digital representations of analogic sounds.

So, what does the Internet mean to public relations professionals and journalists? Before written history, the journalists of yesteryear were men and women sitting around the campfire telling the stories of the tribe, and the historians were the elders passing collective memories down through the generations. Today, our campfires are not only oral but also print- and electronics-based, and our tribes are geographically global. The Internet is the latest electronic medium in a chain of electronic media that started with the telegraph in the late 1830s. This network of computer networks—made possible by developments in personal computers and telecommunications hardware and software—can give a user access to textual and graphic material. For public relations practitioners, the Internet, therefore, represents not a way to do public relations but another way of reaching a variety of publics.

Here are a few of those publics: print and electronic journalists; local, state, regional, federal, and international government officials (legislative, regulatory, executive, judicial); community organizations and leaders, chambers of commerce, neighborhood coalitions; employees and their families; customers, distributors, jobbers, wholesalers, retailers, suppliers, teaming partners, subcontractors; professional societies, trade associations; academic faculty and staff, trustees, financial supporters, students; securities analysts, institutional holders, shareholders, bankers, stockbrokers, portfolio managers, potential investors; special-interest groups (e.g., environmentalists, the handicapped or disabled, minorities, think tanks, consumer groups, health groups, senior citizens, religious organizations).

Do these audiences sound familiar? They should. These are the audiences for all manner of print communications and electronic communications, such as radio, television, and the Internet.

The Internet, though, *is* a new medium. However, the Internet is not about public relations, marketing, or internal corporate communications. The Internet is about information access on a one-on-one scale, potentially. The Internet is about searching through tens of thousands of highly focused newsgroups. The Internet is about highly targeted market segments. The Internet is about creating external and internal Web sites, where potential users can access information and enter into a direct dialogue with the organization offering a service or product. The Internet is about instant communication (via e-mail) on a global scale, instant response (via infobots), and potentially instant customer satisfaction.

The Internet is not a panacea. It is another way for a public relations practitioner to reach an audience. It also takes work, lots of it, to target the right message to the right audience. In the next few years, public relations practitioners, communications professionals of all kinds, and journalists will increasingly embrace the Internet as an extension of their well-honed skills.

PUBLIC RELATIONS PROFESSIONALS, ALL ABOARD!

Organizations (with or without an internal public relations or public affairs function), public relations agencies, and print and electronic journalists all have made increasing use of the Internet and the World Wide Web. While there are no formal numbers, many organizations with Web sites are at least aware that a Web site can be used for public relations purposes. If the United States Agency for International Development (USAID), IBM, General Electric, and Sybase Web sites are any indication, a Web site with a defined public relations strategy consists of information not only for customers but also the media. In an apparently growing number of instances, organizations are setting up sections especially for members of the media.

THE ORGANIZATIONS

For example, the Press Information section of the USAID site (see case study) consists of two other levels:

> USAID in the news: Read more about what's going on at USAID in these recent news stories and find out what editorial pages around the country are saying.

and

> Get the latest information from USAID: You can access press releases from USAID or speeches, Congressional testimony, and op-eds by Agency officials. If you need further information, here's who to contact at USAID.

In effect, each section and subsection is designed to give media professionals quick access to the information sought and, if it's not being sought, to make the media professional aware that the information exists. Overall, the public relations goals are to improve the agency's image and inform the American public of the good work the agency accomplishes.

The United States Postal Service has a complete online file of its news releases, all immediately accessible to the press.

General Electric (see case study) recently redesigned its Web site into three sections, one for consumers, one for businesses, and one specifically purposed for all others, including the media.

IBM (see case study) has various sections for the press, including special events sections. IBM made strategic use of its Web site in 1995 to accomplish a virtual takeover of Lotus. Because IBM was legally precluded from contacting Lotus shareholders directly, it used its Web site to provide information to Lotus employees and shareholders on the rationale behind the proposed takeover. The response was overwhelming. Using barely more than its online presence (and its size), IBM managed to convince enough Lotus personnel of the appropriateness of its offer—Lotus capitulated within a week.

Sybase's Web site contains a separate section titled Communicating with Us by E-mail. In this section are subsections for Product and Sales Information, Technical Support via the Web, Sybase Education and Class Registration, Open Solutions Partners Program, Interested in an Exciting Career at Sybase? and the Sybase WWW Site. If the visitor wants to use the traditional telephone, Sybase provides 800 numbers as well, including one for its Europe User Group.

The growing use of the Internet (i.e., external Web sites) for public relations purposes is corroborated in a recent study by the Institute for Public Relations Research and Education. Conducted by John V. Pavlik, Ph.D. Executive Director, The Center for New Media, at Columbia University, and David M. Dozier, Ph.D. Professor at the School of Communication, San Diego State University, between September 1995 and January 1996, the survey found that the "... most effective use of the Web is to integrate its use into an overall media plan and to recognize that the Web is primarily a communication medium in which users (i.e., members of the public) come to the organization seeking information rather than a sales or marketing tool."

Perry Shoom, Marketing Manager at Canadian Corporate News, at a IABC-Toronto PR, Communications and Marketing Conference presentation entitled "Build a Web Site That Will Draw Reporters" (May 14, 1996), offered the following guidelines for organizations designing a strategic Web site with the public relations application in mind:

> In the case of the media, reporters have tight and short-term deadlines, information requirements which vary from day to day and non-traditional working hours. Beyond the initial press release, a Web site may be the only contact between a reporter writing a story and the organization. The effectiveness of a Web site can shape the views of the reporter covering a story.

Shoom offers several ways to customize a Web site so that it serves to support the media along with other visitors:

1. Utilize links or jumps to facilitate the information flow.
2. Write in a style appropriate for the Web.
3. Don't let graphics get in the way of functionality.

THE PUBLIC RELATIONS AGENCIES AND THE MEDIA

According to the May 11, 1996, download of the Directory of Public Relations Agencies and Resources on the Web site founded and maintained by Impulse Research Corp. (www.webcom.com/impulse/prlist.html), there are 205 U.S. public relations agencies on the Web, 73 in other countries, and several dozen other organizations and resources.

Part of the driving force behind the adoption of the Internet as a public relations medium and the growth of public relations agencies building their own Web sites is that members of the media are using it increasingly in their own work. Frank Ovaitt, a managing director of Ovaitt/Crossover Communications, in "Wired Strategist and the Ten Thousand Dimension Web," points out that, increasingly, not only editors but now also reporters are going online to do their work—not only e-mail but also research, including contact with public relations agencies and public relations professionals within organizations.[2]

The first annual survey of Canadian media Internet use, conducted by Ernst & Young and Canada NewsWire Ltd. in June 1995, attempted to determine the extent to which journalists use the Internet, where the Net is taking them, and when they will be entering the on-ramp. The survey population represented newspapers, radio, television, trade magazines, and freelancers, 1197 (16%) responses were received.

The survey revealed that 38% of Canadian newsrooms are hooked up to the Internet. Of respondents using the Net or online services, 81% do so at least once a week, 39% said research is their primary reason for hooking up to the Internet, and 67% of respondents said Internet usage would make them more productive.

A more recent American survey revealed similar findings. Media in Cyberspace Study II, a survey of the use of computers and the Internet by the print media, confirms and expands a 1994 study conducted by Media Source, The Journalists Information Resource (www.mediasource.com), a service of public relations consultant Don Middleberg.

In the 1995 survey, Middleberg's organization concentrated and expanded its coverage of magazines and daily newspapers. Thanks to an exceptional response rate (about 500 of 2,000 magazines and over 300 of 1,815 newspapers—almost all of them dailies), Media Source was able not only to track overall use of online services but also to gain a better understanding of how editors use these services. The magazine section was the largest survey ever conducted of magazines in cyberspace.

Almost one-quarter of the respondents to the 1995 survey said that they or their staffs used online services daily. More than two-thirds said that they used such services at least once a month. Those totals are significantly higher than those for 1994. Growth, however, has been mainly in daily newspapers; monthly use rose from 44% to a startling 71%. This rise among newspapers was matched by increased use in news libraries staffed by librarians —from 31% of the dailies in 1994 to 61% in 1995.

Furthermore, despite press reports predicting the demise of value-added online services in the face of Internet (and especially World Wide Web) services, the press itself favors value-added commercial services for its searches. Last year, the leader was Compu-Serve. This year, to the surprise of no one who has been following America Online's marketing blitz, AOL surged ahead. Twice as many journalists ranked AOL first (40%) for commercial services and Internet access compared to the Internet alone (20%). CompuServe now ranks third, at 19%, down from first, at 35%, last year. Of course, many use AOL to access the Internet despite its high cost relative to local providers.

According to the survey, once editors and reporters go online, they are interested in gathering reference materials, finding raw data (in particular, government data and corporate biographies), using e-mail, and seeking out new sources for interviews. In that last function, editors and reporters often use old-fashioned online Internet utilities such as LISTSERVs and Usenet newsgroups, as well as the World Wide Web.

According to the report, when it comes to sending artwork, the print media are a year away from total transition to digital technology. Asked how they would prefer to receive artwork two years from now, respondents said they would prefer electronic images by a three to one margin over slides and camera-ready art. At the moment, they say, slides, photos, and camera-ready art are running about even with electronic images.

When it comes to text submissions, news organizations exhibit a bit of a split personality. They want submissions online or on disk from their own correspondents but on paper from outsiders. The correspondents are taught how to code copy for each specific news organization—and everyone does it a different way. Despite the preference for paper now, most say they will want all "media relations" submissions online within five years; in fact, by then only 19% will want submissions on paper.

It should come as no surprise that electronic distribution of newspapers and magazines exploded in the past year. Some 46% of the sample had had no plans to go online in 1994, but that percentage was cut precisely in half, to 23%, in the thirteen-month interval between the two surveys. Some 29% of magazines in the sample are now distributing electronically, and another 31% expect to be doing it by fall of 1997. Among dailies, all but 30% expect to be online within five years; 15% already are online, and half plan online products by fall, 1997.

The 1995 survey concludes: "Not since the late 1960s, when advances in printing technology and list brokerage made small-circulation, specialized magazines cost-effective, has there been such a revolution in the media business. Last year, we called the implications for journalism and for public relations 'dramatic.' This year, we can only say, 'We told you so.'"

SOME RAMIFICATIONS

Increasing use of electronic media, such as the Internet, by media outlets, and on a daily basis by journalists, could change the relationship between public relations professionals and print and electronic journalists. As more and more journalists go online or use e-mail, the direct need for a public relations professional as an informational buffer between an organization and the journalist could be eliminated. This scenario is integral to the paradigm expressed in earlier chapters, that electronic media, in general, and the Internet/World Wide Web, in particular, have had, and can have, the effect of reducing barriers between an organization and its external and internal publics.

Here the advantages and disadvantages of electronic communication media need to be addressed. "The beauty of electronic communication," states John Beardsley, 1995 President of the Public Relations Society of America, and chairman and CEO of the public relations firm of Padilla Speer Beardsley, "is that it is fully descriptive, and entirely noninterruptive. The public relations professional can send an idea via e-mail directly to the journalists. They can discuss it back and forth and, if it's of interest, or the public relations professional piques the journalist's interest, then he can send the necessary information, including text and graphics, directly to the journalist quickly with minimal interruption—the e-mail acts as the phone and messenger/mail all in one."

But, today, a journalist can also bypass the public relations professional and go directly to a Web site to get the basic information required for a story. Does this mean the demise of the internal public relations department? Does this mean shrinking opportunities for external public relations agencies? I don't think so, for several reasons. First, many organizations have already downsized and turned to outsourcing as a way to augment their noncentral operations. In effect, organizations are using more and more outside agencies as consultants to handle their public relations needs. So, for the outside professional, the future augurs well. For the internal public relations executive, the advent of the World Wide Web is a major opportunity. First, a Web site requires strategic planning and internal coordination by an experienced professional. Second, a Web site requires frequent maintenance, in some cases, daily. Apart from the technical requirements, these changes require monitoring by someone. In many cases, that someone is in a corporate communications or public relations department.

NOTES

1. G. Jacobson, "For Journalism Graduates, Opportunities in New Media," *The New York Times*, May 20, 1996, p. D11.

2. F. Ovaitt, *The Public Relations Strategist*, Winter 1995, pp. 17–22.

CHAPTER 9

IBM

ibm.com
Old Orchard Road
Armonk, New York 10504

*We want to personify the company strategy ... we want people to be able
to experience network computing, and they can do that over the Web.*

—Jeff Cross, Director
Corporate Communications

INTERVIEWEES

The Executive: Jeff Cross,
  Director, Corporate Communications

The Renegade: Carol Moore,
  Director, IBM Corporate Internet Programs

The Webmaster: Ed Costello

THE CORPORATE CONTEXT

After many years of black and blue financial returns, Big Blue has been stabilized and strengthened. IBM reported record revenues in 1995, topping $70 billion for the first time. Its rate of revenue growth—12% over the previous year—was the best in more than a decade. It doubled earnings to $6.3 billion, excluding a one-time charge related to the acquisition of Lotus Development Corp. and two special items taken in the fourth quarter. Its cash flow was very strong. It ended the year with $7.7 billion in cash— and that's after spending $5.7 billion to repurchase IBM stock and $2.9 billion to acquire Lotus. One of the best indicators of its progress, and the one that probably matters most to investors, is market value. Last year IBM's market value grew by $6.9 billion, an increase of 16%. Since the summer of 1993, when it announced a re-structuring program, through year-end 1995, IBM's market value has improved by nearly $27 billion.

As expressed by Louis V. Gerstner Jr., IBM Chairman and Chief Executive Officer, the company's strategic imperatives are:

1. Exploiting its technology
2. Helping customers realize the benefits of computing
3. Establishing leadership in the emerging network-centric computing world
4. Realigning the way it delivers value to customers
5. Rapidly expanding its position in key emerging geographic markets
6. Leveraging its size and scale to achieve cost and market advantages

IBM's Intranet strategy is an expression of these goals.

DEFINING WEB SITE STRATEGIC OBJECTIVES

Interestingly, the IBM Web site did not initially have a corporate strategic objective. However, today is a different story. According to Carol Moore, Director, IBM Corporate Internet Programs: "Today [the Web is] the personification of the company's strategy and the personification of the IBM brand. We have five targeted customer groups: large, medium, and small businesses; consumers; original equipment manufacturers; wholesale supplier types; and software solution developers. But we have always felt, at least on the IBM home page, that IBM has such a wealth of content that we are not going to narrow our focus to certain groups. We want to have something for everybody that comes to the site."

www.ibm.com

The IBM Web site is an example of a company with a long, successful history and significant resources working at strategically leveraging its knowledge and expertise base through a new medium. The IBM Web site is oriented more toward public relations and communications than toward sales (as is the case with GE) or customer service (as with FEDEX). In various ways, the IBM external Web site has more in common with the USAID site, which has a definite bent toward public relations.

The IBM home page, probably one of the most organized, least cluttered of Web sites, offers six broad choices: News, Products, Network Computing, Research, Services, Support, Industry Solutions, About IBM, and a link to the official IBM-sponsored Web site of the Olympic Games. Additionally, the Web site offers a news section detailing stories ranging from sports—a story on Wimbeldon, for instance—to an article on Lotus' powerful new Web server.

News. News offers the latest IBM headlines and stories, including current IBM financial information like live IBM stock quotes (on a 15-minute delay), and quarterly earnings. There are also raw data, such as press releases, IBM US announcement letters, and Lotus press releases. Third, there is a rundown of conferences, trade shows, and industry events worldwide, such as the 1996 IBM education worldwide technical conferences and North American trade shows. Last, there is a listing of current job offerings.

Products. This section offers information on Internet products and services, an Intranet and client/server, multimedia, microelectronics, networking, original equipment manufacturing, personal computing, printing systems, research, servers, software and storage to technology for people with special needs, used equipment, voice recognition, and workstations.

Services and Support. This section includes the latest advice on how to use IBM products and receive new upgrades, downloads, and information about how to do business with IBM. A wide array of services is available to customers, ranging from consulting and education to software and manufacturing solutions. Under the heading of Support, there are several choices within the business-to-business and product subsets. Additionally, there are user groups and a choice of nine IBM publications to review.

Industry Solutions. IBM solutions teams are organized into groups that specialize in particular kinds of businesses, including teams that are dedicated to helping customers across all industries according to one's area of interest, which include companies in all industries, divided up into: cross-industry, decision support solutions, solutions and support for small and medium-sized enterprises, and a software solutions directory. Second, there is industry-specific information including, but not limited to, banking, distribution, education, government, telecommunications manufacturing, and travel.

About IBM. This area offers its 1995 annual report, which includes a letter to investors/financials and an assessment of the future of computing. Financial information displays stockholder services, as well as the already offered quarterly results and stock quotations. There are also job listings and other corporate activities, which include IBM and the environment, IBM and the global information infrastructure, and philanthropy.

Official Web Site for the Atlanta Olympic Games. In the period leading up to the Summer Olympic Games in Atlanta, this section emphasized IBM's involvement in the Games, and offered the latest Olympic news, press clips, and an opportunity to purchase Olympic tickets.

Overall, IBM offers a well-formatted, extensive variety of services to those who visit their home page. From general news headlines to investment information to services, IBM sets a standard just as it often does in its own interrelated industry. IBM clearly uses its muscle to market itself positively in related and relatively unrelated areas.

The IBM external Web site went online in May 1994.

STARTUP AND FUNDING

Even though IBM's Web site is externally oriented, its initiation and development were similar to those of many companies with Intranet experience: The Web site started as a grassroots project, then received top management's blessing and support, and grew from there. Proposal to actuality was a few weeks. Initial funding, paltry even by IBM standards, was estimated at about $30,000 to start and $300,000 for the first year. Today, the budget is substantially more. According to Moore: "The Web was a very hot thing and we wanted to drive the perception of IBM as a contemporary company. People were going out there on the Net and we decided we had to as well. It wasn't ordained from on high. It was a grassroots campaign; a few people in the company said 'We're going do this.'"

According to Ed Costello, current Webmaster for the IBM external Web site, Dave Grossman was the first IBMer to set up an external Web site. In the fall and winter of 1993–1994, Grossman was at the Cornell Theory Center as part of his work in support of the SP2 architecture, the parallel SP2 project. As a way to support people, Grossman set up a Web page with information about the SP2. Because he was the only person in the company with any Web experience, he was brought in, along with Carol Moore, to help set up the IBM home page. More recently, Grossman was involved in IBM's 1996 Olympics effort.

The Internet effort evolved to a team consisting of Lori Neumann, a graphic designer from corporate identity and design, two staffers from IBM's Austin, Texas, lab, and another from IBM's Atlanta lab. Moore became involved the day after the first Web site was launched. Said Moore: "We had pathetically few technical resources. We really had almost nothing. At the moment, however, corporate communications is the owner of the home page with more than 100 content organizations on the IBM Web. Each of them has a team, and virtually all of them have a communications person or a marketing communications person at the head of it."

According to Moore: "There's the IBM home page; it's the hub of a giant wheel. There are separate spokes going out to separate organizations. And each one has a team headed by a communications person. For whichever the organization it is, its team takes care of putting its content onto the Internet.

WHO'S VISITING? WHO'S BUYING?

Moore is not quite certain, though, who the IBM Web site's audience is: "We don't seek demographics from IBM home page users. We have statistical software that we've developed called Bean Counter." What kind of feedback is the team getting?: "This week we're going toward 6 million hits. We think that means about 2.5 million visits per week."

When asked if IBM has noticed any change in sales of individual product lines as a result of being on the Internet, Moore replied: "People aren't buying a mainframe over the Internet. They'll buy maybe a PC; they'll buy a low-end, midrange computer; they'll buy software, small-scale software, but they're not going to buy any of our high profit-margin items on the Net.

"Right now, it has catalogs on it, but there's going to be a concerted push to have an electronic commerce strategy that's unified and common to everyone coming in wherever they go on the Web. That will be sometime this year." The Web site does create sales, though: "There was a team that said, 'We were sitting around in the lab one night and we had to buy several laptops and it was you versus Hewlett-Packard. Before we went to the Internet, Hewlett-Packard was the favorite. Until we went to the Net, we saw how much information you had—and Hewlett-Packard didn't have as much—so we bought IBM.'"

SITE PROMOTION

IBM promotes the site with URLs in all its advertising and on some packaging. They put it in traditional media and they advertise certain types of content in the site through banners on other sites.

THE STRATEGIC VISION: NOW

IBM's strategic objective for the Web site has changed since the site's inception. It has gone from personifying the brand to personifying IBM's overall strategy. Lotus was practically bought on the Internet. Moore perceives that the site has finally reached a point at which, as far as public relations is concerned, IBM PR professionals are beginning to think of the Internet before they think of a press release.

Jeff Cross, Director of Corporate Communications, in the corporate headquarters in Armonk, New York, reports to the Vice President of Communications who, in turn, reports to Lou Gerstner, IBM's Chairman. It is in Cross's organization that the IBM external Web site resides.

The Lotus Takeover. Cross expressed IBM's strategic vision for the site by recounting its value during the Lotus takeover: "We view it as an extremely strategic communications vehicle. I think the best example of how we use the Web site strategically was the Lotus acquisition. By law, we were prohibited from approaching Lotus shareholders directly but, with the Internet, there's no way you can stop people from coming to your Web site, and we had, of course, the advantage of planning this takeover in advance, and Lotus didn't know we were going to be attempting to take them over.

"So we put on our Web site information that would be of use to Lotus shareholders when they tried to find out more information about what was going down that Monday morning. And we had posted on our Web site in advance a press release about the takeover offer extended by IBM—a letter from Lou Gerstner to IBM's employees and the text of Lou Gerstner's letter to Lotus' then CEO, Jim Manzi. Later on, we heard that an awful lot of Lotus employees and shareholders and interested bystanders, whether competitors or investment bankers, came to check out the IBM home page to see what news was available that Monday morning.

"Lotus' home page was down because the volume of hits just made it crash. So, starting that day and moving forward, we were determined that the IBM home page would be very strategic. Every major product brand has its home page and a lot of the countries where we do business—159 countries around the world—many of them have a home page. But the corporate home page, which is what Carol Moore is the editor of, that's really the entree or the focal point for coming into the IBM Web site.

Timeliness and Access. "There are other times in the year when we use it as a real-time or near-real-time communications vehicle, so that anyone who's interested in finding out the latest on what our chairman says at our annual meeting or the Comdex keynote address can find it on the Web. Before the Web grew to such popularity, people would have had to wait for their local news on TV or radio or read the newspaper the next morning."

The mission of IBM's Web site today is to personify IBM strategies. Initially, the mission was to personify the IBM brand image, for example, putting on the Web its print ads and TV commercials. In 1995, the mission was changed to personify the IBM key corporate strategy: network computing. According to Cross, "We have a space on the IBM home page where we have content of interest that relates to network computing—things like Lou Gerstner, our chairman's address to the Comdex Trade Show in November 1995. We have a Web version of our annual report. But there is much more than just putting on the Web a print version of the Annual Report. There are a lot of interactive elements throughout the Web version of our annual report, so we want people to be able to experience network centric computing, and they can do that over the Web, whereas it's impossible to do that in a hard-copy magazine or annual report."

Top Management Commitment. Cross underscored top management's commitment to the Web site with respect to it becoming an integral aspect of how IBM does business. "No question about it. We view it as a very strategic communications element. We've talked to Webmasters, Internet people from other companies, in some cases, that operation would report in to product development or somewhere else in the organization. At IBM, it reports in to Communications, and that's testimony to its importance as a strategic communications vehicle. We're using the Internet much more frequently these days for electronic commerce. We're putting our money where our mouth is—with the budget and the head count, meaning the number of people we've assigned to Carol Moore's department, increased this year over last, and obviously last year over the previous year, that is, two years ago, the first time we had a corporate Web site. In personnel, it's up around 40% to 50%. The budget is up nearly 100% in 1996 over 1995. At the beginning of 1996 we had six full-time employees and three contractors—three contract employees who work for an outside agency on our premises. And then we hired one more full-timer this year and a few more contractors. We'll be hiring another contractor, this year, so that staff is increasing close to 50% this year."

Outsourcing. When asked about the use of an outsourcing strategy to support the Web site activity, Cross replied: "Instead of hiring IBM personnel—in the vernacular, the term is 'headcount,' which refers to full-time permanent employees who receive benefits—we also use contractors who work for Sage Communications in New York City. Sage is a placement firm that has people with Internet skills who work for us. We pay Sage and they pay the contractor and the contract employees, and so, outsourcing provides more flexibility to downsize or upsize. It's harder to add full-time employees at IBM because IBM is so conscious of cost-cutting these days; it's difficult to get approval to hire another full-time employee. These program dollars are to hire additional contractors to get the work done. In our case, there's a mix of editorial people and architectural designers, Webmaster techs who know the programming languages and have the computer skills to make the design look the way we want it to on our home page. So it's both editorial and Webmaster skills that we're looking for."

PROMOTING SPECIAL EVENTS

One of the stated goals for IBM's Web site is to make it the place for people to go for to information about the industry. Cross underscored this view by describing some of the ways the Web site is being used to promote special events: "We host events. We want to have our site be known for some cool events. We hosted the Deep Blue Chess Computer versus Kasparov matches in February 1996. Another part of the site hosts the official home page for the 1996 Olympic Games. We're also hosting the Masters golf tournament and the US Open and Wimbledon tennis tournaments.

The Proof Is in the Doing. "How does this pay dividends for IBM?

Because we can do it—we can provide Web sites for these special events. And this is an indication to customers and prospects that we can provide similar kinds of technologies to them so that they can help run their businesses, not necessarily host the events per se on their Web sites, but we can provide electronic commerce capabilities for the Atlanta Committee for the Olympic Games to sell tickets or T-shirts over the Web site. It also helps us get our foot in the door for other prospects who are envisioning doing the same kinds of things. For example, at a recent Internet trade show we had a representative from L.L. Bean stand up with us and talk about our Internet technology, particularly the Net.commerce product that enables secure electronic transactions to take place over the Internet—you can use a credit card on the Internet and not worry that numbers will be bounced around half the world and everyone's got your Visa or Mastercard number or American Express number. IBM technology makes that possible."

THE INTRANET FACTOR

Surprisingly, given the nature of its business, IBM did not launch its own internal Web site—its own Intranet—until early September 1996. More importantly, Cross pointed to the relationship between the strategic vision of the external Web site and the mission of its Intranet: "The Intranet will help with the sharing of information among departments. And I think that whole effort has helped IBM in that it's become the rallying cry for IBM: We're aligned behind the network computing strategy much like people in the '60s were aligned behind the 360 introduction, and that was our Apollo mission, if you will. So this is our newest Apollo mission, to make sure that we succeed in the company and that we know where we're going, we know how to get there.

"I think the external Web site obviously enhances IBM's ability to conduct business 24 hours a day. I think it's lost some degree of personal relation, personal interaction, because you're dealing with a machine, but it makes for greatly enhanced efficiency and there's no question about that."

THE WEB SITE'S FUTURE

Cross looked beyond the near future and speculated on the future of the IBM Web site, particularly with respect to the its multiaudience potential: "We're such a large company, we have so much content. One challenge is to make it easily navigable. I see it evolving into a personification of our strategies rather than just a brand image vehicle. You know, it could just become a repository of stuff, press releases and fax sheets, information about various and sundry products that we market. But we want it to do more, be more, than just that, to really be a source of information—helpful, useful information about our strategies—for people, customers and prospects, the media, analysts, consultants, shareholders, whomever, to help them understand where IBM is going and why we have a bright future."

OTHER VOICES: COMBINING CONTENT DESIGN
WITH STRATEGY

According to Webmaster Ed Costello, "We have some stuff that we're working on to bring up later this month called Other Voices, which is really some cooperative work we're doing with a variety of other media organizations, mostly Web-based. We ask them to contribute customized information on our Other Voices site, and we do not exercise any editorial control over it. I think we'll exercise the right to say, 'You can't put that up,' but, in general, we're not going to edit anything they contribute. They get to put their material up and use spaces about network computing, business computing, and computers in society. We get the advantage that they're putting information up, and basically providing information to us for free. They get the advantage that, assuming that this is successful and draws people to these areas, these guys will get free, basically free advertisements for linking off the IBM home page."

Carol Moore plans to add new features to the Web site down the road: "I think there will be a lot more features that will take you into related information beyond the IBM Web. Headline services, for example. If you're reading a story about storage, headlines will appear about storage, hot stuff in storage that day, and you'll be able to go off the IBM Web site to a content-provider's page and see more information on the topic. We want IBM to become the place where you come not only to learn all about IBM but to learn all about the industry. So we're really making a push to become the one-stop place that you come to when you want to find out about the industry or a certain trend in the industry."

IMPACT ON THE MARKETING AND SALES FUNCTIONS

For the longer term, Moore foresees an impact of the Web site on IBM's marketing and sales functions: "I think that, as electronic commerce gets more and more accepted, and as trust in the security of the Internet grows, more and more commerce will be done on the Internet. I think it's indeed competing with the sales force but, then again, for IBM, our most profitable items and services are not sold and never will be sold over the network. There are always going to be very big systems, you really want to sit down and talk to somebody. So, there's always going to be a place for the traditional salesperson."

CHAPTER 10

USAID

info.usaid.gov
Washington, DC 20523-1407

One of the initial goals was to make our business transactions with the American public transparent ... We are moving our Web site to ... be a comprehensive overview of what the agency does for the American public.

—Joe Fredericks, Legislative and Public Affairs (LPA)
Public Affairs Branch of the U.S. Agency for
International Development (USAID)

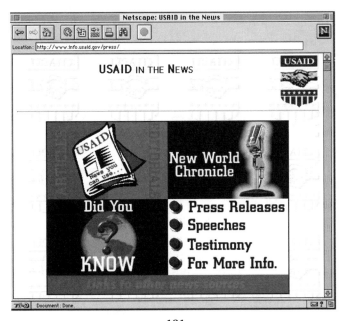

INTERVIEWEES

The Renegade/Father of the Web site: Joseph Gueron,
Division Chief, Information Resource Management

The Renegade/The Executive: Joe Fredericks,
Legislative and Public Affairs (LPA), Public Affairs Branch

The Executive: Joan M. Matejceck, Acting Director,
Office of Information Resources Management

The Webmaster: Jim Russo,
Project Manager for the Internet, Data Services Group at USAID

IN THE BEGINNING: A SURVIVAL STRATEGY, STARTING WITH GOPHER

According to Joe Fredericks, of the Legislative and Public Affairs department (LPA) of the U.S. Agency for International Development (USAID), one of the central motivations for the agency's development of, first, a gopher site and, then, a Web site was survival: survival of the agency in the Washington DC context of government contraction and budget deficit reduction.

Almost two and one half years ago, Joe Gueron, now a division chief in the Information Resources Management department, was the one who saw the Internet as the survival means to the end: "This started in the spring of 1994 as a program-funded exercise. Management was very distracted by some key financial systems that had become a critical success factor for senior management. I went to the health and energy people and I said, 'Look, I think that the Internet has possibilities. How would you like to put money together and we get a machine and one or two people a week to do a gopher?' At that moment, the Web was not as sexy as is it today.

"We started very humbly. I collected about $300,000. I had calculated I would need about $30,000 to $50,000 of capital because, at that time, Unix boxes were a little more expensive than today, so I came out with about 50K on hardware and software and I wanted to be sure that I would have the salary for two bodies: a UNIX type who would be the systems man, and one who would be what I call the soft side, the information side.

"The response was positive in one sense. It took me about three months of intellectual seduction and walking the corridors and kissing tuches and all that but, ultimately, I got the buy-in and I got going."

A Confluence of Factors. Gueron continued: "One usual premise is to use the Internet to create a communications voice for propaganda, for public relations. In this case, we didn't. Instinctively, I went to the global people and said it was going to be more a kind of academic pursuit, R&D, information on development, showing the flag, what USAID was doing. We were very, very far from thinking about the whole Internet gopher exercise as a propaganda tool.

"However, instead, several events took place coincidentally. Our management bureau was trying to do some procurement reform. There was criticism of the agency that we tended to nurture the same type of companies and that a lot of business was going to the same people. So they wanted to create more open competition. At that moment, the boss of my boss, who also was in charge of procurement says to us, 'You have to see what the Veteran's Administration's doing to have a bulletin board. I want all our RFP procurement information on a bulletin board.'

"So, as a good soldier, I didn't even mention I was working on the Internet because that was program-funded and it was scholastic and this was administration procurement. I went to see the VA's bulletin board. It was kind of sexy, but I showed it to him and then took the opportunity to show him the Internet and I said, 'Look, it is true that not everybody is on the Internet, etc., etc., but this is another way to share information about procurement.' We convinced him to allow us, rather than going to a PC-base bulletin board, to use the gopher for procurement.

A $1 Billion RFP to Start. Gueron was very nervous because the first case they gave him was an RFP for almost $1 billion for Eastern Europe. It was the beginning of USAID's aid to Eastern Europe and to the ex-Soviet Union and the Republics. USAID had decided on a vague kind of complex procurement in which there would be a multiplicity of vendors. Gueron recounted: "We were very nervous because everybody else was putting Commerce Business Daily (CBD) notices on the Internet but nobody really was putting the full RFP and we didn't know whether or not vendors were going to protest because the whole text was not there.

Internal Politics. "The problem with gopher was that you could not have images, and so we had many different ways to post the RFP. So we put it on an FTP site as a WordPerfect document. We converted it into ASCII so the vendors could read it. Thank God, everything went all right. There was not a single protest. However, the interesting thing that happened was that, as soon as gopher and Internet started being sexy, there was a fight among many people about who would control the machine, the new medium.

"At that moment, I was flying by the seat of my pants because, from a political point of view I didn't have the experience and I didn't know how to protect the thing and I knew instinctively that I didn't want to have the population people or the management bureau each running a server.

Enter LPA. "So I invited LPA [Legislative and Public Affairs], our external affairs people, to come and join us and create order where there was chaos. It was not a rational top-down decision. It was a happenstance in the sense that there were many forces and many dialogues and meetings, and suddenly LPA took the leadership. I knew I didn't want it. Then we set some procedures about the way we had to clear with LPA, we set up a special mailbox, and we went on. Everything settled down. Now some of the people in technology, in our R&D business, resented this move. Why? Because, in academia, the spirit and the principle of the Internet is that you share information and you just post whatever you please and there is dialogue and all that. And here we created a situation in which everything that gets posted on the gopher gets cleared by LPA. There was a big resentment. One group tried to use the Internet for a specific African project. I said, 'Look, if we have a corporate Web—which was being born at that moment; it had not seen the light yet, but it was gestating—and we have a machine and we have a viable team of contractors and we have not dropped the ball, I don't think you have any theological foundation for giving money to somebody else to create another Web base talking about the ID [international development] business. I raised hell and management supported me."

www.info.usaid.gov

Since 1961, the U.S. Agency for International Development (USAID) has implemented America's foreign aid programs. Spending less than 0.5% of the federal budget, USAID works to promote democracy, free markets, and America's foreign policy objectives around the globe. Every president since World War II, both Democrat and Republican, has strongly endorsed foreign aid. Over the years, ten high-level national commissions set up by the White House or by Congress to review the program have given it backing. U.S. foreign assistance programs have a long and distinguished list of accomplishments. USAID's Web site content reflects the organization's mission.

At the top of USAID's home page, on the right, is the USAID logo. At the bottom is the list of services offered through this site. The wide range of offerings includes: About USAID, International Development Resources, Regional Information, What's New at USAID, Press Information, Business and Procurement, Promoting Democracy, Population and Health, Economic Growth, Humanitarian Response, Protecting the Environment, and Human Capacity Development.

Underneath that, the visitor is able to choose from Search, Phones, Gopher, FTP, and Comments. At the conclusion of this page is the organization's mission statement.

ABOUT USAID

On this page is some background on the organization. USAID is described as a provider of economic aid and humanitarian assistance to advance United States economic and political interests overseas. Established in 1961 by President John F. Kennedy, USAID has achieved a compelling record of achievement, which can be explored through the site. The remainder of the page is a political statement explaining why USAID and other forms of foreign assistance are essential to U.S. interests. There are many polls and statistics that can be chosen to help support this argument in favor of the continuation of organizations such as USAID.

INTERNATIONAL DEVELOPMENTAL RESOURCES

This page lists the sites that may be of interest to people and organizations involved in humanitarian and development efforts around the world. There are a variety of divisions, all of which can be linked via the USAID site. Among the choices are:

U.S. Government (ranges from the Department of State to the Peace Corps and many others)

Embassies (includes the Electronic Embassy Index and Bosnia Herzegovina)

Non-governmental and private voluntary organizations

Government agencies

Internet services in developing countries

General indices and reference information

REGIONAL INFORMATION

The choices at this site include all the locations where USAID's presence is felt: Africa, Asia and the Near East, Europe and NIS, and Latin America and the Caribbean. Underneath this written list, there is also a map that one may click onto to learn about the USAID projects currently under way. For example, after choosing a continent, such as Africa, there is a large selection of choices, including: Africa Dissemination Service, Africa Link, Famine Early Warning System, Greater Horn Information Exchange, Leland Initiative—Africa Gull Gateway, and Natural Resources Management. Thus, it is clear that the majority of USAID's energy in Africa is devoted to preserving the environment and using the land more effectively.

At the bottom of this page is a long list of African nations that are served by USAID. Each country may be clicked on to explore the efforts occurring in that nation. Following that is a Congressional Presentation for the Fiscal Year 1996.

WHAT'S NEW AT USAID

This section includes recent information about developing countries such as the World Food Summit and recent AIDS/HIV developments.

PRESS INFORMATION

There is a USAID in the News selection, in which one is able to read in recent news stories about what is going on at USAID and what editorial pages around the nation are saying about the organization.

BUSINESS AND PROCUREMENT

The choices on this page includes USAID Procurements, USAID's Business Information and Services, the Office of Small and Disadvantaged Business Utilization (OSDBU), USAID West Coast Outreach Program Newsletter, Direct Economic Benefits of U.S. Assistance Programs (by state), USAID Phase I Customer Service Plan, USAID Procurement Regulations (handbooks), Proposal Preparation Resources, Egypt/Commodity Impact Program, and the Office of the Inspector General.

PROMOTING DEMOCRACY

This page is devoted to USAID information on promoting and building democracy and to USAID's strategy. The rest of the page is devoted to emphasizing instances in which foreign assistance has helped to promote democracy in nations such as Mali, Russia, South Africa, and Zambia. If these short articles are not enough, there is an opportunity to click on choices for more information at the bottom.

POPULATION AND HEALTH

This section of the Web site includes information on population and health, HIV/AIDS developments, and demographic and health surveys programs (DHS).

INITIAL WEB SITE CONTENT

Joe Fredericks, of the USAID LPA group, is one of the renegades who initially developed the agency's external Web site. "Two and a half years ago, I realized that they needed to feed substance into the site, that they needed substance very quickly and they came to me and my writers and said: 'Help.' Now it consumes my days. My role is to manage content and to oversee the development of content and the overall flow of the site. When the Web site went up in March 1995, we started out with basic materials."

WEB SITE CONTENT ARCHITECTURE

Fredericks elaborated: "If you look at our image map, we've divided our world up into sectors that we work in. We started out with a page or two on these sectors. We divide our development work into five areas: Economic Growth, Promoting Democracy, Protecting the Environment, Population/Health and Nutrition, and Humanitarian Response.

RFPs on the Web. "One of the first efforts was to put up information describing generally those five areas of effort. The sixth item that went up almost immediately, which actually came from the gopher—and a lot of it still comes from the gopher—was all of our business transactions. One of the primary goals that drove our Web site was to make our business transactions with the American public transparent, so all of our procurement notices went up immediately: Notices about offerings of requests for proposals, requests of all sorts, all of our requests that come in, that go out to the public for information went up immediately; procurement conferences went up immediately. On a dollar volume, we procure goods and services in the range of $5.5 to $6 billion a year. It's all up and available on the Web site now.

"We still don't conduct actual transactions on the Web site. We do provide all the information. For instance, instead of having to come in and formally request the RFP, you can just download it from the site now. That accessibility and that ability to get RFPs quickly and easily are radical changes. We've eliminated some mail, and eliminated some clerks.

EXPANDING THE PUBLIC RELATIONS ACTIVITY

Access. "We wanted to develop a mechanism to expand outside the traditional let's stick press releases in an envelope and throw them out the door and see if anybody happens to pick them up, and get away from the traditional press offices that normally have this list of contacts that they mail to, you know, or they use a list of the top hundred newspapers and media outlets. We decided very quickly that we wanted to increase the access to the press information, as well as provide alternative methods to our established media outlets to get our information. So the press information was one of the first things after that initial first bunch of stuff that went up on the Web. The press stuff went up very quickly. It was, at first, just our press releases. We then started going proactive. The next step was to develop a Listserve function, which is up and has grown dramatically since we first started it. And then we moved to a much more proactive step. What you see now is actually decentralization of the Web function. Dan Israel, of our press office has taken over the maintenance of that portion of the Web, which is a major step for us. We're using him as a guinea pig, exploring having the press office be responsible for the content and for the maintenance and posting of material.

THE MOTIVATION

"One intent was to increase the distribution and the access to the information but, over the past year and a half or so, the agency, like a lot of other agencies in Washington, has been threatened with extinction with the move on Capitol Hill to abolish the agency. We very quickly moved into a very aggressive role in putting out information to defend our existence.

Press Clippings. "One of the ways we did that was to collect and post, collect and distribute, favorable press comments, which you see up on the Web site now in the press information section, a whole series of editorials and articles that provide favorable reviews on the agency and its work. We made a very conscious decision, and our format is actually a little unique because we actually put images of the clippings, not just the text up. And we felt it was very important from a credibility standpoint to take that extra step and utilize that technology that was available to put the actual clipping up on the Web rather than just having a text-based piece of information.

INTEGRATING STRATEGIC OBJECTIVES

"We started out by saying, 'Hey, this is neat. Let's put something up.' And we just started putting materials up. But, like most government agencies USAID does not have a detailed, comprehensive overview of what we do for a living. As you can imagine with something between a $5.5 and $6 billion program a year, a comprehensive overview of our activities would be extensive, but would be out-of-date the minute we published it on paper, and unbearably tough to read. We are moving our Web site to do that, to be a comprehensive overview of what the agency does for the American public.

The Web Site as General Publication. "It's becoming an integral part of our overall communication strategy. The agency does a huge number of paper-based publications, but the publications tend to be very specific on very specific projects and activities that we carry out and fund. What we're viewing the Web site as is the general publication, it's the targeted technical document versus the general mass publication. Our Web site is very quickly becoming the agency's overview document.

THE WEB SITE'S FUTURE: INCREASING THE DEPTH

"What's happening now with the Web site is that it's taking the next step from a comprehensive broad overview of what the agency is doing. We are starting to post information that is very project-specific, that contains much more detail of the nitty-gritty of what we actually do, so you'll notice bits and pieces in our Web site that detail very specific projects. That's occurring at a very rapid rate. These segments are being done very quickly; I reviewed three or four of them yesterday. And so, the next step in our site is to increase the depth and to increase the technical information that's contained in it. Ultimately, what our vision is for it is that it should be a very comprehensive but a very deep document, that it should provide not only a comprehensive overview, but also the depth of detail to support that overview."

THE WEB SITE'S FUTURE: NEW TECHNOLOGY

Replacing Satellite Transmission. Fredericks continued: "We produce a weekly 15-minute radio program, and we are right now actually working with Jim Russo and his crew to start distributing a radio program over the Net. One of the things we're arguing about is what application we're going to use, whether we're going to use real-time audio or Voxware or whatever. But we will digitize our radio program and have it available for download. We currently distribute by satellite. What we're hoping to do is phase out our satellite distribution, if we can get up to near-broadcast quality; then we can eliminate the distribution over satellite and have our outlets that air the program pick it up off the Web.

Video Clips and Conferencing. "We have two video clips up now and, currently, we're just beginning to explore videoconferencing. But we have our public service announcement, up, and we have one other video up right now, and we are in the process of producing four overview videos for the agency, and they will be up on the Web as soon as they're done."

THE OFFICE OF INFORMATION RESOURCES MANAGEMENT ROLE

The Office of Information Resources Management is the centralized information technology organization for USAID. It handles technology planning, technology implementation, and all the strategic and tactical information systems for USAID. Joan M. Matejceck is acting director.

SHIFTING STRATEGIC PERSPECTIVES

Like virtually all those interviewed, Ms. Matejceck observed that, while USAID's initial gopher site, as well as the initial Web site, had one or two central purposes, the vision of the Web site has expanded to include a multiplicity of audiences: "I think there's been

a subtle shift. Actually, I think there was more of a distinction between the gopher and the home page than there has been for the
home page itself. For the gopher, one of the main strategic objectives was doing business through the Web, and secondarily, communicating information about USAID to the public.

"Now the home page is really about communicating information
to the public, to our development partners, to a number of audiences about USAID. By far, now, the areas that have the most play
deal with regional information that we have out there. The International Development page is accessed by government people, and by
university people, by private sector people. Used to be that the primary area was the business area and that was principally accessed
by people who wanted to do business with the agency."

THE INVESTMENT BEYOND LAUNCH

Matejceck continued: "It wasn't a whole lot of additional investment
because, at the front end, what we did was buy hardware, buy some
tools, bring contractors on, which for us was the biggest expense,
and we have an ongoing expense for upgrading tools and things
that is really pretty minor. Our major cost, when you come right
down to it, is the people we are applying to it and I'd say we're probably running somewhere in the $300,000 to $400,000 a year range on
people and that's it. But, when you think about it, I guess, from my
perspective, this office runs around at the present time, with some
development efforts under way, with around 40 million a year as a
total budget, and $400,000 of that might go to the Web. In my opin-
ion, we're getting a lot of bang for the buck out of that."

ENTER INTRANET

Matejceck went on to say: "The thing I'm most excited about is the
corporate Web really. As an organization, we really need that. We
need to be able to share information in a way that this technology
allows us to do. I think our external Web site is going to continue to
do the functions that it is doing. I think it is going to continue to do
them really well. I think we needed to grow and be able to deal with
information differently as an organization internally, and I think
that's one way that we're branching out right now.

WEB SITE STRENGTHS: CREATING AN INTERNATIONAL AND INTERNAL COMMUNITY

"Apart from the public relations aspects," Matejceck said, " another advantage is that this site, along with several others in the foreign assistance community, if you will, has been helpful in pulling together the foreign assistance organizations as a community in a way that we haven't done before. Now we have links to other areas like the World Bank and the Peace Corps and other organizations that we work with a lot and, at the same time, they can get up-to-date information about us in ways that weren't possible before.

"It's my impression that we are working faster, more, and better with other organizations outside our own, and that is really valuable for the people here who do intensive development work. One of the things that I've noticed is that the corporate Web gives us links also to other federal agencies that work in similar areas and that we are working more closely with them and with our own organizations internally to pull information together in ways that we've never done before. Before the Web, we all just sort of worked with blinders on and kind of sent paper back and forth between organizations. This makes the communication much more immediate and much more accessible, and I think it is going to have a long-range impact on my organization as an IRM organization, as a technical organization that's doing technical coordination for the agency. It changes the way we do business. It changes the partnerships we have with people.

"For example, we have dealt for a long time with an organization here that is the corporate history, if you will. They keep the corporate library, paper copies of reports that have been done on development. Every time a development activity is done, it is looked at and studied, and the results of that go into this corporate library, and we've had a long-standing relationship with them that was based on their providing basic data services and things. We've been working with them to make all that library information accessible on the Web internally, and that's going to have a phenomenal impact, but it also creates a different working relationship between this organization and their organization. Because we're now working with them to facilitate their making their information available rather than going to them as a traditional information technology shop and saying: 'Well, let's see, what can we do here?' and doing some kind of limited thing. They own that information and retain that ownership in this environment much more, I think, than they've ever been able to do in the past, and that's good for all of us.

BREAKING DOWN THE BARRIERS

"It's been kind of an old saw for a long time," Matejceck continued, "but it's very true that, a lot of times, the source of distrust and anger is lack of knowledge, and we can't hold onto that anymore because we know so much more than we ever did about the other organizations we're doing business with, and I think that does break down a lot of walls. I think it's the speed. I think it's the ease. I think it's just how rich the environment is for you sitting in your office in front of your screen.

"I have a little story I'll tell you. It's my favorite story about the home page and I think it illustrates for me one of the neat things that has happened for us as an agency since this thing came on. I heard this from the chief of my contracting organization who was out beating the pavement looking for people to do business with USAID a few months back.

"He went to Los Angeles to a trade conference. He went with a trade rep out there. They were sitting in a room with maybe 50, 60 people, and they'd taken a laptop and were showing the home page and showing the place where the business opportunities were, and somebody in the front of the room raised his hand and said: 'But I don't know how I can do business with AID. I don't know anybody at AID. I don't have any relationships with anybody at AID,' and a guy in the back of the room raised his hand and said: 'Can I answer that?' He said: 'I manufacture medical supplies. I happened onto this home page and I looked at the business opportunities and, looking through there, I managed to find three I could bid on.' He said: 'Electronically, I got the solicitation document, bid on all three, won all three; I provided the supplies, submitted a bill, got paid ... and I still don't know anybody at AID.'"

CHAPTER 11

INTERNAL
COMMUNICATIONS
ON THE NET

THE INTRANETS ARE COMING, THE INTRANETS ARE COMING

There is a growing body of evidence that America's organizations (both for-profit and not-for-profit) are discovering the value of building internal Web sites, or so—called Intranets. Intranets, defined as internal web servers used for specific tasks within an organization, are growing faster than the Internet, according to preliminary statistics from International Data Corporation (IDC). The number of Intranet servers totals 70,000 (55% of total servers) and is expected to nearly triple in 1996 to more than 200,000 and to exceed 4.5 million by 2000.[1]

As recently as two years ago, Intranets were virtually nonexistent. Yet, now the market for internal Web servers—the hearts of corporate Intranets—is worth about $476 million, according to Zona Research Inc. in Redwood City, California. Two-thirds of all large companies either have an internal Web server installed or are considering installing one. Netscape attributes more than half its revenue to customers building Intranets.

Forrester Research predicts that the Intranet server business will hit $1 billion by the year 2000.

Zona Research also estimated that sales of software to run Intranet servers will skyrocket to more than $4 billion in 1997, up
from $476 million in 1995. Zona projected that future sales will hit $8
billion in 1998, four times the size of the Internet server business. (A
Forrester Research Inc. survey of 50 major corporations found that
16% have an Intranet in place and 50% either are planning one or are
considering building one). Zona also found that the heaviest informal Intranet application was document sharing (67%), followed by
group communication (17%) and information sharing (17%).[2]

Corporations' internal Web sites already outnumber their external sites. While exact figures are unavailable, industry analysts believe that corporations will soon deploy ten times as many internal
Web servers as external ones. At IBM, the ratio has hit 30 internal
servers for every external server, according to comments posted to
an online discussion group.

An Intranet connection on every desktop is an idea whose time
seems to have come. Anecdotal and reported internal Web sites
also point clearly to the rapid adoption of Web sites as an internal
corporate communications tool by many of North America's largest
and mid-sized companies. To draw a clear picture of the current impact of technology for employee communications, Cognitive Communications Inc. and Xerox cosponsored a survey in the spring of
1996 of 731 corporate communicators primarily from Fortune 500
corporations. The response rate was 23%, with 165 communicators
representing 162 companies responding. According to the report,
"While the primary focus [was] on employee communications, this
report provides senior executives, employee communicators, technology and line managers with insights on how technology may be
used strategically to provide a competitive edge for employee communications."

Among the key findings of this survey, 95% felt that employee
communications must take a key role in assisting their companies
in technology upgrades. This is up from 79% in 1994. Another finding was that "The use of electronic media (e-mail, electronic
newsletters, Intranets) for internal communications is overtaking
print faster than expected." The report further states: "The overwhelming acceptance and expansion of e-mail within corporations
in the last two years, coupled with the explosive growth of Web

technology, has made electronic communication the primary medium of choice for communications professionals at many corporations. Currently, survey participants use electronic media 21 percent of the time and project that by 1999 electronic communications vehicles (e.g., Intranets, electronic newsletters) will represent 40 percent of their communication mix." In contrast, the respondents predicted that they will depend on print communication only 29% of the time three years from now, versus 52% at present.

Of the survey respondents, 85% are currently implementing or planning an Intranet site. Further, the respondents report that this new electronic medium has opened additional career paths for them and for their staffs as cross-functional strategists, team leaders, and content architects. Further, more than half the communicators have reached out to establish formal ties with their company's information services departments in order to implement these technologically driven communication strategies, a finding consistent with the analysis in Chapter 15.

Other results confirm observations made elsewhere in this volume—communicators continue to report that the use of these electronic technologies for employee communications speeds up decision making, shortens the communications cycle time and reduces costs. Also, 64% of survey respondents said that these technologies helped flatten their corporate hierarchy. They overwhelmingly agreed (92%) that technology is essential for the effectiveness of their departments.

SPECIFIC EXAMPLES

With respect to the growing use of web technology for Intranet purposes, a broad range of Intranet examples abound, including: the Xerox, Sun Microsystems, and US WEST cases in this volume, systems integrator Mitre Corp., consulting firm Booz-Allen & Hamilton Inc., IBM, USAA, MCI Communications, Sybase Inc., PanCanadian Petroleum, and Chevron Inc.

For example, in the summer of 1996 Visa International Inc., will have connected its 19,000 member banks to an Intranet in the hope it will reduce, if not eliminate, the more than 2 million documents the banks collectively send Visa each day.[3]

At Sun Microsystems, 22,000 computers are hooked up to an internal TCP/IP network with 500 internal Web servers. These servers reside inside the corporate firewall, though certain information such as e-mail is passed across the network. Each department has its own home page, while the network is also used for research and development, including testing of Sun's networking products.[4]

Drugmaker Eli Lilly and Co. is linking 16,000 of its 26,000 employees. The Indianapolis company plans to use its Web page as a gateway to corporate databases. At MCI Communications Corp., departments, such as engineering and advanced technologies, have set up home pages to discuss breakthrough technologies and to get ideas for product development.

At Sybase Inc., the $1 billion software maker, departments from engineering to personnel have put up home pages on the company's internal network to share information about what they're doing. In addition to department-sponsored home pages, employees are setting up individual home pages with personal and career information. Sybase has more than 3,000 desktop computers hooked to more than 20 proxy servers on a global firewalled network. Sybase employees use their internal network for engineering support, technical training, and documentation. The Sybase Web site provides an excellent example of the blending of external and internal organizational communications. The site offers a link to employment, such as: "Interested in an exciting career at Sybase? Send your resume ... to be considered for a position at Sybase." At the resume page, prospective employees are asked to submit their resumes to the company electronically. In effect, the external Web site is a virtual recruiting site, providing yet another example of how Web sites (both internal and external) are eliminating barriers between customers (or, as in this case, prospective employees) and the organization.

At Chevron, the company's Intranet is moving to include things like policies, procedures, and employee listings.[5] 3M's global network depends on timely economic analysis to prepare business plans and stay competitive. The company can quickly disseminate its corporate economists' quarterly reports to employees anywhere in the world, instantly and securely.

At the real estate services firm Cushman & Wakefield, the corporate Intranet gives its 700 brokers access to a wide range of competitive information.

At National Semiconductor, engineers can enhance their productivity by using an internal Web site called Community of Practice, which serves as a highly secure forum from which engineers can share confidential knowledge and ideas with their colleagues.

With more than 300,000 employees, AT&T comprises more people than many medium-sized towns. To find each other, employees can use a Web page interface to a database of employee phone numbers, addresses, titles, and organizational information.

Cadence Design Systems, the world's leading supplier of electronic design automation software and services for the development of sophisticated electronic products, is using its corporate Intranet to educate its sales force about new sales strategies and processes and to provide them with the resources to help them sell.

Electronic Arts is a fast-growing interactive entertainment software company known for some of the best-selling computer games in the world. Headquartered in Silicon Valley, the 1300-employee company has embraced the multimedia capabilities of the Web to enhance employee communications.

Home Box Office is using an Intranet to access vital data for making television programming decisions and to provide its sales force with tools to help sell HBO's premium television services.

The 11,000-person Douglas Aircraft Company builds airplanes for over 200 airlines around the world. In addition to delivering airplanes, it delivers a staggering volume of aircraft service bulletins, documents that provide crucial information on how to modify and service the company's airplanes. The average bulletin is 25 pages long. The company now distributes service bulletins electronically.

There are examples at the other extreme of organizational size. Jones Hall Hill & White, a 14-attorney law firm in San Francisco, specializing in municipal financing, built an internal site in October 1994 to allow employees to communicate. Its internal site has features from legal resources to lifestyle information, including links to online news, databases, and computer support information.

THE SHAPE OF THE INTRANET IN THE FUTURE

A March 1, 1996 Forrester Report, entitled "Network Strategy Service," from Forrester Research, Cambridge, Massachusetts, made this prediction: "Over the next four years the Intranet will be enhanced with new services [beyond document sharing] that will thrust it into the limelight as the key component of corporate networks. The rise of a standards-based 'Full Service Intranet' will come at the expense of proprietary network operating systems (NOS)." The report concludes:

> By 2000, the Intranet will grow far beyond a TCP/IP network that just supports the Web. It will have five core standards-based services—directory, e-mail, file, print, and network management—that will overshadow proprietary NOS solutions from Novell, Microsoft, et al.
>
> Corporations will migrate from proprietary NOS to Full Service Intranets to get the benefits of easy connections with the outside world, multiple competing suppliers, and lower costs.

The report surmises that all this will happen because of several market drivers, among them, that business is committed to the new customer connection, that a horde of vendors see gold in the Intranet, and that open systems are cheap, cheap, cheap. Other factors will help evolve the growing Intranet phenomenon, Forrester predicts that directories will consolidate identification and security, Internet e-mail will penetrate the corporation, file service will jump to the Web, shared printers will be dragged off the NOS, and network management will stay the course.

THE INTRANET EVOLUTION: CORPORATE CULTURE AT WORK

As attested to in Chapter 15—"The Politics of Constructing an Effective Web Site"—and in the several cases in this volume, both Internet and Intranet Web sites evolve through various stages. In the early going, a narrow focus Web site is launched, usually by someone in a middle management role. With time, though, top management gets into the act, and the Web site moves from a niche application to a broad strategic vision.

Virtually every case described in this volume matches this scenario. The Intranet model is somewhat different, however, from the Internet model. Perhaps because an Internet Web site is externally oriented, it is usual for one department to have coordinative control over organizing the content and working with the various content providers in the organization. An Intranet, on the other hand, perhaps because it is internal to the organization, requires a different collaborative design. More departments are involved on a more regular basis, and the chances for initial conflict among departments are livelier.

A range of scenarios may play out. At Xerox, three renegades developed an Intranet, but only after it was sold internally did top management give the site its full blessing. At Sun Microsystems, even after an Internet and Intranet were launched, management wanted to shut them down. Only after much effort by several internal zealots did the sites survive. At the United States Agency for International Development, a conflict among departments arose for control of the Web site. The Legislative and Public Affairs department was finally given control of the site but only after one senior renegade fought hard to position the Web site in the right place. USAID has also just launched an Intranet that, ironically, is creating a more harmonious community of colleagues, domestically and internationally.

Some companies, though, get stuck. PanCanadian Petroleum Ltd. is Canada's second largest oil producer and its third largest natural gas producer. The company is engaged in the exploration, development, production, and marketing of crude oil, natural gas, and natural gas liquids. Primarily active in western Canada, the company is growth-oriented, with 1994 production of 130,000 barrels per day of conventional oil, synthetic oil, and field natural gas liquids, and 547 million cubic feet per day of natural gas.

PanCanadian Petroleum's internal Web site, launched in November 1995, functions as a corporate public relations vehicle and is used to reach eight field offices. The Chief Technology Officer is interested in partnering with another oil company, or possibly a university, to research oil and gas exploration. PanCanadian sees the Web as a vehicle that can be used for that research. Only since November has there been a significant number of people in the firm seeing the potential of databases (the firm owns IBM PCs with Sun servers and Sun workstations in the exploration area).

According to interviews with Val Mellesmoen, former Senior Analyst, Internal Communications, and Rick Barry, Senior Technology Analyst in the Technology Management Group, in early 1996 PanCanadian's Intranet was launched within a few months of the concept's being presented. Its Intranet was initiated as a direct result of the confluence of two factors. First, in 1995, top management, after years as a company with an authoritarian, bureaucratic style of management, decided to create a corporate communications department. Mellesmoen was one of those hired to create the department. Second, the company had conducted an employee communications audit. A clear statement from employees was that they wanted to get news about the company directly from the company rather than reading about it in the media. They also made it clear to management that they wanted this information in electronic rather than print form. Simultaneously, Rick Barry, of the company's Technology Management group, was already investigating the opportunities presented by the Internet. These streams combined to create the company's Intranet.

However, according to a more recent interview with Hollie Zuorro, Director of Corporate Communications, Ms. Mellesmoen has left the organization and the Intranet is in limbo. There appear to be two reasons for the stalled forward movement: one, top management is somewhat ambivalent about the Web site's value and, two, concerted effort is needed on the part of various internal departments to coordinate a cohesive strategic vision for the Intranet, a step that Ms. Zuorro is anxious to accomplish. Until that happens PanCanadian's Intranet seems destined to remain a half-born communications tool.

On the one hand, an organization's corporate culture will either nurture or squash a potential Intranet. If the corporate culture is open to the concept, it is likely that an Intranet will gestate and survive. If the corporate culture is highly centralized and rigid, an Intranet is most likely not to happen. On the other hand, if an organization is somewhere in between these two cultural poles and is lucky enough to employ an innovative renegade or two, an Intranet may just appear and contribute strategically to the organization's future survival.

Corporate culture notwithstanding, the vast majority of organizations already have the telecommunications infrastructure in place. The cost of acquiring a computer with server capacity is nominal, as is the cost of software to program the computer and create a Web site. It is more than likely that the content and technical expertise reside in-house to accomplish the necessary initial steps.

But what most often prompts a wavering management to come down on the side of an Intranet is the news that the competition down the street is launching its own strategically defined corporate Web.

NOTES

1. PR NEWSWIRE, Feb. 5, 1996.

2. A. Morri, "Intranet Outpaces Internet Growth," *Multimedia Producer*, May 1996, p. 11.

3. *InformationWeek,* Jan. 29, 1996, p. 15.

4. K. Maddox, "Building Internal Web Sites," *Interactive Age*, May 8, 1995.

5. A. Bilodeau, "One—Utilitarian Intranets Get the Message: Design Counts," *Web Week*, Feb. 1996, pp. 26–27.

CHAPTER 12

XEROX

800 Long Ridge Road
Stamford, Connecticut 06904

The initial objective for the Xerox Intranet was to create a knowledge base that contained all the information Xerox people need to do their work in the world of Xerox.

—Cindy Casselman, Manager of Interactive
Employee Communications

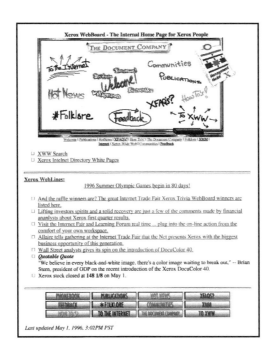

INTERVIEWEES

The Renegades:

Cindy Casselman, Manager of Interactive Employee Communications

Malcolm Kirby, Manager of Applied Collaborative Technology
Department of Information Management

Rick Beach, General Manager, Advanced Technology
Business Services, Xerox Business Services

The Webmaster:

Michael Joseph Ryan, Internal and External Web Site Webmaster
Palo Alto, California

XEROX'S INTRANET: REFLECTING COMPANY VALUES

In 1995, the Xerox Corporation (the Document Company) achieved almost $16.6 billion in sales, compared to approximately $15.1 billion in 1994 and $14.2 billion in 1993. Xerox is clearly a growing concern. Xerox's approach to the world of documents, the role of people, and the overriding theme of community as expressed in its 1995 annual report is also reflected in the scope and tone of the company's Intranet.

For example, Xerox expresses a belief in "creating productivity through the document." In other words "The document transforms information into knowledge and knowledge is power." Xerox, the leader in the $200 billion global document market, provides document services that enhance productivity.

Xerox perceives that "... the document is the heart and soul of the business process. Whether in paper or electronic form, the document structures, communicates, and preserves critical information. It provides the essential links between the people who manage processes. It binds work groups together and enables them to communicate ideas. And, because documents are an important connection to customers, they can be used to differentiate and create a competitive
advantage." Xerox's approach is that "People want to use and manage knowledge—not be buried by unnecessary information."

Xerox views the document as a complex, evolving tool that people use and reuse. Their strategy is to add value to the document across its entire life cycle: input (receipt and capture), management (archiving, retrieval, construction, summarization, abstraction, authorization, authentication, accounting, and work flow), and output (electronic distribution, printing, viewing, and use).

The company also expresses a strong sense of community. According to Paul Allaire, Chairman: "We are building a special community where Xerox people contribute, grow, and have fun. Our community is global and diverse. We see diversity as a business opportunity going beyond numbers and targets. Because we are diverse, we bring fresh ideas, opinions, and perspectives to the creation of solutions for our customers. We appreciate the value of each individual; this is a key factor in our growth and success.

"Our community is based on the principles of the ethic of personal responsibility, the need to anticipate and adapt to change, our commitment to quality, the ability of each of us to draw what we need from our community, and the company's obligation to respond to our need for information. This is an 'empowered workplace' that is team oriented and line driven, in which each of us reaches for more and contributes the maximum. We are market driven, action oriented and committed to absolute results. Xerox people are developing a deep understanding of customer needs, creating value, and doing what's right for the customer. We will add value at the right time and in the right way for customers and shareholders."

The company's Intranet is a direct reflection of these values. On the basis of in-person interviews with several Xerox executives directly involved in the creation and maintenance of Xerox's Intranet, it is clear, that without question, the overriding theme of Xerox's Intranet is the creation of community, very much in keeping with the company's strong and institutionalized "teamwork" approach to the conduct of its business.

The initial objective of the internal Web site at Xerox was to create a knowledge base that contained all the information Xerox people would need to work in the world of Xerox, such as business processes, benefits, forms, information and news about Xerox, and competitive news.

The Intranet Web site was launched in mid-November 1995 and

even though Xerox is a much larger company, the initiation of its Intranet was very similar to PanCanadian's experience. The initiative for the site did not come from top management but rather from Cynthia Casselman in corporate communications and two technology-oriented employees, Malcolm Kirby and Rick Beach and, ultimately, Mike Ryan in Xerox's Palo Alto office.

Although the concept for the Intranet did not begin with top management, it ultimately received full support from top echelons. On November 15, 1995, Xerox held its annual Teamwork Day, which acknowledges the work of Xerox employees in teams. The Xerox Intranet became part of the keynote address by Paul Allaire, Xerox's CEO, who made it very clear that the internal Web site was a key answer to what the employees had asked for—timely information accessible to everyone, knowing about what was going on in Xerox before they read about it in the press, and enfranchising people who were no longer in Xerox offices but in virtual offices.

Mr. Allaire's remarks are telling in that they echo the central themes of this book: that the Internet creates an environment in which people can connect directly and have timely access to the information they need to be productive.

Allaire said: "For the first time we have the technology available that will let us give you access to people and information in a virtual place—an online office. This technology allows us to deliver instant information to you directly—'democratically.' It supports lateral communications across all business lines and allows you easy access to the outside world of our customers and competitors. It supports the concepts behind empowerment by enabling instant access to the information you need to do your job—when you need it and where you need it."

Clearly, the Xerox Intranet is an extension of its teamwork approach, not only to doing business but also to working with employees.

Again, just as in the PanCanadian experience, only a few months elapsed between the proposal for an Intranet and its actual launch. Also similarly, a partial but significant impetus for the Intranet was feedback from a communications audit Xerox had performed in the spring of 1995. In that survey, employees indicated that they wanted information that was "timely, accessible, and honest." An Intranet seemed to be a natural solution to this employee need and to provide employees with a "connection to the corporation."

THE RENEGADES' VISION

According to Cindy Casselman, the leading Web site renegade, the initial objective for the Xerox Intranet was twofold: To create a knowledge base that contained all the information Xerox people needed to do their work and create a virtual community within Xerox. The Web site (www.internal.xerox.com) was launched on November 15, 1995. The company calls their Intranet "The Xerox WebBoard" after the ubiquitous whiteboards located in Xerox offices.

As expressed in *READ_ME.DOC*, and ad hoc newsletter, the Web-Board is "an entry point to a growing database of Xerox knowledge and information." There, employees can find up-to-the-minute news and information about Xerox, including the latest competitive information, or can explore the Xerox Management Model. The Intranet home page also has links to the Internet, Communities, Hot News, Folklore, and XFAQ's?. There is also a Welcome link in several languages.

The WebBoard is located on the internal portion of the World Wide Web (inside the Xerox firewall) because "of the sensitive nature of some of the information." Xerox employees have access to the Intranet from within the Xerox network using a Web browser, such as Web Surfer or Netscape. They also have secure remote dial-in access to the Xerox Intranet.

When asked, "How does the Web site fit in with the overall corporate communications plan? How does it integrate?" Ms. Casselman replied, "We regard this as a pull model for corporate communications, as opposed to the push model, which is what we were using prior to this. So now we have both the push and the pull."

THE CORPORATE ANGEL(S)

Who in the company godfathered the project? According to Web site renegade Rick Beach: "That's a very fascinating question and the simple answer is no one, and the more complicated answer is there were four or five godfathers. What Cindy did, to her credit, was conceive of this idea and explain it to a number of people in management, and then, I think, she was surprised at how generous they were in supporting it. So, if you're talking about it in terms of godfather, the godfather never had the idea—we did—and Cindy enrolled management in supporting it. It'd be more like a theatrical angel, a backer in the theater. We got support, cover, and financing from a set of people at the management level."

While top management ultimately gave their full support to the project (as reflected by Chairman Allaire's Team Day remarks), in the early stages, the Web site had to be sold. There were many presentations and meetings and conversations over a period of a couple of months.

Malcolm Kirby adds: "I think that understates it. Essentially, Cindy could have had these people enrolled in a vision in about a 15- to 20-minute conversation about what she had in mind. And it was generally a one-on-one presentation format. But the way I heard the story told, the presentations were much more engaging conversations than 'Here we are—you need to make a decision.' It wasn't like that. It was, 'How can you help me make this happen?' and people came along with money, and lots of things happened."

The timing of the introduction of the Web site to Xerox was fortuitous, however. An employee communications audit conducted by Xerox earlier in the spring of 1995 provided a dynamic foundation on which the Web site could be proposed. Cindy Casselman observed: "The groundwork had already been laid because we had just finished doing a communications survey of Xerox. And the results of that survey really pointed out a number of needs from the employees that this medium could answer, such as timely, accessible, honest communications."

Two central themes in Ms. Casselman's presentation helped turn the corner: "One is that we expressed the inevitability of this medium happening, and that we thought we should go after it strategically, with some objectives in mind. The other was that we were hoping—and are still hoping—to build a community that Xerox people would feel a part of, particularly if they were connected to the corporation only through their laptops."

As of early 1996 the question of evaluating the site's effectiveness was still in contention. Ms. Casselman indicated that Xerox has not set up any kind of an evaluation or measurement tool to gauge the effectiveness of the Web site at least in the short term, but it was planned. So far, the company is looking at the number of hits to the site.

Kirby added: "Before you leave the comment about what the messages were that people reacted to, I think you have to appreciate that this appeared as a credible solution to the problem that was evidenced by the survey."

FUNDING

At the outset, funding was almost nonexistent. The Intranet renegades at Xerox used existing hardware and software resources. The early budget was in the tens of thousands. Today, even after only a few months' use, all departments that contribute content to the Intranet also contribute partial funding.

It is fairly consistent with the development of Web sites at other companies that funding for the initial site was small or even nonexistent. Casselman recounted: "There was no budget. It came piecemeal from many departments. From the information management community, it came from the worldwide education and training community, and it came from corporate communications. It didn't come from marketing, because that's really the external Web site, and I'm only talking about the internal at this point. Human resources hasn't contributed to this moment, because it has its own proprietary software applications that it just finished creating that's being used. And so we haven't put that application on the internal Web site yet."

Casselman underscored the incremental nature of setting up an internal Web site—most organizations already have an internal telecommunications network infrastructure. In many instances, server hardware and applications software are cannibalized. Casselman recounted that, because of the nature of Xerox's business, the hardware was already in place. Malcolm Kirby added: "We've built an extensive Web infrastructure throughout the company. And so, this site was really just another site on top of that. We did all the design internally on a shoestring. We're talking tens of thousands of dollars." Casselman stated: "We now do have a budget for the site but, last year when we got it up, we had practically no money."

CONCERNS

Casselman reviewed some of the internal concerns with respect to the organization itself, and technical and financing problems in the early stages: "I wouldn't say we had any resistance. I would say there was concern, and there still is, as to how this is going to enable people to be more productive. I think some people are concerned that it's a waste of time, or that it hasn't been fully developed yet, so it's not really very useful—there's a lot of garbage out there, and it just hasn't reached a point where they feel that it's really going to add to our productivity. I'm sure there are people who have the concern that, yes, people will get on the Internet and just use it for e-mail all day long and do no work. There may be concerns, but there hasn't been any resistance. We have been fully supported."

INITIAL DESIGN AND CONTENT

When asked if the content that went on the initial Web site was material that came from existing materials or was newly created graphics and content, Rick Beach recalled: "Because we're thinking of this as a delivery mechanism in which there are existing materials, the building up of the knowledge base in Xerox is one of the motivations for this Web site. That's taking existing material and presenting it. But perhaps the most interesting aspect of this is creating a sense of community among the employees and management. And that's happening. There's new material presented and there are ways to use the Web site in order to enable moment-by-moment contributions."

THE TEAM AND THE COMMITTEE

Since the Web site launch in mid-November 1995, management of the WebBoard has evolved into a production team and a content committee. Said Casselman: "The corporate communications and public relations people put together a process that deals with some aspects of the daily maintenance, but not all. We are refreshing the site on a daily basis with daily headlines."

Rick Beach said, "Corporate communications people, if you will, take the editorial role. Cindy, Malcolm, and I are the ones who nurture the site, nurture the vision. And then we have a steering committee, representatives from various organizations. Xerox is a large organization. There are about 15 people on the steering committee. It meets once every couple of months. It has an irregular schedule. The Webmaster, Michael Joseph Ryan, is in Palo Alto, California."

PROMOTION

How does Xerox promote the site around Xerox? According to Beach: "There are a couple of ways. It's actually an insightful question, because we've talked carefully about how to take advantage of it. One answer is that, for new installations of software done by the information management people who load up the software on a new PC to make it work for a salesperson, for instance, the Web server configuration with all the network addresses and so forth is the default home page.

"There are some coordinated announcements. But probably the most effective is word of mouth. In November 1995, Xerox had a significant event called Teamwork Day, which acknowledges the work of Xerox employees ... in teams, obviously. And we were given a few minutes on the podium to describe our team's activity in that context. And because of the survey Cindy mentioned, it became part of the keynote address by the CEO shortly after our presentation in which he made it very clear that this was a key answer to what the employees had asked for—timely information accessible to everyone, knowing about what was going on in Xerox before they read about it in the press, enfranchising people that were no longer in Xerox offices but in virtual offices. There were some very significant comments made by the CEO, indicating that this was the way to go. So there's been a lot of reinforcement of that, as you indicate, in various print mechanisms and certainly dedication to keeping the production process informing employees."

RESPONSE

Casselman pointed out the interactive features of the Web site: "The response has been very positive. We have a lot of interactive features on our Web site [such as a specific Feedback section], so we get feedback. And that's how we're gauging the response. We have a lot of submission forms that people can use to comment and ask questions in a very simple fashion."

Rick Beach added that response to the Web site has had an impact on internal communications: "It's already changed the agenda because it's now clearly on the agenda. We're seeing evidence that everything we believed in is happening."

Casselman reflected on the Xerox Web site's strategic orientation in the context of other organizations that have set up their own Intranet: "It is my understanding that most of the internal sites out there have been kind of ad hoc. We really went after it with some real objectives in mind, particularly around building a community for Xerox people. And I think, in that area, we are ahead because that's one of our primary objectives.

Has Xerox seen an impact of the Web site on other traditional media, such as, print and other electronic communications like business television networks, and videocassette networks? According to Ms. Casselman: "A lot of people who now understand that this is another way of communicating are factoring that thinking into their communications. Do we think there's going to be a decreased emphasis on the use of print as opposed to electronic media for the Web site? We don't really think so—no. That question reminds me a lot of 'Do we think that there are going to be fewer face-to-face meetings because we have all these electronic ways of communicating?' We haven't found that to be true."

Kirby added: "There's a context you should keep in mind about Xerox. We call ourselves The Document Company-XEROX, and everybody takes that very seriously. So the basic model is that a document is a collection of information structured somehow, and there are different distribution methods and different media for conveying that information. And, as you know, a Web browser may be one, and printed documents may be another. But, at some level, we're looking for a transparency, a transformation of the content.

And then people will use the right delivery mechanism, depending on what they're trying to do."

THE FUTURE

When asked to project some sense of how they thought the Web site was going to evolve and what kind of features might be added, Casselman responded: "I believe we will get a lot more content on, in terms of publishing and distribution of really relevant information: benefits, job postings, those kinds of things. We will continue to develop the community aspect of it. And begin to put the processes in place that will enable this to go and grow."

CHAPTER 13

US WEST

1801 California
Denver, Colorado 80202

My objective is that the people inside our company that are running it everyday—whether it's the personnel installing the phone or the person who takes an order or my accounting people who pay the bills—understand the industry and,to do that, they must understand the Internet. My objective is that they use it on a regular basis.

—Margaret (Peggy) Tumey, Vice President Financial Operations
US WEST Communications

INTERVIEWEES

The Executive Visionary: Margaret (Peggy) Tumey,
Vice President Financial Operations, US WEST Communications

The Renegade: Sherman Woo,
Director, Information Technologies

Founding Team Member/The Webmaster: Suzanne Mullison

A COMPANY IN TRANSITION

Broadly speaking, there are two strategic elements to US WEST's Intranet: the Intranet's application as a competitive tool to deal with a changing business environment, and the manner in which management introduced the Intranet to ensure its long-term success.

US WEST Inc. is in the connection business, helping customers share communications, entertainment, and information services in local markets worldwide. The company's major subsidiary, US WEST Communications, provides services to more than 25 million residential and business customers in 14 western and midwestern states. US WEST Communications was created from three former Bell telephone companies: Mountain Bell, Northwestern Bell, and Pacific Northwest Bell. The company's mission is to be a leading provider of integrated communications, entertainment, and information services over wired broadband and wireless networks in selected local markets worldwide. US WEST also owns companies involved in regional, national, and international markets. For 1994, US WEST had about 60,000 employees and reported revenues of nearly $11 billion.

As a regulated utility, US WEST is going through a cultural change. It's never had to get into the competitive arena and differentiate itself from new potential competitors to provide phone service. For the first time in its 100-year history, US WEST has to worry about competition. Part of the response is the Global Village Project, an Intranet designed to foster, enhance, and augment the competitive advantage inherent in US WEST and develop information for the Intranet that will create value-added services and opportunities for employees so that they can become more adept at reacting to the competitive environment.

US WEST began as a traditional telecommunications company created from three former Bell telephone companies. Today, though, it has extended its reach beyond a 14-state region to national and international markets. In a manner of speaking, management has moved the company aggressively not just to respond competitively in a shifting economic climate but also to shape its future deliberately in this environment. The Intranet is evolving as a strategical tool integral to providing employees with the informational tools they need to compete collectively in the emerging telecommunications market.

In a subtle but effective stroke, top management, working initially in concert with Peggy Tumey, deliberately did not take an aggressive, top-down policy position with respect to the US WEST Intranet in order to allow the Intranet to take hold on a grassroots level and grow organically. In a meaningful sense, this was an insightful human resources approach to a potentially disastrous corporate culture problem. When an organization's employee population has spent years working under the assumption that its product or service is a given and then suddenly finds itself without boundaries— either to reach beyond the boundaries to seek new markets or to allow competitors to reach in to take a bite out of its heretofore protected market—this can be disconcerting, to say the least.

US WEST top management took the risk of not dictating adoption of the Intranet as a communications tool but rather allowing its employees to discover it gradually and directly. Sometimes, the fastest way to get from where you are to where you want to go is to lose the map. As Peggy Tumey, Sherman Woo, and Suzanne Mullison all detail, this approach—while certainly not perfect and far from complete—allowed for a genuine adoption of the Intranet communication medium by an employee population steeped in structure, regulations, and tradition. It is also clear that Tumey had to make a case for the Intranet. But from the interviewees, there is a strong sense of an enormous release of excitement and enthusiasm for the Intranet, fostered in no small part by top management's deliberate decision to keep its "official" hands off initially.

HOW IT BEGAN: RESPONDING TO THE COMPETITIVE ENVIRONMENT

US WEST's Intranet was originally the vision of Margaret (Peggy) Tumey, Vice President Financial Operations, US WEST Communications, as a direct response to what she viewed as the emerging competitive environment: "Over two years ago, it became obvious to me that the vast majority of the people in our telecommunications business did not understand how much the industry was going to change. Now an awful lot of that change has already occurred to us or, at least, it's much better understood by people who are in the industry who realize that all sorts of different products will be made available to customers, that it will be real competitive, and that something called the Internet is going to change how we even think about business."

Tumey commented on the impact of the shift from a protected business climate to a competitive one: "Coming from the Bell System, it was pretty easy for people to believe that, if we decided that somebody wanted a product, we could develop and then sell it to them but, somehow or other, we maintained a modicum of control. The thing the Internet proves is that you cannot control things, and that we have to work in a business and in an industry where people have all sorts of choices and the media themselves are something you can't control.

"For two weeks, I didn't sleep thinking about this because I could not figure out how I was going to explain to the leaders of the business what I meant by what I saw coming at us, which started looking like an avalanche to me. So Sherman Woo and I tried to articulate these concerns. In the old days, everybody knew how to use the telephone. Then we determined that our industry was largely about computers and we insisted that most people learn how to use a computer. To me, the next generation of that was that everyone needed to learn how to use the Internet.

"Sherman and I spent some time together, and he went off and thought for a while by himself and came back and said, 'We need to use the Internet inside, just like it exists on the outside.' This is when Mosaic was available, around November 1993. Our internal network is configured like the external Net, which allowed us to use Mosaic inside our business."

A GRASSROOTS, RENEGADE MOVEMENT STRATEGY: TACIT TOP MANAGEMENT BLESSING

Together with top management, Tumey developed an internal communications strategy not only to launch the Intranet but also to secure its long-term viability. She made appointments to talk to the president of the company about these concerns. Said Tumey: "Two and a half years ago, people didn't get it, largely. But I knew we had to start it quietly and on our own and not insist on the top down support for something that, at that point, was radical. It wouldn't have worked, even if the president was supportive of my doing it.

"At that point, we started on our own and a lot of the officers knew that I was doing it on my own and that I was paying for it out of my own budget. We bought some computers, but I could not buy fancy furniture and space. So our Global Village has a very homespun feel to it. The furniture is from the flea market and the computers sit on orange crates."

THE GLOBAL VILLAGE: THE FIRST CUT

US WEST's Intranet started as a way to communicate changes in the business to the work force in general. According to Sherman Woo: "When we began using the Web, we were not attempting to demonstrate the use of the Web as much as we were trying to use the Web as a way of communicating information about business changes that we felt were on our horizon in the telecommunications business."

US WEST's Intranet was launched in the spring of 1994, making it one of the oldest Intranets in the United States. Said Woo: "We did get a big head start on a lot of people. When we first started, for example, most of the lists out there had less than 100 businesses that could be seen. And this was way before any of the indexes got built. And it was approximately three months after Mosaic was introduced that we began using pieces of this for our own internal purposes."

The site has at least three purposes, the first being communications. The second was information, the third computing. As Woo describes it: "You basically have a variant of a telephone network, except this turns broadcast on its ear and deals with narrowcast instead. As a communications vehicle, the Web is actually teaching people a different way to communicate. There are lots of words written about computer-mediated communications, but it is about relearning things that have been lost to us as participants in this culture. We believe the work force has been the product of many years of broadcast programming, basically, where we've been taught to sit by the electronic campfire every night to take lessons from the market. It gives us both our economic and our professional dreams.

"And we've built an economy that uses this broadcast mechanism to manage and stabilize our buying habits, and our production habits. And it's worldwide. We've all been products of this broadcast culture. I think what the Web teaches us is to relearn how to write and how to form ideas and to communicate those ideas in a way that actually emulates the advertisers and the other broadcasters. I mean, we've seen that over and over again, where a group or an individual wants to use the Web that way. And I think, after some experimentation and some feedback, there are probably an infinite number of ways in which the Web can be used to communicate at different levels, which is going to enlarge either our concept of what broadcast is or my concept of what narrowcast is."

FROM INITIAL FUNDING TO ONLINE

Tumey provided less than $100,000 to get the Intranet going. It took a few months to go from proposal to actuality. Currently, Woo has a client-funded budget, representing perhaps 30 departments that is in the millions. According to Woo, clients see the Intranet as an investment: "What they're investing is the use of the Web for their own business purposes. And so the business value that they want out of it has been justified on the basis of the program that the particular business unit's working on." Currently, about 20,000 people out of the Communications company's 51,000 employees have access to the Intranet.

CONVINCING EMPLOYEES: THE WEBMASTER ROLE

Webmaster Suzanne Mullison was one of the five founding team members. She commented on her early Intranet role, which continues to this day: "One of the things I do is give tours, which are about an hour and a half presentations to groups of 10 to 20 company employees, letting them know a little bit about the Internet if they don't already know. We look at some of the reasons for the rapid growth of the Internet, and then how we might apply that internally. And we look at some of the sites. I try to find out where these groups of employees work and, if I have information that relates directly to their group, we stop and look at their site. If not, I show them some general kinds of tools that can be helpful to them in doing their day-to-day jobs."

Proselytizing. The current tours are an outgrowth of the proselytizing work Mullison and Woo did in the early stages. When they first started the Global Village, very few people knew of the Internet. Said Mullison: "Employees would pick up the newspaper and never read anything about it. Maybe they'd find an article once every month or so, and we'd be so thrilled, we'd cut it out and save it and paste it on a board here because it was so seldom that we'd hear about it. Consequently, none of our employees knew about the Internet. So we brought them down just to let them know about this new technology and that we were building the same thing inside the company.

Response to the Early Tours. "We got tremendous response because people found it so fascinating. At the time, I was the one who answered the Hot Line we'd set up. It's a recording, and I'd come and pick up the messages every couple of hours. The message mailbox was almost always full. Sherman Woo gave the tours at the time and we would run two to three a day. That's how much response we had—with about 20, 25 people attending each of those tours.

"I think the external media probably had something to do with it. I also think that, because we started it as a grassroots effort—from the bottom up—we were seen as rebels. And that was attractive to technology folks inside the company, who always had to follow standards. They now saw this as a way of expression that didn't have all the rules and regulations that traditional Bell System companies had. So, of course, they were thrilled with it."

GROWING THE INTRANET

US WEST's Intranet has grown organically. Woo observed: "The surest way to have scotched the whole thing was to make it official. If it's perceived as being official, then everyone connected with it expects official support and funding, and they won't really get off their butts and do anything with it until they get all the paperwork signed on it. When you make it a grassroots effort, what you attract are basically the disenfranchised and the highly motivated."

The step from concept to actuality was also enhanced by the fact that much of the technological infrastructure at US WEST was already in place. Said Woo, "There was a way for us to leverage what we had in terms of a technical network. We were able basically to place in a lot of hands the tools for authoring, for publishing, and for becoming visible rather quickly. It was all done internally. I had hired some consultants, but they didn't know any more than we did at the time. So we collaborated and worked on building this thing. Technically, I knew pretty much what had to be done."

US WEST'S INTRANET: A DESCRIPTION

US WEST's Intranet launched in the spring of 1994. As of the end of June 1996, there were 136 servers, of which the information technologies department has over 60.

The information technologies department has one of the strongest presences on the US WEST Intranet, with different sections covering various angles of the business. This is no accident. Sherman Woo, one of the founders of the initial US WEST Intranet, is part of this group. Beyond individual departments, the US WEST Intranet has a section called Online with IT, which allows employees to go in and choose whether they would like to write to an officer or ask a question via a radio-buttoned list of the officers in the department. In this manner, an employee receives a one-on-one response. Another portion, called The Rumor Mill, also allows an employee to write to the officer. But the response is not just to the individual employee; it's online so everybody else can read the answer as well.

According to Webmaster Suzanne Mullison: "It's very efficient. Years ago, I worked on the employee suggestion plan and, at that time, I had a particular person with a problem and spent a lot of time trying to resolve that issue for that man. In the Rumor Mill, I read the other day that another man had the same problem and was asking for help and, again, somebody spent a lot of time trying to help that man. Well, now it's online, so the next person who has the same question can refer to it. It's almost a FAQ [frequently asked question]."

There is an online employee directory, as well as a section entitled the The Virtual Secretary, originally created in print form by Webmaster Mullison. This site has information for the Denver area and covers such topics as: Who do you call for copy paper? Who do you call for catering? Who do you call to get an annual report? How do you get from building to building? Some suggestions of things that good caterers do, and driving directions.

The public relations department plays a large part in the Intranet's content and, according to Mullison, will be an even stronger player when the Intranet's graphics are redesigned: "The PR people manage the employee news bulletin online (EMNET). They will be having a couple of discussions groups of their own, which aren't up yet, like stock quote information and a lot of the things that are relevant to employees day to day. We have an internal directory that hits against our human resource database about once a week and provides employees with a way to access information about their co-workers in a relatively accurate manner rather than in an often outdated paper format."

RESULTS: CULTURAL AND QUANTITATIVE

The Intranet has exceeded Tumey's expectations,"particularly in our ability to access library kinds of information and talk groups. But we also use it to access critical business data that's locked in our legacy system, such as what we call the facilities check. That's the ability for salespeople to find out, when they're on the phone with you and you ask for three lines, if they have the inventory at the time they're speaking to you. Other telephone companies may not know that. Our legacy system did not have a way to deliver that current information to the front-line salesperson."

The problem with legacy systems is similar to the GE experience: Mainframe computer technology is not designed for today's Intranet/Internet applications. Legacy systems are big systems built on computer mainframes that cannot talk to one another. What US WEST is attempting is to create interfaces that will allow it to tie into all those systems and allow those systems to talk to one another so that it can pull up information instantaneously, respond to a customer service question, or provide customer service or a new connection to a residential or business customer and do so in a very timely fashion. US WEST is attempting to answer a question, fix a problem, or respond to a new order in a much more timely fashion than its competitors.

Tumey continued: "We're using Web technology to access information so that we can have a valuable conversation with the customer. Before the Intranet, we would say, 'Yes, I'll be happy to sell you three lines,' write up an order, and then come back four days later and say, 'I only have one.' That's a big problem. Nobody wants it to be that way. It's not that we're idiots; it's just that the systems have not allowed easy access to information that exists but is buried way in, practically in the code. Now that information is on the salespeople's desks or however they are accessing. They have Netscape and we've configured it to ... we have a search engine of our own beyond it that we've built that works for these kinds of systems and the interface looks like anything else you're doing on the Internet. It just is a nice little window, and you put in the address and whatever you're looking for, and it goes in and has logic and searches in our older systems and brings back the information."

TOP MANAGEMENT'S OPEN EXPECTATIONS

Another result is that top management has now openly expressed high expectations for the Intranet. According to Tumey: "There is a belief that we can leverage this to meet a lot of short-term needs in creating access to information that is currently locked in nondatabase types of systems, and that's the highest expectation because it is so leverageable. There is such value to our business in those kinds of applications, and we have a lab where we just experiment with these little ideas as much as we can, and Sherman essentially runs that lab and we stretch it to look for answers across our entire business.

"There is also an expectation but less of an understanding of the value of the communication aspect of it, and that is, I think, that when the leaders are very focused on real business, today's business needs, access to the data is the aspect that interests them immediately. We also want to have impact as leaders over a longer term,
mobilizing people to understand business issues, to behave in ways we need them to behave, to understand what leadership needs, to understand what leadership is willing to do to support them—all those kinds of almost social contract things that we do with people—that's a lot of what my focus is for the Global Village.

"It's a little bit harder to get people to focus on the long term, and by long term I mean nine months or a year. This is the next thing I'm working on with the leaders of the business. At the lower levels, especially in areas where people tend to be technically real confident, they have no trouble using this medium at all. They use it for all sorts of things. It's getting at higher levels and leveraging it for the ability to really create the community of the business that I'm looking for next.

"I think that it is easy to underestimate the power of this medium, the usefulness, what it can do, as far as connecting us around the world and with all the things that we read about, and, secondly, the power for us as individuals inside a business to use it to communicate with our people, to help them move into the year 2000, to create community. In our businesses today, we have way too much disenfranchisement through downsizing, through all the things that we've been through in the last five years across American industry."

INTIMACY THROUGH TECHNOLOGY

In line with her perspective on the communications value of the Intranet, Tumey commented on the connecting characteristics the Intranet inherently provides: "There's a great sense, I believe, of disenfranchisement, and people need to feel connected to their leaders and one of the real valuable ways we can help people be connected—it's not the only way, but it's one of the valuable ways—

is how we communicate with them using this medium, which can have a much more intimate and personal feel to it. You know, you can write to your Vice President and get a message back or you can have a chat group going on and the leader can come in and make a comment and be part of what's happening."

Sherman Woo's experience of the impact of US WEST's Intranet echoes Tumey's but also parallels the Xerox Intranet experience: "The biggest part of what we're doing is not the demonstration of technology at all, it's the demonstration of community. That's the interesting part. We started with one server and now there are something like 60 servers [in the Technology Department]. And they are at group levels and at department levels. And what my team does is basically help other people learn how to master the technology and the information so that they can put together rather quickly a site ... a system in whatever business project they're working on."

Numbers of Employees Online. Mullison estimates that probably about 12,000 to 15,000 users out of a total of 51,000 employees are currently on the Intranet: "We're at a point where we're trying to get more mainstream employees involved and interested. The typical employee says, 'Oh, I don't know anything about that computer stuff and I don't want to mess with it.' So we're trying to figure out how do we get those people—how do we present enough about value that would make those people want to take the time to configure a browser or load a browser."

Line Service Employees. There is an inherent reach problem with US WEST typical of other companies with technically oriented employees who work in the field, and that is access to the technology where they work. Within the regulated side of its business, about 30% of US WEST's employees do all the line service work and don't generally have access to the Intranet. US WEST is trying to address that problem through either departmental computers or kiosks or some other solution.

The Paperless Environment. Because they're out in the field, they don't have access or need for computers. So they don't naturally migrate or come back to a computer to look up certain things. What US WEST is attempting is the model that many other companies like Apple and others have used, and that is the paperless environment, to force people to use Web technology versus trying to go find a manual someplace. This is in keeping with US WEST's desire to reduce costs of newsletters and manuals and other associated activities that people may or may not even use and that aren't current. With Intranet access, US WEST can make everything current, and a field employee can get access to the most current information instantaneously, without having to worry about incorrect data or using the right form.

Converting Print Content into Electronic Form. US WEST is clearly a company looking to reduce its reliance on the traditional "print"-oriented communication system. US WEST might be able to reduce the costs of human resources activities if for no other reason than a reduction in the inventory and the process of filling out forms. US WEST is working on putting forms and the process of filling out forms into electronic format, where they can be submitted and managed electronically. As with most organizations, US WEST has pallets upon pallets of these forms sitting in warehouses. Managing this inventory is a tremendous and costly job. Working toward eliminating mountains of paper and the numbing process of filling out paper forms suggests a dramatic culture change in the making.

Along these lines, Woo commented: "Here's a cultural change from a staid company that perceives that everything has to be run by the book to one that wants to free up the energy and the creativity of all its employees. There is a hurdle that has to be cleared here between managers who look at time clocks as a way of understanding productivity to managers who look at results as a way of calculating whether their team has been productive or not. I think that's a big change. It has to do with concepts of what it is to actually be a learning organization. And how to provide information for that learning that takes place on the job. We think the Web is actually assisting us in understanding that and making it happen."

Corporate Memory. On the more positive side, it is Woo's opinion that the Intranet is helping to create a corporate memory and allow employees to see the corporate big picture. For management this could mean employee communications nirvana: "An employee has the ability to go to a server in a department and actually go back and look at information items over time. The requirement to publish as soon as you begin to become visible out there allows you to see many more projects and things in progress, if you will. And it becomes a way for us to keep up with each other on a daily basis, as opposed to quarterly or weekly, or whatever it takes to go through the other venues in order to become visible."

TUMEY: PREPARING FOR THE NEXT STEPS

Tumey pointed out that US WEST is preparing for the next phase in the Intranet's development with the true blessings of the organization's leaders, some of whom use it regularly. Tumey observed: "We have some leaders who absolutely understand it. That's no problem but, for general use, it's like getting officers of a business to use a computer when they have a secretary. That's a hard leap. My objective is that the people inside our company who are running it everyday—whether it's the personnel installing the phone or the person who takes an order or my accounting people who pay the bills—understand the industry and, to do that, they must understand the Internet. My objective is that they use it on a regular basis.

"They may not absolutely understand that, when they use the Internet, what they're doing is learning about the industry, but it's like using the telephone when I started as an operator. For the people to use it on a regular basis to get all the information about their benefits package or to communicate with the vice president of their department or whatever it is, the leaders have to be broadcasting information for them to respond to. It has to be a two-way street. That engagement needs to go on, on a regular basis, and that's what my next objective is—nurturing that engagement."

Chapter 14

SUN MICROSYSTEMS, INC.

2550 Garcia Avenue
Mountain View, California 94043-1100

It was a main part of our business, a main part of the way people were get-
ting information on competition, on customers. It was starting to be a ma-
jor communication tool. To try to shut it down was like saying, "We'll cut
off your phones at the end of the month."

—Judy Lindberg, Internet Program Manager

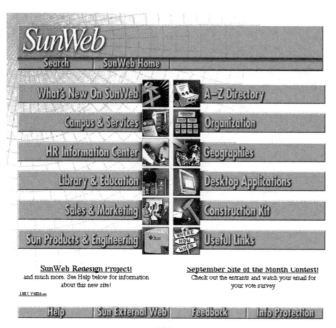

THE INTERVIEWEES

The Renegade: Judy Lindberg,
   Internet Program Manager

The Intranet Webmaster: Debra Winters

The Trainer: Jerry Neece,
   Enterprise Training Programs Manager, SunUniversity

THE SUN MICROSYSTEMS INTRANET: EXTERNAL SUCCESS, INTERNAL WRANGLING

A singular vision—"The Network Is the Computer™"—has propelled Sun to its position as one of the world's leading providers of enterprisewide network computing solutions and industry-leading Internet technologies. Structured as a group of six discrete, focused, and flexible business units, each delivering open, scalable, and powerful product and service offerings, Sun has earned a reputation as one of the world's best-managed companies. Founded in 1982 and headquartered in Mountain View, California, Sun employs approximately 15,600 people worldwide. It is ranked number 244 on the Fortune 500.

With annual revenues of more than $6 billion, Sun continues to enhance its reputation as a leading provider of products and services that enable customers to build and maintain open network computing environments. Recognized as a proponent of open standards, Sun is involved in the design, manufacture, and sale of products, technologies, and services for commercial and technical computing.

There is no doubt that Sun Microsystems is a leader in the new age of communications, particularly with respect to the Internet. Various brokerage firms recommend Sun as an investment. It is paradoxical, then, that the story behind the Sun Internet home page, as well as its Intranet, is one in which a group of very bright and talented Sun employees, obviously highly enthusiastic and passionate about the Internet's potential, met with overt internal resistance to the concept from management. From the interviews conducted for this case, what emerges is the story of a company whose public position was strong support of the development of the Internet while, internally, management resisted, for some time, the notion that the Internet was a useful communications medium.

The Internet/Intranet renegades, who have prevailed in this case, took strategically effective steps to make sure the innovation worked, steps that are echoed throughout many of the cases in this volume: formation of a team of various experts to get the project going, decentralization of responsibility for information sites on the Web site, and formation of a network of gatekeepers and Webmasters to manage the ongoing flow of content. The originators made the strategic decision to evolve the Intranet so that it fit into Sun's normal course of business rather than attempting to inculcate the new technology in a aggressively fashion.

The other story that comes out of the Sun case is the company's use of the medium for training. Leading the charge is Jerry Neece, Enterprise Training Programs Manager, SunUniversity, a bright, articulate professional with a passion for what he is doing. Neece worked out a system that takes advantage of Intranet technology, including technology developed at Sun, while working around the Internet's current disadvantages, namely, insufficient bandwidth for motion video and for complex graphics and download speed.

Overall, what emerges from the interviewee comments is that Sun is a company full of bright, talented, imaginative, technically adept, and determined people. Managing this kind of employee population must be a task indeed. But an employee population with this kind of profile, while somewhat unruly, can also innovate. Sun's Intranet is just such an innovation.

IN THE BEGINNING: A BUMPY ROAD

In the early stages of Sun's external Web site (and then its Intranet), management in this company was not convinced about the viability of the Internet or its use as a central internal communications vehicle. It is apparent from the interviewees' comments that Sun's evolution as a leading proponent of Internet technology for its own use has been an uphill climb for the renegades and zealots at Sun who are leading the charge.

THE EARLY STEPS: THE FORMATION OF THE TEAM

Judy Lindberg was one of the team leaders and original founders of the Sun Microsystems Internet site, which led more recently to the development of its Intranet. According to Lindberg, she was told to go on the Internet in mid-January 1994 to develop a Web site to be launched in April of that same year.

It is universally true of the development of an Internet or Intranet site that the effort requires a team of people with a range of expertise and experience. The creation and evolution of an Internet or Intranet is a classic example of the ad hoc project team paradigm emerging in many organizations today as a way of getting work done.

The original Sun team consisted of:

1. Andrew Barker, SunSoft
2. Jerry Meed and Wil Shelton, product marketing
3. Teresa Lau, worked for Coleen Troy in Marketing Communications; a large chunk of corporate information was on the Marketing Communications database
4. Carl Meske, a main driver on technical aspects, architecture, and setting up and working on Information Resources and security; now works for Engineering.
5. Hassan Schroeder, programmer, had worked with Oslo Net during the 1994 Winter Olympics.
6. Dr. Eric Schmidt, provided internal project support
7. Burt Sutherland, Sun Labs group (Sun's R&D lab group)
8. Jennie Trickle, Sun Labs, secured the room in the Sun Labs building in which the team holds Web team meetings
9. Daryl Sano, graphics designer, has written a number of books; subsequently went to Netscape
10. Jacob Nielson, former adviser to Daryl Sano; performed usability testing

Lindberg pointed out that the initial team was a grassroots effort, consisting mostly of a lot of people working on the Web site in their extra time. Said Lindberg, "It was something they passionately wanted to do."

AN INTERNET PRODUCT LAUNCH LAUNCHES INTERNAL EMOTIONS

Lindberg's manager at the time was Bill Lee, vice president of network engineering, which had a new product launch scheduled for April 6, 1994. Lee suggested putting up some Web pages for the launch. Sun had a product called the Voyager, which Lindberg described as "... kind of luggable—I hesitate to call it portable—but a cute little product." Lindberg described her early steps: "I started talking to legal and Irwin Berzinsky, and we started an alias right away. My machine and that alias has over 1,000 people on it now. Within the company, we have 1,800 information servers. But I had to go to legal because there were copyright and intellectual property issues that had to be addressed, and security—like don't bring home any stray software programs and potential viruses.

"We had to come up with policies and guidelines fairly early on because people would be going out over the Internet. The MIS organization at first said 'Over our dead body,' and then our management said we would have to charge anyone that used the Mosaic browser that was available at the time $50 a person per month, and all the engineers were sending flame mails and were all upset and saying, 'How dare you!,' like they had an inalienable right to the Internet. There was a big flap over this."

USING TRADITIONAL TECHNOLOGY TO PROMOTE NEWER TECHNOLOGY

The Teleconference. Lindberg called a teleconference meeting with 24 hours' notice and invited everybody to come and air their differences. According to Lindberg, Dr. Eric Schmidt participated, as well as Terry Keely, Anesh Ibrawall, and Terry Lenahan. Lenahan was one of the IR [information resources] people helpful in setting up the policies and guidelines that they wrote.

A New Internal Structure: Gatekeepers and Webmasters. Lindberg added: "We had to set up a way to manage this. We had to come up with a whole new way to do things. So we set up a series of gatekeepers and Webmasters. The Webmaster term is now part of the policies and guidelines. That title is reserved for the technical people who belong in Information Resources in Enterprise Network Services.

"Information resources people maintain the Webmaster title but we set up a series of gatekeepers. There are major gatekeepers for the Operating Company and, if you're in a business unit, every person in that business unit that has information or reports that they want to publish has to go through the gatekeeper or they're all on a gatekeeper alias and they talk about issues and how to do things or what the policies and guidelines are. The main gatekeeper is responsible for screening out inappropriate content or identifying legal issues in the information that's provided."

MANAGING WITH LIMITED RESOURCES: DECENTRALIZED RESPONSIBILITY

Lindberg's team did not have a lot of resources, so they formulated a distributed way of managing the site: "The vision was to have each group that's publishing information responsible for publishing that information on the Web, so that we don't set up a whole huge infrastructure. And so, the Web site's not a separate operation; it's part of normal business. That was our initial vision, and I think that's where it will continue to go because it fits into the organization better that way. You're not creating new things to compete or fight with other things. Not everybody was eager to do all this and we're still trying to get more participation in this in the company although it's pretty widespread now."

"SHUT IT DOWN!"

Sun's first Internet station cost $1,000 with one T1 line for the entire company—a very modest initial investment. However, according to Lindberg: "They said they would shut down the Internet activity at the end of the month and at the end of the quarter so that it wouldn't interfere with the financial reports. Within about six months or so, when it came time for them to try to shut it all off, everybody screamed because now it was a main part of our business, a main part of the way people were getting information on competition, on customers. It was starting to be a major communication tool, so that's like saying, 'We'll cut off your phones at the end of the month.' The Web site had become a critical business tool."

ALL HOMEGROWN

Despite the early resistance, Sun was among the first to create a major corporate Web site. Lindberg recounted: "I think Silicon Graphics put its page up a day before or a week before we put ours out on April 6th. But they only have one product on their Web site. We went around to every product manager of every product. We have hundreds of products."

A TWIN BIRTH: THE INTRANET

Sun Microsystems' internal (Intranet) Web site went up in March 1994, almost simultaneously with the external Web site. This is counter to the IBM experience. At IBM, the Intranet has been slow to evolve and was not scheduled to launch as an organized Intranet until the summer of 1996. At Sun, the external Web site and the Intranet were launched at about the same time because the initial Internet team had the vision to realize the communications value of an Internet Web site. Lindberg explained: "One of the good things about having your complete product line published on an external site is that most Sun employees had never seen the entire product line in one place. If you wanted to get a look at that product line, you would have to go over to marketing and pick up all the several hundred product brochures and, even then, maybe they didn't all have a brochure or something. Sometimes, it's very difficult for companies to distribute that information inside."

Lindberg also outlined the process the team went through to determine what content should be organized on the Sun Intranet: "Jacob Nielson had joined the company at that time and he had done some advising to Daryl Sano. Jacob did some usability testing, we had some cross-functional teams, and we brainstormed what kind of information employees would want to know, what kinds of things were problems, and what we were doing inside the company that we wanted to publish.

"We had people from SunSoft, Sun Federal, marketing, engineering, the library; we've always had a good representation from the IR, MIS kind of people. We brainstormed a big list: What is the kind of stuff you want to let people know about? We put those on cards and did some human factor studies, usability studies. After the cards were sorted into piles, we came up with what the major buttons on the Intranet would be. We ended up with 15 buttons initially."

THE INTRANET'S STRATEGIC VALUE

Lindberg defined the strategic communications value of the Sun Intranet: "The real advantage of having complete product information available to all employees is that they don't have to look it up and ask a lot of people but, of course, you don't know what that process was costing you in the first place. But, with the Intranet, you have people spending their time and you spending your money on things that are more productive than running around trying to find information.

"Because Sun is so high-profile, we had to be very careful about commerce and security. But I think that full electronic commerce is going to be very real. And what we're looking at is how do we make this more of a business-to-business selling tool, creating an environment for our partners, creating the virtual external corporation for solutions for customers. I think that's where it's going. I'm not sure that's what everybody at Sun thinks, but I think you'll see more development of this as a sales and marketing tool. Right now, it's kind of passive, but you can qualify sales leads, save money on literature fulfillment, put telemarketing scripting on the Web, and provide all that information to help develop sales leads before your salespeople even get in the door. You can provide forms online where customers can say what they're interested in and what their situation is with respect to buying. You can look at the sales cycle and see how much of that you can put on the Web before a customer even comes in, so you get them closer to a sale."

The Sun Intranet experience echoes some of the motivations for US WEST's Intranet, particularly with respect to providing employees with competitive information, and saving on administrative costs. Says Lindberg: "When you have a complicated product, customers have to be educated as to how they can use it and what it is. So, looking at it from the standpoint of how we can solve a lot of these business problems and move customers closer to the buy decision can be a tremendous saving in time and money and in resources. Plus, you can tie that into financing and funding the customers and linking them up with partners and improving the partner relationship. So you can say, 'Here's the solution.' You can give examples of solutions that include partners, and link directly to their pages of how to buy their part of the product. Using it more as a business tool, outside and then inside on the Intranet.

"What we're seeing already is Phase I in the evolution is publishing and providing information to different people in groups. You can save a lot of money there. For example, I've published a bunch on how Sun saves time and money on the Internet, articles on the outside that you can look at. One, titled "SunTea," is about how we do our expense reporting online. And they're going to be Java typing that tool. Before, you used to fill out a form and then you'd have to have an administrator or somebody carry it around to the approval people, who often weren't in their offices. It'd get left on a desk and then you wondered what happened to it and it'd get lost and then you'd have all this frustration of running around trying to get that closed. Now you fill it out online and it won't let you submit it unless all the fields are correct and then, once you summit it, it's e-mailed to all the approvers, and you know exactly who's approved it and who hasn't, and the whole thing occurs online. If it's an expense report, finance can write you a check and the turnaround on those checks is much shorter. I think they're saving at least 50% or more over the cost of doing it the old way. And what you don't capture on that cost is everybody's time wasted when you have to redo a form or it gets lost—or you know the time of the person running around and doing this, but you don't even capture that because you don't know how much you spent on it in the first place."

STILL A BUMPY ROAD

Lindberg's experience nurturing the Sun Internet and its Intranet to their current status parallels in part Peggy Tumey's at US WEST. While Tumey had tacit top management approval, Lindberg had an uphill struggle getting the technology (that Sun has a high reputation for) applied internally as an effective communications tool: "This Intranet infrastructure is important, but it's taken this long to get recognition going, and in my case, they told me to go push this, but I'm in engineering. They get driven by how much hardware they're moving. They don't make the link between creating the demand that this Internet project has created and the perception of Sun as a leader on the Internet. They don't link that with what we've been doing. So I'm being told to not do the stuff that helps the whole corporation because I work for the group that's pushing the hardware. They want me to do something else, but I don't want to do something else.

"You see the potential, but they're saying 'What good does it do for us to do general Internet talks when we're trying to sell network products?' I'm hoping I'll get on with one of the groups that are doing something on this, but it's been very slow to get out there. The same is true for Jerry Neece. Jerry was extremely powerful in this and we had given proposal after proposal in this group. He got frustrated and went over to sales training. Jerry said, 'I may go down in flames, but I light the way for others.'"

TRAINING ON THE INTRANET

Jerry Neece, Enterprise Training Programs Manager, at SunUniversity, had an early Internet role and did a lot of evangelism in 1995. But he decided it would be better if he actually tried implementing Web technology instead of just talking about it.

The Distributed Network Training Model. Neece explained that, since he's a university professor in the evening and has done training jobs in the past, he accepted a job to reengineer Sun's training into what is being called a distributed network model. Currently, a lot of the training is done at headquarters. Because Sun sells in 147 different countries, it flies salespeople in to spend a week or two on training. Says Neece: "There's really nothing wrong with coming to headquarters. Sun salespeople really should know what headquarters is like and later, when they bring customers in for briefings, they'll know the lay of the land."

Huge Potential Cost Savings. Neece observes, however: "There are tremendous cost savings involved if the number of trips a typical salesperson makes to headquarters is reduced from four a year to three a year by delivering one of those classes that they might have taken place at headquarters onto the network. Now they are not doing Web-based training, but they are a step beyond that already.

The Web's Too Slow. In the spring, Neece encoded a piece of video that Sun's founder, Scott McNealy, created in which he talks about "the zero administration client," or the Java terminal, the network computing box. It required 300 megabytes of storage to encode that in MPEG. Neece remarks, "My contact in our MIS group told me several months ago when I took over this project that he would shoot me if I tried delivering 300 megabyte MPEG movies across his network, even if it was Scott McNealy."

Local Classes. It became apparent that there would have to be a solution that didn't involve the wide area network but still had the capability of delivering video. Says Neece: "One can deliver what is called the 'big stuff' locally, meaning that, with a combination of a Netra Web server in a Sun media center, one could actually deliver a stream for the MPEG one video and audio files at high speed over a switched 10 ethernet.

"The cost of upgrading the branches from the current 10-based ethernet, where everyone shares 10 in a branch, to a dedicated 10 megabits for every desktop is actually quite low. It's less than $10,000 per branch. So, over the next two and a half years, the company is changing all the branches worldwide, about 200, to switched technology from the shared technology."

CD-ROM Training via Netscape. Another common goal at SunUniversity is to design for the lowest common denominator, defined by Neece as one of his new salespeople in the People's Republic of China. They are not connected to the Sun wide area network, so training down any kind of network base cannot be delivered. Neece was forced to use CD-ROM, and he now delivers a package of ten CDs to a new hire on the first day. When the new hires load onto a CD drive on their laptops, they will be able to be trained just as if it were on the Web because the graphical user interface (GUI) to get to that CD is Netscape.

Neece comments: "It looks like the Web because the data comes up instantaneously on a hyperlink, unlike a search and fetch operation. When MPEG movies are clicked, for example, Scott talks about a new network computer. The MPEG starts running instantaneously in a 4- by 5-inch window in the middle of the browser. There is no latency involved, so one does not have to pace one's study to include the elapsed time. How long might it take me to fetch a 300-megabyte file? Days probably, so that's not an effective way to do it. The video is extremely effective; to watch the founder of the company actually share his vision on this box is something that every employee, not just the new hires, should see. The only way to really do this is to deliver it on a CD so they can read it from their laptops, somewhere in the branch or with the model that puts a Netra and a video server in each branch."

Netra is an acronym for a Sun product line of network-attached devices. It is a platform that does one thing and does it well. In the case of the Netra Internet server, what Netra does is Web-serve. Its best feature is that it gives the user connectivity to the Internet. Can you load Oracle on it if you want to, like a hardware platform? No. It was built to serve the Web only and to give interconnect. Sun believes that there is an emerging market for inexpensive (less than $20,000) specific-purpose devices. They can't be used for a general-purpose server, but whatever is put in that box is optimized to run a particular thing. The Video Server is an example, the Netra Internet server is an example, The Sun Screen Security product is an example. Neece comments: "We just introduced a box called the Netra NSF 150. All it does is serve NFS, nothing else. We've been able to produce a function-specific box at half the cost, and with three times the performance."

According to Neece, "I'm just teaching everything as a data type. I don't care whether it's video or audio or GIFs or whatever, it's just bits to me, and the way I distribute them out to those branches is a software distribution internal to the network called Softdisk, short for software distribution, and that's a mechanism that's been in place for years and years and it's the way, in the client/server environment, we ship the next, the latest version of Netscape out to all the branches or the latest version of whatever processing tool we use."

Neece, in effect, is using the network to update training content on a weekly basis during off-hours. Because this is a store and forward model, he doesn't have to do it in real time at 10 o'clock in the morning when the network is all plugged up. Late at night, when the network is not being used, he shoves the content over the network and gets it out to the furthest location within about three days.

"In the branch, they sit at their workstation and, from their desktop they take the training. It is served onto their desktop in the branch. People obviously want to take it home, and that's why it's also available on a set of ten CDs that you can just plop in, read on your laptop, and play at home as well."

SYSTEM COST AND JUSTIFICATION

The cost of the combination of hardware and software at the branch, the local delivery mechanism with the video server, the Web server, and all the software needed to run and manage it, plus or minus ten grand, is in the $50,000 to $60,000 range per U.S. branch. "To put that in perspective," says Neece, "this is the justification we used to fund it. If, for example, there are $3,000 salespeople in the field and the average cost of a trip for a week to take training from Europe is about $2,200 and from Asia is about $3,000 and the number of trips those 3,000 people take is reduced by one each a year, take the 3,000 multiply it by the $2,500, and that's how much money Sun saves. Just in reducing the air travel cost and hotel expenses, it more than pays for the network. In terms of Intranet applications," Neece concludes, "the one that will pay for itself fastest is probably training, simply because it has such a large cost elimination associated with it that is travel."

"It won't eliminate people coming to headquarters, but it will reduce the number of times they come. There are many things that can be done better at headquarters because these people are real subject matter experts." Neece is in charge of training new hires and the sales curriculum. The real focus right now is on new hires in the sales and technical force.

The Old Training Model. Neece is using a combination of class-room and network-based training to accomplish what is currently happening only in the classroom. In the old model, 42 different pre-senters would present their area of expertise over a four and a half days. That included all the product lines, all the markets they were sold in, and all the resource groups people could call on to help them get the sale. They all delivered foils and on Tuesday after-noon, the first people were starting to fade. "By Thursday," Neece recalls, "if the retention rate was 10%, I was lucky. It was just a fire hose. It was great training. In fact, it is. The people that came in say, 'Hey, your training the people you have in front of us here are really the best I've seen in the industry, but it comes at us so fast, we can't retain it all.'"

The New Training Model. What Neece needed was to take the in-formation presented in class and distribute it through a delivery mechanism that would allow people to read more at their own pace. That's where the network and these CDs helped. Neece could actu-ally take 75% of the content from class and shift that to various pre-sentation formats, using a combination of audio and video and a lot of HTML text. Now, trainees study before getting to class. When they get to class, they still come for the week, but they are doing two and a half–day real-life case studies based on real customer sit-uations.

Neece explains, "What I'm doing in the educational model of pre-senting information, modeling the way you want it done, discussing it, practicing it, and then providing some sort of assessment and feedback to individuals on how they did—that's the model we've adopted at Sun." In that model, Neece presents and discusses a lot of the information using the network but actually assesses and pro-vides feedback on a lot of it in class, where he is better able to do that. He puts senior salespeople in front of the class and watches how they present case studies. He also does some real-time feed-back: "I just don't see how you can eliminate that using the network. However, I can turn off that fire hose that we've had for seven years, and now I can let students set their own pace for training."

International Trainees. "I've got 147 different countries. The people from Korea and Italy seem to be the ones with the weakest English skills and, for them, being able to pace their own training is very important." It is quite a modular-distributed model and, up front, it uses a lot of artificial intelligence. In terms of localization for foreign countries, Sun is working with a company called Net Phonics, which has developed a technology that voice-synthesizes HTML. By dialing in through a PBX port, one can listen to a Web page in whatever language the voice synthesizer is for. Or one can record his or her real voice, and attach it as a file on a certain page so that when various numbers are pushed on the telephone keyboard one can hear a real person's voice recorded. One of the features of a trial software package called Teleprompter is that it takes a Web page and scrolls for the user. So a person that reads in English and speaks in German can record an audio file that's attached to the page. A trainee coming from Germany will be sent German content. Neece foresees: "Written German content will be sent, but right now this will certainly make a big difference for someone who can read English and listen to German. He will pick up 20% of the words he currently doesn't pick up, which are often the words that best describe what is really expressed."

Vertical Markets Training. According to Neece, Sun is going after five vertical markets: manufacturing, telco, government, education, and financial services. As a result, the training model is built around people selling into those industries. In fact, Sun has five separate case studies during the week, one for each of the major markets. Neece is doing almost all the product training on the network, for products from servers, desktops, and graphics to all the different product areas Sun sells.

Neece has a whole other set of training modules around the industries for what are called the horizontal solutions. For example, one horizontal solution is software development in the manufacturing and telco industries. A total of ninety-nine modules will be completed in Neece's first push out the door in a couple of months.

Selling Skills Training. Neece says, "We pretty much assume that new hires have sales skills before we hire them. Recently, we've been hiring quite a few people from IBM that have anywhere from eight to fifteen years of industry experience. So, whether they need the skills or not, coming from that environment, they are probably going to say 'There is nothing you can teach me about sales that I don't already know.' From an assessment standpoint, they prove themselves during the case study and, if they can use presentation skills, I note that they can do that, but the presentation skills course is one of the courses delivered down at the branch level. Each of the branches has someone it works with locally that teaches a presentation skills class. The branch brings the people in and they are treated as a group. That kind of training in the distributed network model is a kind of training Sun recommends to be delivered out in the field location."

TECHNOLOGICAL DEVELOPMENTS

What needs to happen technologically for the Internet and the Intranet to become even more integrated into the training sequence? According to Neece, the growth of the Internet needs to slow down or the speed of putting bandwidth into the backbone of the Internet needs to speed up. Until that happens, the recent problem will continue: The Internet is just too slow to surf. Neece has largely stopped surfing. Neece teaches a class in electronic marketing in the Santa Clara M.B.A. program. To get the kind of bandwidth for the surfing he needed to complete his class, he had to go into his office at 7 a.m. on a Sunday morning. He couldn't possibly do it in the middle of the afternoon during a weekday. It's just too slow. "That," Neece notes, "was one of the reasons we saw very early that we weren't going to be able to use the Web for training. We would have to go to the store and forward model."

Because the Internet is Sun's business and Sun has been living it, Neece and others at Sun realized that the Web wouldn't work for training purposes. There are technologies that have the ability to deliver terra bytes per second, and they're actually in the labs right now, Neece said. He had seen prototypes of a technology called phototonics, which uses light pulses rather than anything electrical or electromechanical: "At those kinds of speeds, using phototonics, you can actually ship terra bytes (a thousand gigabytes) per second through the network. After terra bytes is Peta bytes, and I've actually heard people discussing Peta bytes already, primarily in terms of data storage."

Neece said, "We are going to see those kinds of numbers, and it's all going to be accessible." There was a study done by the ATM

Forum, which is a users' body around the technology called ATM (asynchronous transfer mode). Forum members interviewed RBOCs and PTVs around the world and concluded that, by the year 2004, ten years from the time the study was done, for the same $30 a month that Sun pays to RBOCs PAC Bell, for example, or NYNEX, Sun could get 2.4 gigabits per second."

With that kind of bandwidth at home, Neece remarks "You can deliver anything. You can deliver multiple strains of very high quality video to high-definition television sets if you've got the money to pay for it because, by then, we'll be paying by the bit instead of any kind of distance thing. It's just a matter of when. It's no longer a matter of if. There are a lot of people competing to bring you that last hundred feet to your house. And that competition will drive it to happen a lot sooner than it would have happened normally."

CHAPTER 15

THE POLITICS OF CONSTRUCTING AN EFFECTIVE WEB SITE

T he evolution of a Web site—from the gleam in someone's eye to daily content refreshment—moves through various stages. There are consistent organizational and management issues and factors all organizations must face when building a Web site. Also, surf enough Web sites and, eventually, you will observe common elements that support effectiveness.

WEB SITE EVOLUTION

A Web site evolves through several stages as organizations address such factors as:

1. Attention: Renegades At Work
2. Before and After Launch: Formative to Strategic Objectives
3. From Ho-Hum Interest to High Collaboration
4. Web site Management: The Team, The Committee
5. The Budget: From None to Sum
6. Outside Resources: Used Sparingly

ATTENTION: RENEGADES AT WORK

At the outset, the vision for a Web site is typically formulated by one to three evangelists who take the time to propose and develop the site. In other words, the initial impetus for an organizational Web site normally does not come from top management; it is usually a renegade operation that grows, in a relatively short period of time, to involve the entire organization. One reason for this is opportunity. In economic terms, the cost of an organization's entry into the Web site world is not prohibitive. The hardware and software to create a Web site is highly accessible. In many organizations, personal computers with the capacity to function as a Web site server are plentiful. The programming software is relatively inexpensive. Most important, the telecommunications infrastructure is in place. Organizations already have a network in place (for an Intranet, at least), and the world's telecommunications infrastructure is evolving daily.

Expertise is also available. Organizations have on their staffs telecommunications and information systems professionals with training and experience in networks, computers, and software. Many have been dabbling in Internet hardware and software for some time. Then there are the content experts: professionals in corporate communications, public relations, marketing, sales, human resources, and training. When these two disparate groups, content and technical professionals, meet on the common ground of the Internet—to build an external Web site, an Intranet, or both—it is an opportunity waiting to happen.

In a few instances, timing is the crucial factor. For example, the organization may have just concluded an employee communications audit that called for a modification of organizational approaches, or a market analysis required an adjustment in tactics, or top management decided to reorient the corporate culture. In effect, the organizational environment was ripe for the introduction of a new communications medium. Add a pinch of entrepreneurialism, a spirit of experimentation, and a willingness to achieve a goal, and the result is a combination of forces that leads to a proposal for a Web site.

For example, AT&T's external Web site was launched from Bell Laboratories by two individuals with financial assistance from the company's chief information officer and the public relations department. At IBM, the external Web site was started as a grass-roots campaign: a newly hired employee from corporate identity and design and two people from IBM's Austin Texas and Atlanta labs. At FEDEX in the early stages, the Internet steering committee consisted of a marketing person and two program developer types. Now there are rarely less than 15 people at committee meetings; the core production team is composed of personnel from marketing and the Information Technology Division. The original Pathfinder production team at Time Inc. consisted of four people. The current production team is at least double the size.

At PanCanadian, two departments initially joined forces to create an Intranet—corporate communications and information systems—essentially, two individuals in the middle ranks who then sought top management approval. The company had just concluded an employee communications audit. A similar pattern evolved at Xerox, which had also just concluded an employee communications audit. Three individuals initially joined forces: one from corporate communications and two from technology departments. These individuals are still involved in the Intranet's development, assisted now by the Webmaster. US WEST's Intranet was initiated by a vice president in the finance area who joined with one individual in an information technologies group. The former served as an evangelist for the Web site concept and ultimately garnered top management support for the concept.

Overall, the time from the initial proposal by the renegades to an actual launch is usually several months.

BEFORE AND AFTER LAUNCH: FROM FORMATIVE TO STRATEGIC OBJECTIVES

In the main, the motivation for launching a Web site moves through two stages. In the first stage, before launch, the motivations are various: for the sake of experimentation; "other people are doing it"; or for some general communications objective. Once the Web site is online, however, management wakes up to the tremendous potential of the Web site and begins to articulate specific strategic objectives. In a few instances, though, organizations have a clear idea of its strategic objectives from the outset.

For example, at IBM, its external Internet Web site was perceived initially as a "very hot thing"—IBM wanted to drive the perception of IBM as a contemporary company. According to IBM's Carol Moore, "People were going out there and we decided we had to as well." Initially, there was no strategic objective. Today, however, the Web site is geared to becoming the personification of the company's overall strategy and the IBM brand. Further, it is the company's intention to make the IBM Web site the site to surf for expert information about the computer industry. The most significant before and after scenario at IBM is in the perception of the Web site's objective initially as a "neat thing" and later as purveying the company's overall strategy. There is a push on to have an electronic commerce strategy that is unified and common to everyone coming to the site.

At PanCanadian Petroleum, there were two reasons for launching an Intranet. First, in 1995, top management decided to create a corporate communications department—in a company with a long-standing authoritarian, bureaucratic style of management. Then an employee communications audit showed clearly that employees wanted to get news about the company directly from the company rather than reading about it in the news media. The Web site appeared as a suitable answer to management's desire to reflect its new attitude and, at the same time, to employees' needs. But strategic goals were not defined initially.

In all these instances, while a case could be made for the sites, an evolved strategic objective was not forthcoming until *after* the Web sites' launch. In effect, an early step in creating an effective Web site is to decide what its strategic objective is. More to the point, an effective Web site must be an extension of an organization's business. For example, FEDEX's Web site is a place where customers can conduct business, not only making decisions about FEDEX as a carrier, but also providing customer information, logging in pickups, and tracking packages as they work their way through the FEDEX system. The company experienced well over 1 million package tracks in 1995. With the Web site, the costs savings—the use of the FEDEX 800-number—is enormous. The company also saved money from distributing its tracking software to over 100,000 people over the Internet rather than mailing diskettes.

In AT&T's case, the "after" is in the future. The company views its external Web site as the "800 number of the future," suggesting the Internet's tremendous transaction potential and implying AT&T's potential to dominate the Internet as it does the 800 number business today. At US WEST, it's Intranet is helping to evolve the corporate culture from a "by the book" organization" to "a learning organization." It is also perceived that the Intranet is helping to create a corporate memory by allowing employees to see the corporate big picture.

An external Web site is not only a place where customers, potential customers, and employees (along with prospective employees) can access information about the organization, it is also a place where they can interact with it. An effective Web site is a way for Web surfers to get to know the organization and for the organization to get to know them and to conduct business—to connect direct. If the Web site is not designed for this kind of strategic orientation, the process should be aborted until a strategic vision is articulated. If, on the other hand, a strategic objective is articulated and is a direct extension of an organization's activities, then the process should, by all means, go forward.

FROM HO-HUM TO HIGH COLLABORATION

Generally speaking, before a Web site is launched, there is some corporate commitment to the site; typically, only a few understand the site's potential. After launch, however, many managers see the potential and join in numerous collaborative efforts to expand its strategic usefulness. Thus, a Web site encourages highly collaborative effort.

An effective Web site can be an integrating force. In the very early stages, a content person and a technical person get the Web site going. The usual initial combination is someone from corporate communications or marketing working with someone from computer or management information services. After launch, departments that once did not speak to each other are, in relatively short order, interacting, primarily because a Web site is a place where everyone can come to gain an overview of the organization as a total entity. The Web site is reminiscent of the experience of astronauts who have had the rare good fortune to view the earth as a single entity from space. The Web site, whether external or internal, is everyone's opportunity to view the organization as a total entity from cyberspace.

WEB SITE MANAGEMENT

Once a Web site is launched, a management structure is created on two levels: a committee to oversee the Web site's strategic objectives and a team (headed by a Webmaster) to manage the Web site's day-to-day operations. The committee is a direct reflection of the collaborative environment a Web site creates and of the integrating nature of the Internet. The Web site team is also a collaborative structure.

Following launch, it is usual for a steering committee to evolve, which meets to review the site on a periodic basis. Someone, usually from a corporate communications department, is tapped to manage the Web site's content. A two-function team manages Web site refreshment—someone from a department like corporate communications and someone from an IS function. E-mail response is usually handled on a decentralized basis.

For example, AT&T's external Web site is managed internally. There are 18 people listed at the Web site as part of the Web site management team. Because there are 250 to 300 separate content suppliers to the Web site, the managing Webmaster uses a spreadsheet to track project status. New content can be placed on the Web site within hours. IBM's content and technical team handles the Web site refreshment work at both the headquarters and divisional levels. At FEDEX, e-mail sent to the Web site is handled by several people. One person acts as a mailbox administrator, but the e-mail is actually routed to as many as four or five people who deal with it on a part-time basis. The content partners at the Time Inc.'s Pathfinder Web site have a great deal of control over the look and feel of their individual Web pages; in fact, the core production team has a hard time enforcing any style guidelines at all.

The Xerox Intranet is refreshed daily and is guided by a steering committee of 15 or so Xerox employees. Updating is handled by an editor on the East Coast (Stamford, CT), who sends the edited content electronically to the Webmaster group in Palo Alto, California. US WEST's Intranet is also a highly decentralized effort. There are 50 individual servers. A team helps departments learn how to use the technology.

This two-tiered structure (the steering committee and the Webmaster team) is a seeming paradox: one the one hand, the Web site creates a collaborative, integrating environment with a steering committee having strategic objective responsibility; on the other hand, while there is a team directly responsible for managing the site on a daily basis, e-mail response and content development is a highly decentralized activity. Budgeting is also highly decentralized (see the section headed "The Budget").

Despite the paradox, the structure makes sense: While the Web site creates a demand for a high level of coordination and collaboration on a strategic level, it also calls for a decentralized effort on the operational level. If content changes were not managed on a decentralized basis, it would very quickly become unwieldy—Web sites can be complex.

There are other considerations, such as the longer-term ramifications of a Web site for the various functions of the organization. If it is correct that a Web site creates a large opportunity to connect directly with customers and employees, what does this mean for the structure of various departments in the organization? The answer to this question is found in several of the previous chapters: For marketing and sales, it can mean a change in the role and function of 800-number clerks, call-center clerks, and salespeople; for advertising executives, it means the need to develop interactive media skills and a reorientation to the ramifications of customer interactivity at the speed of light on a one-to-one basis; for public relations professionals, it means an evolving relationship with print and electronic journalists and a need to view a Web site (regardless of strategic role) as a public relations opportunity; for internal communications managers, it means, for the first time in the history of organizational management, having an opportunity to interact with all aspects of the organization for the benefit of employees and in support of the management's strategic goals.

THE BUDGET

Funding for a Web site usually starts relatively small. In many instances, the initial budget is nonexistent. However, after a Web site is launched, budget commitments grow dramatically, but line items are decentralized among user departments. Within a short period of time, though, every organization within the firm is contributing to the Web site but in a decentralized form—again, with a corporate communications department managing the content and an MIS department handling the translation of the content into Web site form. The highly decentralized nature of an organization's Web site budget follows the decentralized nature of content contribution to the Web site.

There is a strong relationship between a company's size and the relative size of the overall, decentralized Web site budget. For example, at AT&T, the estimated initial budget ranged from a low of $100,000 to a high of $1 million (although it is probable it was in the low six figures). It is highly likely that there is no single line item for the external Web site—with several content suppliers to the site with separate servers, the Web site budget is highly decentralized.

IBM's initial budget was $30,000 for the initial design and hardware and $300,000 for the first year (launched in May 1994). The current budget is substantially more, although it appears that there is no specific budget line item and that the overall budget for the external Web site is decentralized among content contributor organizations. At FEDEX, there was virtually no budget at the outset. Initial content was already in electronic form. Hardware already owned by the company was borrowed and repurposed.

Xerox's initial Intranet budget for hardware and software was in the tens of thousands. Much existing hardware and infrastructure was used for the project. Currently, all departments contributing content to the Xerox Intranet also contribute partial funding. In effect, funding is (again) highly decentralized. And, at US WEST, a sympathetic vice president of finance provided less than $100,000 to get its Intranet going. Currently, there is a client-funded budget representing approximately 30 departments that is in the millions— again, though, the budget is highly decentralized.

OUTSIDE RESOURCES

Overall, outside resources are rarely used, particularly in the case of larger companies. When outside resources are used, they are related to design as opposed to strategy. In the main, Web site development is done in-house. The Webmaster function, in particular, is handled in-house.

At AT&T, an outside firm, Neographics, was chosen to help redesign the Web site in the early stages. IBM used an outside designer to help create content design at the outset. They are still working with the company. Most of the production work at FEDEX, except for graphics, is done in-house. The company will use outside consultants, who "… are pushing the envelope." PanCanadian used an outside firm to help design the initial Web site. Xerox used no outside resources, while US WEST worked with some outside consultants but, basically, "… they didn't know any more than we did at the time." GE, on the other hand, retained META4 Design not only to work on its external Web site redesign, but also to manage the day-to-day maintenance of the site.

The apparent scant use of outside resources—which runs counter to the trend of outsourcing as a strategic management objective—may be a function of several factors. As we have seen, organizational Web sites are homegrown entities. Further, the expertise to at least launch the site is available internally. Where outside design or consulting firms have been used, it is to provide support to the internal resources, not strategic management or objective setting. Further, it makes sense for the day-to-day management of the Web site operation to be internal to the organization, particularly with respect to an Intranet that contains sensitive and even perhaps proprietary information meant for employees' eyes only.

CHAPTER 16

REALIZING THE STRATEGIC VISION: THE WEBMASTER FUNCTION

In this period of downsizing, rightsizing, organizational flattening, and job elimination, there is one function that is appearing more and more often on the evolving organizational chart: the Webmaster function.

Just a few years ago, this "job" didn't exist, even unofficially; today, though, it is becoming de rigueur for any organization with a Web site of any complexity. Most organizations host their Webmaster function internally. A few, though, like General Electric and Reebok, use outside resources for this function. From the cases described in this volume, Webmaster units range in size from small (one or two people) to large (dozens). Some expect to remain the same, most expect to expand their size in response to the growing demands of their function, which includes such activities as Web site maintenance, e-mail traffic, creating links for new organizational Web sites, Web site graphic design, testing new technologies, and counseling and advice.

Beyond the organizational renegades who cook up an initial Web site, and the organizational angels who nurture the process, the

Webmaster function is a significant factor in realizing an organization's strategic vision of its Web site, whether external or internal. Like the telephone system and the telecommunications infrastructure before it, an organization's Internet organization and the people who manage the operation are important links in the effective maintenance of a Web site.

The Webmaster function has, in a short time, developed its own professional publications and organizations. It has also rapidly evolved job descriptions and salary definitions. According to Al Boss (ALBBOS@HBSI.COM) in a June 13, 1996, posting to the PRFORUM (on the Internet) dealing with salaries for Web site coordinators, "Salaries for Web site coordinators are all over the place. You can hire a student to bang out HTML at $10/hour, but the professionals should cost you the same as their counterparts in other media (though, if they don't know that, you can hire them for less)." Kristin Zhivago (kristin@zhivago.com) editor of *Marketing Technology*, estimates that a site coordinator/administrator would make $35 to $45K, a designer $45 to $55K, and a technical expert $60 to $75K. A Webmaster turned publisher or Web architect could make $75 to $100K. Despite the information below, most Webmasters, says Boss, do wind up combining the roles listed below into one person's job.

In her newsletter and online, Zhivago has elaborated on a job description model created by Kathy Doyle, a consultant in Branchburg, New Jersey. Following are job descriptions for a Web champion (publisher), site coordinator, site designer, and technical expert:

Web Champion ("Publisher")

The overall manager of the Web site. Has the final say, takes full responsibility. Is the ultimate "owner" of the site. Combines technology and marketing experience. Probably started out as a Webmaster. Political ambassador to other managers; able to have a peer relationship with them. Understands new technologies and is passionate about promoting new site functionality. Especially important now that the Web is shifting ...

from its "static distribution" phase, where printed materials are simply placed on the site, to a "universal transactional medium" with links to corporate databases. All departments are now affected in addition to marketing, and political resistance is sure to become a serious factor ...

Site Coordinator

The person everyone would turn to when they want to add/ remove/change/enhance site content or when they have a new idea for the site. *Nothing* would be put up on the site without the site coordinator's involvement. The coordinator would be responsible for maintaining consistency (of language and navigation) and making sure that deadlines are met, as well as overseeing and possibly writing copy for the site. The coordinator would maintain contact with the PR person at the company, assuring a flow of timely new releases, awards, testimonials, and approved article reprints. The coordinator should be responsible for answering Webmaster e-mail or forwarding it to the appropriate people. As you all know, those accessing Web sites assume that the Webmaster address is the best link to the company itself, regardless of their question, request, or complaint. They expect response within 24 hours. Very few companies are currently equipped to handle this level of interaction. For the Web to continue as a viable communications vehicle, a human being has to be held accountable for timely response to Webmaster e-mail.

Site Designer

A person who works with the coordinator to integrate new graphics and create the appropriate environment for new site features. The designer also maintains logos and other graphics for the site. In companies where head count is tight, a graphics designer from the marketing services department could be assigned to this position, but it could quickly become a full-time job.

The Technical Expert

The one with the technical skills and the authority to actually alter the contents of the site. This person loads the new content (provided by the site coordinator and the site designer), resolves space conflicts, and backs up the coordinator's HTML software with more sophisticated Web authoring tools. He or she should be capable of handling minor text changes, as well as major additions like a new area on the site. The technical expert should also measure traffic and generate reports on page visits and click-throughs. The person doing the technical work should be separate from the people doing the routine text updating and the design. Many companies have been hoping to find one person to do it all, but it is extremely rare that one person is adequately skilled in design, writing, and technology. Those who have this rare combination of talents own Web site development companies and are making more money on their own than they ever would working inside a corporation.

What follows are descriptions of the Webmaster functions at FEDEX and General Electric (marketing/customer service Web sites), IBM and the United States Agency for International Development (two Web sites with a strong public relations orientation), and US WEST, Xerox, and Sun Microsystems (the three Intranet Web sites). These Web sites are described in this chapter with reference to Webmaster function, staffing and operations, Web site maintenance, e-mail traffic operations, future technologies, strategic perspective, and Webmaster growth prospects.

FEDEX

THE WEB SITE ORGANIZATION

The internal organization that handles FEDEX's external Web site is quite evolved, primarily because the company has been working at it for some time. Says Robert Hamilton: "Marketing and IT for 10 years have been jointly shaping these Power Ship offerings of various kinds. The marketing guys have had their heads wrapped around network computing and issues of customer interface and things like that for a long, long time. So although there is a department inside the Network Computing Department of FEDEX that reports to the CIO that does indeed steward the operation function of the Web site and does the actual loads of content, deals with the mainframe issues, etc., the Webmaster mail that would ordinarily go to the Webmaster actually comes to a department of Marketing.

"There's another group inside the company, also in the IT division of the company, that is instrumental as a coordinating function, and that's the customer automation department. They're the ones who really have been the stewards of the whole Power Ship program for all these years—sort of the central point of coordination—and, as the Web site has touched more and more departments inside FEDEX, those internal coordinating mechanisms have gotten more and more important, so now we have a steering committee coordinated by this customer automation function at which marketing sits and network computing sits and legal and data protection and all the usual suspects inside the company sit, and it is that mechanism that actually enables us to set up priorities and actually allocate development resources."

WEB SITE MAINTENANCE

Webmaster Susan Goldener pointed out that her group checks to see if there are any press releases that need to be posted and makes sure that all the applications are up and running, although her group is passing that over to an operations group so that it can be freer to develop new technology and projects for the Internet. Goldener explained that her group works with customer automation and FEDEX's marketing departments, because they're the primary users for the Internet site, to determine what new requirements there are and how to put these features together so that she can bring new features to the home page.

Other users include public relations, which uses the Internet as a medium to put press releases out and to update all its customers on what's going on at FEDEX. For instance, over the Christmas holiday, which is FEDEX's peak season, it had a daily operations update on the Web site about the weather across the country.

E-MAIL TRAFFIC

For FEDEX e-mail, which is an essential feedback loop from customers who find the site useful, is critical to setting priorities. All the answers to the Web mail are coordinated by FEDEX's marketing function. FEDEX's e-mail is approximated at about 150 a day: "It's quite a responsive thing," notes Winn Stevenson. "If there's ever a hiccup at all with any of the functions, then obviously the Web mail surges by the hour and we can track it."

For the 80% of the questions that come in repeatedly, FEDEX has designed a set of e-mail templates that let it answer back very quickly. The marketing department has relationships with the departments that have specialized responsibilities; for example, if there's a deep operational issue, a customer service department liaises with marketing in sending the Web mail elements that touch on that issue. The customer service department can also track its responsiveness. Likewise, if someone wants to talk to someone in the Software Department or has enhancement suggestions, FEDEX has specialized targets for those Web mail messages.

The first-line filtering is done for the questions that fit in the 80 percentile profile that FEDEX already has template-formatted answers for. They will, in effect, skim those off and turn the answers right back around immediately for the customers, leaving the remainder of those questions that don't fit a given template. The issue is then researched, or the group digs into or contacts the customer by phone. The group spends most of the time with the 20% of questions that don't fit into the 80 percentile of solutions.

FEDEX uses an auto responder that acknowledges receipt of e-mail immediately, however fast a customer is connected to the site. FEDEX also has an internal standard of five business hours to close out a customer issue and resolve it to the satisfaction of the person who wrote the e-mail.

FEDEX still has a huge component of frequently asked questions, many of them compliments about the site. People ask specific operational questions or want even more information than has been given to them about tracking. People convey anecdotes about usage and how the Web site has saved them somehow. Stevenson commented: "It's a wonderful set of testimonials. There's a relatively astonishing set of anomalies people write in about."

AN E-MAIL ROLE FOR THE AGENCY

FEDEX uses a combination of 5 or 6 people in-house and external resources to handle its e-mail traffic. Since the e-mail function has
been structured with templates, the flow, depending on the issue, is
placed in one organization or another for response. Stevenson com-
plains that he has been short-handed because things have grown so
much faster than they've been able to add staff. FEDEX will actually
take a bundle of the 80 percentile questions and posit those with
the agencies to craft the response and get responses out from a
fedex.com domain address.

The Wells Hanley-Wood agency in Minneapolis, one of FEDEX's
creative agencies, is involved in the Webmaster mail. The agency is
not the total depository of it but only one resource coordinated by
this group. How does it work, with FEDEX in Memphis and the creative agency responding to e-mail in Minneapolis? "It's very easy. In
effect, we get a feed," Stevenson answers, "The feed of e-mail, of
course, comes to the site, and then we'll mirror the feed. We collab-
orate every day about which ones we're sending to customer service inside, which ones are going to ground ops, etc."

GENERAL ELECTRIC

THE WEB SITE TEAM

According to GE's Susan Moyer, "What we originally started out
with was called Team Internet within the company, which included
both marketing and tactical people who were key players in the
whole scope of what the site was going to be, and we worked with
them on trying to figure out what this would all be. Team Internet is
sort of a cross-business, a cross-functional team. It grew out of Corporate Marketing Communications but, realizing that we really did-
n't know a lot about it and we needed to involve all the businesses
on both the marketing and technical sides, we decided to get together as a team. And they've been like a steering committee. There
are about 30 people on the team."

Moyer continued: "We realized the need to really capitalize on
the new marketing medium, and we obviously weren't doing it with
the site that we had, so we have a network of marketing communi-

cations people from all classes of business that we contact and communicate with on a regular basis. We started with them, and we also tried to get a technical person from each of those businesses and we brought, I think 80 or 100 people together in one room, and we brainstormed and came up with, I think, eight different sub-teams. Navigation strategy was one, and all the different areas that we want to focus on. It became clear that there needed to be some-body for focusing the advertising firm. So then, after we chose META4 Design in August 1995, I was appointed initially to get the Corporate part of it up."

IBM

THE WEB SITE TEAM

Ed Costello is Webmaster for both the external Web site and IBM's Intranet. His group is constantly changing. "My role," Costello says, "is to guide the technical team for the IBM home page group, of which Carol Moore is the manager." Costello has two people work-ing for him. They take care of the reference server and provide tech-nical support for the editorial team, as well as providing technical guidance for other IBMers throughout the company that develop content for the other Web sites, of which there are close to 100. Alex Wright is the head of the editorial staff, assisted by Abigail Collings. Collectively or functionally, at one level, they provide corporate in-formation on the IBM home page and publish information on the IBM home page. They also give technical and editorial guidance to other IBMers.

THE HARDWARE CONFIGURATION

According to Costello, "While the IBM home page is reserved for top-level corporate content, there are about 100 decentralized servers throughout the organization." One of the recent trends at IBM is server recentralization to some extent (a similar trend is oc-curring at Sun Microsystems). For example, the Software Division has been centralizing all the software pages onto one or two servers, whereas they were spread all over creation before. To give them a common look and feel and make it easier to retain the management, the group has its own programmer and editor.

SOFTWARE TOOLS: NO STANDARDIZATION

Costello's group is using a wide mix of tools, including UNIX, OS/2, and Windows. They also have a couple of Macintosh users. Costello points out that most of the graphics are done on Macs using Photoshop. Most of the editorial content is done using OS/2 and Windows. There isn't any one package that people use. Costello notes, "We haven't found anything that's the holy grail for the god of HTML and we even have people who just use a simple text editor to do the HTML work."

NO HARDWARE DICTATES

Since Costello began overseeing the IBM Web, he has never sent out a document telling users that they shall use this and that. Most of the servers are IBM RISC systems, running AIX. There are a few odd systems, but there are some other systems like the AS 400 division that have an AS 400–based server. The system 390, the mainframe division, uses a system 390 for its server.

Costello recounted the worldwide growth of the number of servers at IBM in the context of the growth of the Internet between 1995 and 1996. In June 1995, there were 10 or 12 systems on the Internet. But, as Costello thinks back, "It was really after we did the Lotus takeover and showed how you could use the Internet for marketing and public relations that it exploded and grew quite rapidly. Some people saw what IBM did with Lotus and saw that we got a lot of value out of it and wanted to get up on the Web and I think, there were some people that were taking their time planning out their Web site, and it just happened that they all came on in a relatively short amount of time."

MAINTAINING THE SITE

Describing the process of getting new content on the Web site, Costello says, "Typically, what happens is that, if it's considered a corporate announcement, there is already a press plan in effect. Internet stuff is considered part of that now. Alex Wright or Abigail Collings work with the lead press contact either to get the raw press releases or to work with them in some way to get the raw information needed to get the story up on the home page."

HANDLING E-MAIL TRAFFIC

IBM Web site e-mail is handled in a couple of ways. People can simply send mail to the Webmaster at www.ibm.com; about 2% of the mail is sent that way. Webmaster mail is under 100 notes. Some days it's very low, and some days Costello gets 100 to 120 notes. The average is around 60 notes a day.

Much of the mail consists of questions about products or services. Another group within IBM, originally set up in the spring of 1995 to answer the 800-number information lines, has access to all the information necessary to handle questions submitted through e-mail, the Web being one possibility. Using a form that you can click on from anywhere on the IBM Web called Contact IBM, the user is asked if the question is about the Web or if it's a question about products or services. A first-level filtering is done there. If the user clicks on a question about product or service, it automatically goes to this group, which handles all those questions, so Costello's group doesn't even see that mail. This volume is around 100 to 150 a day.

NEW TECHNOLOGIES: FUTURE IMPACT

Costello referred to some of the newer technologies in the Internet environment and speculated on their effect on IBM's Internet activities: "From a technical perspective, Java is certainly going to have a big impact and we're just beginning to exploit it. A lot of what people have seen and used Java for has been glitzy-type stuff, and we have been trying to find some more practical uses for it. We have been doing some work to provide a dynamic map of the IBM Web, a graphical visual of how the IBM Web is laid out. The user can click on and see little page icons, click on a page and get some information about that page and, depending on the browser, double-click on it and navigate to that page. It works in theory but, when we try scaling it up to the size of the IBM Web, it turns out to be harder than we thought it would be."

USAID

THE WEBMASTER FUNCTION

Jim Russo, Project Manager for the Internet, Data Services Group, manages USAID's Internet and Intranet's day-to-day operations. The group also provides project support to USAID development projects that have an Internet or Telecom component to them, such as the $15 million Leland Initiative, the goal of which is to put Internet hubs in 20 sub-Sahara and African countries over the next five years with the idea of promoting two of USAID's strategic objectives: democracy and economic growth.

There are five people on the Webmaster staff: Russo, a UNIX systems administrator, a Webmaster (whose job is the day-to-day running of the external Web), an individual dedicated to the corporate Web, and fifth individual, who is assigned graphics work and a list server.

Russo was one of the team members originally involved in the initial gopher site. He started with two other individuals on a gopher site that predates USAID's Web site.

THE HARDWARE AND SOFTWARE CONFIGURATION

USAID started with a Sun Microsystems Sparc 10 and then upgraded to a Sparc 20. Now it's running Solaris OS, which is Sun's version of UNIX. "It has 128 megs of memory on the machine and about 10 Gig of disk storage." Russo elaborates: "We back it up to tape, but we don't have a double system. The server's on-site. There were a number of factors that went into this decision. At the time Internet service providers (ISPs) were a relatively immature industry and they weren't as readily available as they are now."

MAINTAINING THE WEB SITE

According to Russo, there are some general guidelines: "Tell us where you want the information to go and who is the intended audience for the information. How do you intend to maintain it? How long do you want it to be posted?" USAID requires the conversion to be in HTML or ASCII. The customer has the responsibility for getting the information into appropriate form. There are some exceptions, however. In the case of first-time clients, Russo will have a conversation with them, perhaps a meeting, determine what their resources are, or what their technical capabilities are. As a last resort, Russo's group will do the work but will try, as much as possible, to push it as far down into the organization as they can.

E-MAIL TRAFFIC

There is a Webmaster postbox that comes across Russo's desk. It used to be that he actually attempted to answer the mail. But he doesn't do that anymore. Now, there is a Public Inquiries box. Russo will screen it and, if it's a technical question about the Internet site specifically, he'll take care of it. Otherwise, the query is sent to the Public Inquiries box, which is managed by the public affairs office.

Volume is about 10 to 15 notes a day, five days a week. A large part of the e-mails involve procurement questions because all USAID's procurement information is on-site. A number of inquiries are about specific procurements, although they get a number of inquiries about jobs—people sending resumes, college students looking for opportunities in the development field. The other broad category is specific questions about USAID's programs, such as, What is USAID doing in the democracy area in Bulgaria?

THE STRATEGIC VISION: THE WEBMASTER'S PERSPECTIVE

"The Web site does so much for us," Russo explains. "With the gopher site, we were limited to text and now, with the Web site, we have full multimedia capabilities. The quick-time movies and graphics give us a lot more ways to tell our story and convey information. Real audio is another area we're looking into to actually put radio broadcasts on our corporate Web. We have actual radio broadcasts and recordings on our site."

Russo continues: "The other big thing is that the Web has made the Internet accessible to the everyday user. Before, it was mostly UNIX techies who used it for Internet relay chats and to have conversations—it was a fairly arcane mechanism, and its applicability to the general public was limited. But the Web really opens it up and makes it an easy-to-use universal tool for communication. I think, most Americans don't really know what the U.S. Agency for International Development does and I think that our press office feels that the Web site has been an effective tool for explaining what the goal of foreign assistance is and what USAID's role in it is.

"USAID has profiles of the kinds of people that come in and use our site, and they tend to come from the commercial sector, the university sector, and the government sector. The government domain accounts for about 34%, the commercial domain about 26%, and the university domain about 18%. The .org domain is 5%. The .net domain is 11%. The country domains account for 6% of the traffic."

FUTURE VISIONS

According to Russo, "Once the telecommunication links become fast enough and the compression software becomes good enough, USAID will be able to put movies and more audio types of information out there." Russo believes there's real potential for distance learning applications, particularly in developing countries. "I've been in the computer business for quite a while. I don't think I've ever had as much fun doing something as I've had doing the Internet-related work, because it's so broad—it's not a narrow, technical niche. The user really has to understand the business function of the organization he works for and has to understand about information management as opposed to just technology management. I interact quite a bit with end users and people who are not in the technical field, and the whole graphic, multimedia aspect of it combines in my mind to make it a whole lot of fun. That's why it's attracting a lot of people."

Russo concludes, "People in the Internet world talk about dog years. Well, in the Internet, one month of Internet time is a year of normal time, and this thing has just taken off so fast. Two years ago, the Web was just kind of coming into being, and now it's everything. Who knows what's going to happen in the next year or two?"

US WEST

MAINTAINING THE PAGES

The Webmaster function, run by Suzanne Mullison, maintains US WEST's Intranet pages. When a new site is created, the Webmaster is informed, and the site is them linked to the Intranet home page. The Webmaster function controls the home page and the graphics there, but each individual site beyond the initial home page controls its own graphics and tools. Responsible for these functions are so-called departmental computerists, although not every area has one. Mullison's unit relies heavily on the department computerists.

Mullison's people don't decide what groups are going to create, but they do give them guidance on whether they think a site will be effective or not; it is the originating groups that decide what to do. Says Mullison: "A Human Resources person says 'I think it would be a really good idea if we had this tool.' Then the HR people get together and decide yes or no and create the page if the answer was yes and have us link in. We don't set any standards—all we offer is advice." US WEST has a Ph.D. type analyzing the Intranet to determine what improvements can be in design, links, and content architecture. Presumably, the results of this home page redesign will have an impact on the overall linkages among departments.

HARDWARE AND SOFTWARE CONFIGURATION

US WEST has a lot of links to authoring tools online. The company's Intranet uses GIF and HTML primarily, with a few PERL scripts for mailers. A Graphic Converter converts other graphic formats into GIF tools.

E-MAIL RESPONSE

The Webmaster answers about 5 to 8 questions a day but hands off other help questions to technical specialist Lee Lloyd for a one-on-one response. Feedback forms are PERL scripts sent via e-mail. There are a few FAQs, but Mullison and Lloyd are working on the process of how to gather more.

Webmaster Mullison looks forward to new features that will be added to the US WEST Intranet: "I know that we'll expand on discussion groups as soon as we start getting the folks using them—learning how to use them." Sherman Woo [one of the original renegades] has a crew of developers. And they are very excited about Java and those kinds of tools.

"We're in the process of having the internal help desk folks pick up our help questions. As we grow, we need to have somebody who's able to deal with larger quantities of question seven days a week, 24 hours a day. Our group is so small—it's just Lee and me. We're concerned about what will happen, when we grow to our ability to respond to our internal customers. Of course, we are such a large company, we already have help desk operations set up for other systems. They can just pick up ours and answer those technical questions as well."

FUTURE VISION

Mullison, though, had a different perspective with respect to the use of the Intranet: "I see us growing—growing in usable tools that can be obtained on the Web, such as forms—putting forms out there. And growing as we provide more value on the Web—growing in number of internal company employees who will have a need to come and use the Internet to do their day-to-day business. Forms is the one application that comes to mind now. But we've got the EM-NET directory, which is the employee locator. To me, that's a valuable tool. We have a learning systems course scheduled online already, so that, if someone wants to see what kinds of classes they can take here, inside the company, they can find that online. Soon they'll be able to enroll online, so that they won't have to talk to a representative from the learning systems organization. When we get more and more of those kinds of things, policies and procedures—things of that nature—as we grow those, I believe the value will grow."

Mullison pointed out that it is one of their success points that they've been able to remain small, cost-effective, and in operation: "The fact that our group is small is attractive, and so, growth probably would depend on whether we change from that grassroots effort. If an officer says 'OK now, everybody will use the Global Village,' and makes it a mandatory tool, then, yes, I think we'll have to grow. But, as long as we remain a grassroots kind of effort, we probably will not try to grow."

XEROX

WEB SITE MAINTENANCE

With respect to software or materials to get content into the site itself, Xerox has a variety of tools for HTML Web production. A production team in Palo Alto, California, does this as part of a Xerox business services offering. This was one of the pilot production activities. They've done some work for the Xerox public Web site, and they've done some work for some pilot customers. The collection of tools they use includes HTML Webweaver, Top Quad, Top Medal, Microsoft Word Internet Assistance, various image-processing tools, like Adobe Photoshop, and a program called Debabelizer.

According to renegade Rick Beach, the Web server is a server on the Xerox Internet. It can be reached both for updates and for access anywhere on the Xerox Web. Obviously, it's under security access control, and the updates are made by the production people by accessing the file system underneath the Web server directory tree. The Webmaster and the production people coordinate their production processes, and so that happens in a reliable fashion.

With respect to managing traffic, Beach stated: "You have to understand that the Web infrastructure is quite extensive inside Xerox. There is a multitier proxy structure and the Web server. At the moment, we've only needed one of them." The Web server—a Sparc Server 20—is located in California.

The site is refreshed daily and is guided by a steering committee of approximately 15 Xerox employees from various departments. And there is significant impetus to expand the Intranet's offerings.

Updating the site daily is handled on both the East and West Coasts. An editor on the employee communications staff on the East Coast reviews material to be included in the Intranet. That person then edits the material and electronically—via Xerox's internal network—sends the material to Webmaster Mike Ryan's group in Palo Alto, which then HTMLs the material for inclusion into the site.

SUN MICROSYSTEMS

THE WEBMASTER FUNCTION

Debra Winters, Intranet Webmaster, assumed her role about two and a half years ago. She was the very first titled Webmaster at Sun. Prior to her tenure, the Webmaster position had been a grassroots function. Everybody who brought the Sun Web online actually had full-time jobs aside from that.

GATEKEEPERS AND CONTENT PROVIDERS

Winters described how the Sun Intranet was structured by operating company. The data is actually owned by the VPs or CIOs of the operating companies. They appoint high-level gatekeepers. There could be a structure of gatekeepers under those gatekeepers that looks very much like an organization chart. Winters works with a good dozen and a half high-level gatekeepers and knows that one of them has anywhere from 30 to 50 gatekeepers under her. Some of those are content providers as well.

THE WEBMASTER ORGANIZATION

There are 12 people in Winters' group, but they're staffing up to around 20 in fiscal year 1997. Most are involved in the Intranet, with a couple devoted to the Internet site. In the one department, there are two distinct groups: Operations, and Technology and Electronic Commerce.

The Technology and Electronic Commerce group is in charge of researching Web technologies, for example, search engines, Web servers, and cache servers. This group selects browsers for Sun's wide area network like Netscape, for example. They do all the technical testing and packaging and push it out on the networks so that it's available to all employees worldwide. The Technology and Electronic Commerce Group actually does the first implementation, the first application, the testing and the tweaking, and the feasibility testing of a program running on Sun's network. Once it's installed and running smoothly, the operations group picks up the ball.

In terms of positions, on the technology side, there is a Program Manager who manages the projects. Then, there is a developer, who is extremely Suncentric in his skills but is also very technical.

On the operations side, most are people persons though they have solid technical backgrounds. Winters has a background in mainframe and PC programming, with two or three years of work in the Sun environment in a very technical capacity. Winters supported spreadsheets on the Sun environment, so she has a good technical background but doesn't do nearly what the technical people do. She focuses more on writing architectural documents, sitting with VPs, and groups of people to try to get them online, and working with artists.

E-MAILS AND "ASK THE WEBMASTER"

Winters has an ISDN line at home but, whether she's at home or at her office, the first thing she does is check e-mail, and usually there's mail from European countries. Winters gets statistics on cache servers that explain how hard they are being utilized by how many users. She also gets reports, some of them daily. Winters gets a series of e-mails on a day-to-day basis. A technician who supports her takes care of most of them.

AN EVOLVING DEPARTMENT

Winters looks forward to an expansion of her department, as well as a switch in roles. She explains, "I'll probably move to Manager of the Operations side. Then, the Technology Program Manager will likely be Manager of the Technology side. That right there opens up two spots. And I have a technician working for me now. We will double that position, so we'll get another technician, which is badly needed now. We need technicians to support the Webmasters big time because of the little technical nickel-and-dime questions."

THE FUTURE OF SUN'S WEBMASTER FUNCTION

A Consulting Role. Winters says, "I see it growing to a staff of around 30 people and us getting into more consulting services. I see us even doing some Web development. I heard from a very high level VP the other day that he felt it was a missed opportunity for our group not to have consulting services. So I think that might be coming down the road. Our sales force and Sun Integration are all over us like flies to try to get us to meet with their customers. I think that once I become more like the Manager of the group and the group starts running and we staff up to more people to handle more of the work, I will be branching off and doing more work with the customer visit center, as well as Sun Integration and Sun education in helping them to develop classes, so we can actually make some money off our Intranet expertise."

Policy Content. At some point, there is going to be a lot more business mission-critical policy enforcement. Winters predicts that Sun is going to be more Webcentric in the way it is running its business: "There will be policy implemented at some point. For example, corporate policies and procedures might reside on the Intranet and might be made available on the Intranet. The employee handbooks are there already. A lot of corporate mission-critical stuff is already there, and there is going to be a lot more corporate-owned information sitting on corporate-owned and -maintained Web servers."

Sun IntraWeb Service. It is estimated that there are close to 2,000 servers at Sun Microsystems. The IntraWeb Service is an attempt to consolidate and manage the Intranet infrastructure. According to Winters, "We're not the only company that's faced with this. Everybody is asking, 'What are you doing with all your desktop servers?' So what we're doing now is building an IntraWeb Service, so we have, let's say, 20—off the top of my head—servers with huge disk drives. ENS would add more disks and then we wouldn't have so many machines just sitting on secretaries' desktops and everybody's desktops. It's a support nightmare."

CHAPTER 17

REALIZING THE STRATEGIC VISION: WEB SITE DESIGN CONSIDERATIONS

THE DESIGN PROCESS

If everyone has done his or her job and is paying attention to internal and external feedback, a Web site's initial strategic design will become irrelevant within months. It is axiomatic that the redesign of an organizational Web site begins the moment it is launched. A Web site is dynamic. It is not like a brochure that, once done, has a shelf life of six months. Or a print ad that, once run, is not repeated. Or a radio or television ad that once completed, can rarely, if ever, be modified.

A Web site not only can be modified at will but should be modified. Some companies refresh their Web sites daily. The corollary to this is that managing a Web site is not a part-time job. To be effective, a Web site must be managed by someone on a daily basis.

THE SURFER AND THE WEB SITE

Putting a Web site up to market your product or service is challenging. Unlike other marketing tools (e.g., direct mail), the marketer has relatively little control over intruding on the customer or potential customer. Instead, the potential consumer must find you. A marketer currently has few definitive ways of measuring or defining an Internet audience (although this is highly likely to change in the near future).

Although it is possible to find out how many hits are made to a site, it is not possible to identify who those hits came from and whether the hits came from separate individuals or someone revisiting the site several times. The latter is probably more usual. Despite this dilemma, the Internet is a valuable place to be, simply because the competition may be already there or heading there.

CHECK OUT THE COMPETITION

Before designing a site, get on the Internet and check out what your competition is doing. What do their Web sites look like? What kind of features do they offer? Do you have something unique to offer? Is there something awkward about their sites you could improve on?

It is also beneficial to look at the sites of different segments of your industry and related industries. For example, if you are a tertiary hospital, don't just look at other tertiary hospital sites; look at community hospitals, medical schools, pharmaceutical companies, medical supply companies, and volunteer ambulance corps.

GATHERING WEB SITE CONTENT

Once you have articulated a strategic objective for your site, check out the competition, and put together a team to develop the Web site. Gather all the appropriate content resources you already have available. These might include:

- Digital material

- Videos

- Photos

- Artwork

- Literature

- Press releases

- Articles

- Advertising materials

- Marketing materials

- Promotional materials

- Research papers/results

- Transcripts/speeches

- Annual reports

- Other relevant sites to link to within your site

Keep in mind, though, that content on the Web site must support a strategic objective or it is not relevant.

POTENTIAL LEGAL ISSUES

While you gather the different elements for the Web site, it is important to address legal concerns:

Is the material proprietary? Does it need to be protected by copyright, trademark, or register mark?

Does permission to reprint need to be obtained?

Does photo credit need to be included?

Are you repurposing material that is not covered by electronic rights?

Are there liability issues with other sites linkable from your site?

Do you need a disclaimer regarding the material contained in your site or other links to your site?

CONTENT ARCHITECTURE

Once information is gathered, an outline, blueprint, or content architecture needs to be created. This will be a guide to constructing the Web site. More importantly, it will help you map out all the site's pieces to ensure that no information/department is left out, to show all the cross-links to be made, and to avoid duplication.

While you're creating your blueprint, the technical infrastructure needs to be selected. This means choosing a computer server that can handle both the information you put on the Net and the inquiries you get back. This is very important if the Web site is to offer an e-mail address for inquiries, an order form for the purchase of products or services, a guest book, a survey, or membership form.

Similarly, if a phone or fax number is offered, an appropriate bank of operators or fax machines must be in place. There's no bigger turnoff to a customer than not getting through.

CONTENT DESIGN

Organization. Sites in which the material is thoughtfully presented, both in terms of leading the user through the site in a logical way— that is, providing an outline or a table of contents, and in terms of carefully chosen graphic support, are winners.

When a site is organized in a neat, clear way, the graphic element has impact. For instance, a flowchart style of graphic with topics in different boxes, beginning with broad topics and filtering down into boxes with more specific information, makes a Web site accessible.

Visual Appeal. Quality Web sites are visually appealing. They look exciting and dynamic. A Web site's home page should immediately draw you in. This involves the use of color, though not every color in the crayon box need be used. Plenty of appealing sites use only two or three colors and are very appealing visually. Besides, too many colors only slow down the download process. Bandwidth problems and modem speeds notwithstanding, the last thing you want is an impatient Web site visitor waiting minutes for a glorious graphic to download.

Sites can be equally effective through careful choice of fonts, use of capitals or initial caps, and color of text, along with a logical architecture consistent throughout. This is similar to the outline format we learn in school. Each line in the outline is laid out in a specific order, beginning with a roman numeral, then a capital letter, then an arabic number, and so forth. Once readers become familiar with the pattern, they can easily locate the information sought.

Tone. A Web site's tone also needs to be considered. Is it going to be strictly informational? Or does it need to be upbeat or warm and friendly? It depends on the site's strategic objective. Again, we return to the beginning of the process: What is the Web site's strategic objective? What business will customers and potential customers conduct at your site?

Table of Content Links. Another feature that makes for a well-organized site is table of contents (TOC) links within the site. Let's say a home page has 10 areas to visit within the TOC. You want to see sections 3 and 7. You click on section 3 and explore it until you are satisfied. Now you want to go to section 7. Instead of having to back out of section 3 with the "back" option to the home page, a menu at the bottom of each page in the site automatically links you to section 7. This is a time-saving and convenient tool for any Web surfer.

Quality Content. Now that you have a site that is aesthetically inviting and well organized, the quality of the content must be addressed. The more thorough the information contained in the site, the more appealing and relevant it will be to the user. This is not to say that the information contained in the site should be the length of the *Encyclopedia Britannica*, but it should be thorough. Surfers searching for information want to be able to get either the full picture or be guided by cross-links to additional information. This is another way to make a site accessible.

Using Graphics. There are other types of graphics that make a site dynamic and exciting. These graphics usually personalize or demonstrate the text. Text can be personalized with graphics by including a picture of key executives within a site's organization.

Interactivity. Another element that makes a Web site accessible is the ease with which a surfer can interact with the site for more information. The most common method is simply to provide a phone or fax number or an address to which one can write. Some sites include an e-mail address in order to obtain or impart information or ask a question. In its most rudimentary form, the surfer would take down the e-mail address, exit the Net, and send an e-mail via her e-mail software. More sophisticated sites allow the surfer to click on some portion of the "For more information" line, which will automatically bring up an e-mail memo on which to send the request.

Other sites offer surveys and membership forms or guest books to sign. Some of these need to be printed out and then mailed to the organization; others can be completed online.

There are sites that identify the Webmaster and how to locate him or her via e-mail. This is an excellent direct link if a surfer should want to bring something to the Webmaster's attention or to ask a question that only he or she will be able to answer.

Different Browsers. When you are preparing to put your site on-line, it is important to keep in mind that different browsers will present your material differently than you designed it. For instance, The University of Iowa's *Virtual Hospital* entire site is beautifully laid out and organized when viewed in Netscape. However, when viewed through America Online (AOL) (version 2.5), it appears as a long listing of information that seems never-ending and difficult to navigate.

A tool that some sites contain is a record of the number of hits to a particular site as of a particular date. There is some debate as to the value of including this information. For the marketer, the use of e-mail addresses, surveys, membership forms, order forms, or guest books helps give some insight into who is visiting a site.

TESTING

Before putting your site online, test it, test it, test it! Before putting its site online 1-800-FLOWERS spent weeks ordering flowers from its online service to work all the bugs out.

WEB SITE FRESHNESS

Keeping the information on a Web site up-to-date and fresh is very important. People want new information, not yesterday's news. Like a mystery novel, read it once and there really is no reason to read it again. But a reference book with continuous updating rewards revisiting. A one-line statement as to when the page was last updated indicates to the surfer the timeliness of the information.

Identifying New Information. Some sites alert surfers to new information with some kind of graphic. The choice of color is usually yellow and red. For instance, the word *new* is in red against a yellow background in the shape of a rectangle or a sunburst. Usually, surfers can click on this graphic area and go directly to the new information so that they won't have to search the site to try and figure out what has changed. Still other sites suggest you check with them on a periodic basis.

GENERAL ELECTRIC: A MARKETING WEB SITE

THE MOTIVATION BEHIND THE REDESIGN

In the latter part of 1995 and prior to April 15, 1996, Web site management at General Electric realized that the external Web site was not structured in a way that served "customers" visiting there. The original Web site's content and navigational architecture was a reflection of GE's internal organization—by business unit—rather than a design that accommodated various customer groups.

Susan Moyer, the Internet program manager, commented on the company's approach to developing the Web site's redesign: "We're [taking] a new look at it—what consumers' needs might be, a general consumer from the home, and what a business customer might need. Then, of course, the third audience is the shareholders, the press, students, people looking for general information about GE. So we're thinking about our market in that way and then looking at the fact that we have district home telemarketing centers; the GE Answer Center, which focuses on consumers; the GE Business Information Center, which focuses on business customers—we're talking to them about what types of questions we could answer online at the Web site that are easy and frequently asked. The Web site could begin to divert a lot of the call load into those areas.

"We have 70-plus businesses and we can provide basic information about each of those 70 businesses—who they are, what they offer, and how to contact them. That's the corporate part. And then each of the businesses can add additional applications that might be more finely targeted, and a lot of businesses are working on that."

INVESTMENT IN THE REDESIGN

There were many reports in the media that GE planned to invest $5 million in the redesign of its external Web site. According to Richard Costello, manager, corporate marketing communications: "That's an overestimate. I'd say it's less than half that. I'd say we've spent between a quarter and half a million dollars on the stuff that was up there before, somewhere in that range. But the current redesign is less than half of $5 million."

HOTWIRED: AN ADVERTISING SITE

SITE DEVELOPMENT

HotWired developed its site internally. CEO Andrew Anker recalls the early software problems: "We were, to some extent, one of the first commercial companies on the Web. We were actually out before Netscape. So there wasn't anything off the shelf that we could pull from, and there was very little out there. There wasn't a commercial browser, so we put on a large software development effort. We built a lot of the stuff in-house. We do a lot of stuff by hand or, now, by a process that we've developed in-house ourselves. And, even now, a year later, when there's stuff out there, most of the stuff that we're seeing isn't as good as what we're already using that we've developed ourselves."

SOFTWARE TOOLS

Senior Designer Jonathan Louie's department uses primarily Photoshop but also Illustrator, BBD Edit, Debabelizer, Director, and Shockwave. Louie reiterated CEO Anker's view that the site is moving closer to an interactive television medium. Says Louie: "Streaming audio and video. We're doing experiments now to find what the limitations are and, as those limitations become disbanded, we'll be using them more."

THE DESIGN GROUP

According to Louie, in the last three or four months, the design group has stayed the same. But about three months ago, the group increased by five designers, and Louie foresaw that, in the next three or four months, there might be another increase. What's driving the growth is the production of more content: "It's coming from great ideas happening here and great ideas that we want to put out."

THE READERSHIP AND PAGE DESIGN

Louie notes, "I'm surprised at how many of our readers are coming from home. I had assumed that many are visiting us from business, but we're finding that many of HotWired's readers are coming from home and they're coming on 28.8 modems and the sizes of their monitors are smaller than I had imagined. They have 14-inch rather than 15." This makes a difference, says Louie. When HotWired designs a page, they have to make sure that a reader can see it, that the whole page works well at a 14-inch monitor, so that the visitor doesn't need to scroll to catch a glance at what a home page is.

As HotWired develops more and more programs that have deeper and deeper content, it becomes more difficult to let people know what's going on inside its content area. Louie explains that HotWired wants to offer content that somebody is not just going to take a look at and turn around and leave and hit the back button but is going to go down deeper and further. Yet, if people are coming in at 14-inch monitors and there's a lot of content both broad and deep, it's very hard to fit all that in and have compelling content and snaz appeal, all in a 14-inch monitor.

According to the HotWired staff, 70% of visitors come in through Netscape; America Online is approximately 4% to 5% at most. This seems very odd to Louie because America Online holds a very large proportion of online users. Up to this point, America Online has not supported things like tables and frames, but now America Online supports Netscape browser use. Louie hopes that this will change, but they really haven't been concerned about America Online users because America Online hasn't been at the vanguard of Net design publishing. Now that America Online users are coming to HotWired or at the very least, have the capability of seeing them in a more advanced way, "Hopefully," Louie wishes, "they'll start to visit more and we'll start designing more for that audience."

THE DESIGN PHILOSOPHY

Louie explains that there is no black book, but there is a point of view. HotWired has always tried to pay attention to technology and to use technology to further the communication message but not to become reliant on it for visuals. HotWired wants to avoid looking like computer Star Wars. HotWired is a large group with a lot of ideas and a lot of discussions and a lot of heartfelt inner conflict, just trying to develop content, and they want that to come across in their pages. They want Hotwired to look like it's a site made by humans not by computers. And these are human thoughts and human feelings going on a computer screen. "So," Louie continues, "if there's any black book edict that HotWired has, even though we use computer technology, it will avoid computer technology, gizmos, hudads, all of those things."

PUBLIC RELATIONS SITES

IBM

Redesign, No Scroll. IBM has also gone through a process of re-designing its home page. Since the end of April 1995, right at the start of Internet World, IBM redesigned its home page. According to Webmaster Ed Costello, "It wasn't much of a drastic redesign. But, over a year ago, IBM had a very horizontal layout. There was a masthead on the top and stories, and then there was a list of navigational links at the bottom. The problem with that was that, as more stories were added, it pushed the navigational links off the bottom of most people's screens and, as sad as it is, through very unscientific testing, we found basically that no one scrolls or that, out of the number of people who use the Web, a large majority of them don't scroll."

According to Costello many people use PCs that have a more horizontal than vertical layout. For example, Costello uses an RISC system, which is more vertical. The first redesign IBM did was in August 1995, when they made their first use of tables. IBM moved all the navigation categories to the top of the page, which led to the concept of rotating stories. Thus, basically, every time visitors hit the home page, they could possibly get a completely different set of links. That design enabled IBM to have many different stories that could be linked directly off the home page without filling up the whole page with 10 or 15 or 20 links.

"Redesign," Costello says, "worked well through the past several months." But, in January 1996, IBM started to look at it and said it wanted to consider redesigning it again to keep it fresh and changing. So Costello's group looked at moving some of the information around and worked with another company to do some testing of its current layout and several proposed layouts to get an idea. The testing was very simple: It was just eye-tracking, tracking where people's eyes moved as they looked at the page, but it effectively validated the design that IBM already had because it showed that, in the previous design, this was a very compact design that worked very well.

Story Emphasis. The eye-tracking showed that people saw the graphic, which led them to see the stories, and then they would click on. It also showed that there were some dead spaces in the navigation areas. Costello's people took the feedback from the eye-tracking testing and used that to feed into redesign. They wanted to de-emphasize some of the navigation, not too much, but they wanted the lead story to have the main emphasis. Also, they had a new brand campaign called network computing that became very prominent on the home page.

They have not done any hard, statistical analysis yet, but just by looking at some raw numbers, it seems that traffic has increased. The goal now is to drive people into the stories and into the brand campaign material. Costello indicates that he has "… just a gut feeling that it has worked, not in terms of hundreds of thousands of people, but moderate growth … It looks like about a 5% increase. The way we measure growth on a week-to-week basis, IBM's traffic has grown between 5% and 10% anyway."

USAID

Web Site Design. According to Joe Fredericks, of the organization's Legislative and Public Affairs Department, USAID went through a number of prototypes before settling on one. They started with a simple image file and a series of links but then settled relatively early on a front-page image map. USAID is a very decentralized organization, with operations in over 100 countries. One of the things USAID has tried to do is maintain a design standard so that its Web site is identifiable, no matter where it is entered. Fredericks commented "It was very important that, no matter where you enter our Web site, either through the main page or coming in from underneath in one of the subdirectories, the design remain consistent."

PUBLIC RELATIONS AGENCIES

An analysis of several dozen public relations agency Web sites turns up some observations about how the agency side of the Internet public relations application is shaping its sites for strategic effectiveness. Almost half the 32 Web sites reviewed contain a graphics logo at the top of the page; four are centered on the top of the page; the remaining 13 logos are located at the top left of the page. Generally, the home pages that omit graphics logos use large, bold lettering. A few have a shaded background, or white lettering within a dark background. The background feature adds a more professional look to the logo. Two of the agencies using graphics logos have the descriptive words from the icons in the logo as categories to click on for information. These categories are located either in the text and underlined, or in a horizontal row and underlined.

Use of icons on the home page for click-on information was infrequent in the 32 sites analyzed; there were only 5. But icons were used repeatedly for contact information (usually a phone or envelope) and Web sites under construction (typically a road construction sign). One unique icon was a door with "Come on in..." printed below it. The one visual element that nearly all Web sites share is the use of vertical bold lines across the page separating the different sections of each Web site. A few Web sites contain dividing lines with a design, creating a pleasant effect. Also, a dividing line that is centered on the page but does not extend completely across it has a separating effect, yet it is more attractive. It also sets up a stream-like visual rhythm.

Half the Web sites contain a large, boldly lettered "Welcome," which creates a friendly environment. It is usually located directly below the logo in the opening text or, in the case of Edelman, within the graphics logo. The "Welcome" in the opening text is of normal letter size and thus, does not have the same impact as the larger greeting. Other viewer-friendly terms found on a small percentage of the Web sites sampled include "We hope you enjoy your visit"; "Please get in touch"; and "Thanks for visiting." There are also helpful suggestions, such as *Starting Points for Internet Exploration.*

Only two companies offered a choice of languages in which to read the Web site. Fleishman-Hillard offers English, Spanish, French, and German. Also, Fleishman-Hillard had the only Web site that offered cross-ethnic marketing in its "Capabilities Brochure." A second company, Zwart & Partners, based in the Netherlands, offers Dutch and English. In the English version, a picture of the office building is provided.

One company displays itself as being the "pick of the week" from an organization or company called "NCSA/GNN." This is directly below the graphics logo, at the center of the page, in bold lettering and underlined. Other Web sites include *awards* as a click-on feature, a few firms list annual billings, and others mention in the text their "Fortune 100" clientele.

Only two publications are quoted on a PR Web site, *The Wall Street Journal*, reporting a "235% return on investment for PR." This quote from a financial authority is used in the Web site as a benchmark of success that the PR firm aims for—and beyond. *The Vancouver Sun* is cited as saying that a local PR firm is "one of the city's most effective." Also, half the companies have click-on information for some of the following categories: client list, case studies, press releases, alliances, and experience. Some of these categories are worded in a friendlier manner, such as "See what our clients have to say."

A few click-on categories that attracted attention are: *What's New; Hot List; Technology News Tips; Events and Conferences;* and *Special: Working with the Media: A Primer for Entrepreneurs.* One other unique attraction is a company that consults with those who want to handle their own promotions; they offer a few consulting how-to lessons, with a list of consultation fees. Another unique concept was a company with a monthly interactive contest called "Quandary" for communications professionals and students. Fictional PR dilemmas are presented, for which the viewer can propose brief solutions interactively. One PR agency uses its home page to promote its own products, speaking engagements, and seminars; it uses small pictures of the actual books it is marketing. One of the most interesting Web sites is an up-to-date example of a communications company's project: *Virtually New Orleans: An A to Z Internet Guide to the City of New Orleans.*

Although every Web site gives its e-mail address or click-on access to it, only 15 sites provide a telephone, fax, and/or mailing address. A few of the larger firms list the cities where their offices are located. A few Web sites offer miscellaneous information, such as the last update of their home page; news of more information to be inputted shortly; and the number of people that visited the Web site "this week" or "this year."

Some of the most effective public relations Web sites were those that succinctly defined themselves within the first paragraph, thus allowing the visitor to know quickly if the company concentrates its PR within a specialized area or, at the very least, what the company has to offer. Some of these sites also use strong, motivating language that attracts the viewer. Some of the motivating phrases include: "Develop and implement effective marketing"; "Our mission"; "Unconditional commitment to excellence"; "Generating quantifiable results"; and "We help our clients harness the power of communication."

Many web sites offer in-depth background about the company, its owner, the partners, and the staff. Some sites provide pictures of the owners giving the site a more personalized appearance, thus, allowing the viewer to relate to the firm.

AN INTRANET SITE: SUN MICROSYSTEMS

INTRANET REDESIGN: DIRECTION FROM THE TOP

"I'm going through a redesign right now," says Webmaster Debra Winters. "What's motivating the redesign? The business is changing. Also the Intranet was originally a grassroots effort. It was done from a very bottom-level employee perspective. Now, however, my direction is coming from the Executive Management Group (EMG), which are all CEO Scott McNealy's direct reports. And they are now saying 'Okay, what is the message we want our employees to carry with them?' This is a push from above rather than a push from below.

"For example, at one time, we thought we needed an engineering button, and we thought that would be really hot. Well, ... guess what? The engineers weren't so excited about participating in our Intranet. They have their own Web servers and they could care less. So that button really gets no attention. It's time for it to go away. It's time for new buttons to be brought on."

Sun Microsystems' Intranet top page has never been redesigned. Similar to USAID's Internet home page, it's one big bit map. Says Winters: "It's not like I could just move a button off it because it doesn't belong there anymore. We actually needed an artist to come in and take care of this for us. So this is the first time that we've actually done that. Now, on the second-level pages, many of those have gone through a metamorphosis of sorts. There was a page called 'Functional.' Three years ago, that was supposed to serve different functions at Sun. It has evolved into a giant yellow pages. The button's name is going to change."

Appendix

INTERVIEWEE BACKGROUNDS

FEDEX

ROBERT G. HAMILTON, MANAGER, ELECTRONIC COMMERCE MARKETING GROUP

Robert Hamilton has been manager of Electronic Commerce Marketing for the last two years and is responsible for the establishment and marketing of all aspects of FEDEX's online interactive customer technology, including FEDEX's award-winning World Wide Web site on the Internet, America Online, CompuServe, and Microsoft network sites. Prior to this, Mr. Hamilton was Manager of Information Systems Marketing, responsible for such customer technology as FEDEX Ship desktop shipping software, PowerShip 3 shipping terminals for small business, PowerShip 2, and FEDEX Tracking software.

WINN R. STEVENSON, VICE PRESIDENT-NETWORK COMPUTING

Winn Stevenson is Vice President–Network Computing for FEDEX. He is responsible for the analysis, design, implementation, and administration of telecommunications, including voice, radio, video, and data communications systems and service to support the company's package business. Stevenson is also responsible for the development of the software systems, support for the company's PowerShip series of products, and development of, and support for, the FEDEX Internet and Intranet.

Stevenson joined the company in 1979 as Manager, Communications Software. He was promoted to director of telecommunications in 1982 and Vice President Telephone/Radio Systems in 1985. In 1987, he was named to his present position. Stevenson attended Memphis State University.

SUSAN GOLDENER, INTERNET TECHNOLOGY MANAGER

Goldener is the Manager of the Development Group responsible for the programming aspects of the Web site—CGI, some basic front-end page work, and actual installation of Web pages on the Web site. Goldener took her position in May, 1995, six months after the site was launched.

GENERAL ELECTRIC

D. RICHARD POCOCK, GENERAL MANAGER, MARKETING COMMUNICATIONS, GE PLASTICS

Mr. Pocock manages Advertising, Sales Promotion, Press Relations, and Customer Communications in North, Central, and South America. He has led numerous communications initiatives, including the launch of GE's presence on the World Wide Web in October 1994. His 22 years of experience at GE Plastics include roles in product management, marketing management, sales management, and venture development. Prior to joining GE in 1973, Mr. Pocock held several sales positions with Union Carbide's Chemicals and Plastics Division. He holds a B.S. degree in Mechanical Engineering from Rensselaer Polytechnic Institute and an M.B.A. from Case Western Reserve University.

RICHARD A. COSTELLO, MANAGER, CORPORATE MARKETING COMMUNICATIONS

Richard Costello joined GE in 1980. Since that time, he has taken a leadership role in the development and implementation of many key marketing programs, including the award-winning "We Bring Good Things to Life" advertising campaign, GE's two companywide customer service centers—the GE Answer Center and GE Business Information Center—and the introduction of the company's global identity program. Today, Mr. Costello has oversight of all the company's communications to customer and consumers. He is currently focused on development of an Internet marketing strategy for GE, the consolidation of communication suppliers and the professional development of GE's internal marketing communications talent. Born and educated in London, England, Mr. Costello started his career in the British advertising industry. He moved to the United States in 1973. Prior to joining GE, he was Vice President at McCann-Erickson, Inc., in New York. Mr. Costello lives in Norwalk, CT, with his wife Linda Olson and their two children, Anna (age 5) and Luke (age 2).

SUSAN MOYER, INTERNET PROGRAM MANAGER

Susan Moyer is responsible for the redesign and launch of GE's Web site in April 1996. The launch included focusing 72 diverse GE businesses and partners. The new site included 8,000 pages at launch. In addition to the current Internet marketing initiative, Susan leads diverse and global teams to implement other corporate initiatives, including Supplier Management.

Prior to being appointed to her current position in October 1995, she managed GE's Corporate White Pages Program and Corporate Accessibility programs. Also, as Communications Director for the GE Business Information Center, Susan was responsible for marketing GE's business-to-business customer center. Susan joined GE as part of GE's Advertising and Public Relations Training Program. Following assignments at Electrical Distribution and Control and GE's Advertising and Sales Promotion Operation, Susan joined A&SPO as an Account Supervisor. While there, Susan developed and implemented communications programs for Semiconductor,

Transportation, Drive Systems, and Power Systems, among others. Susan graduated from the University of Florida with a degree in Advertising and Marketing.

ALBERTO BLANCO, PRESIDENT AND FOUNDER, META4 DESIGN

Blanco has been at the forefront of multimedia and PC-based technologies for over 16 years. As early as 1980, he was writing media planning and budgeting software for ad agencies. In 1981, Blanco founded GS&B, a general-market advertising agency that specialized in financial and retail. Under his leadership, GS&B grew to a $20 million agency in just three years. Its success quickly caught the eye of managers at Lintas Advertising, which subsequently purchased the fast-growing agency. In January 1984, the very first Macintosh computer was unveiled. In it, Mr. Blanco immediately recognized a tool that would one day represent a medium by itself. In 1985, Blanco was at William Esty Advertising as agency Creative Director and an early champion of cutting-edge graphics and computer production technologies—long before it became the thing to do for ad agencies. He discovered innovative tools and endorsed their use: among them, the Scitex for retouching photos, the first Avid system in 1986 for editing commercials, and the early Silicon Graphics workstation for three-dimensional logo animations and special effects.

In 1987, Mr. Blanco left the Esty agency to start The Team Works, a company specializing in recruitment of high-level freelance creative talent for ad agencies. Computer technology was a key element of the Team Work's business plan. A proprietary database was developed to give recruitment personnel easy access to a candidate's profile via a local area network. In 1987, the company added a laser-based multimedia catalog to the service. Now a candidate's entire body of creative work could be seen, including digitized commercials, radio spots, and personal interviews. Since then, Blanco has been involved in the development and marketing of hundreds of multimedia products ranging from online application to CD-ROMs.

HOTWIRED

ANDREW ANKER, CEO, HOTWIRED

In Anker's own words: "I am President and CEO of Hotwired, the pre-miere Web site. Mostly, what I do all day is send and receive e-mail and go to meetings. Not that bad, actually. Before joining HotWired, I worked for the investment banking firm Sterling Payot Company for two years. I was involved with a number of companies at Sterling Payot, including Metricom, Pacific Telesis and, of course, *Wired*. Prior to Sterling Payot, I did a year at a start-up firm named AdExpress Company, where I was Director of Development. I was in charge of front-end software development and was responsible for an application named SAVIE, which helps to sell cable television research and ratings data, and was eventually sold to A.C. Nielsen. Before that, I spent five years working for big Wall Street investment banks—First Boston and PaineWebber. I went to school at Columbia University, where I got a B.A. in Economics. I'm married and have three future HotWired employees: Zach (age 5), Dagmar (age 3), and Astrid (age 1)."

RICK BOYCE, VICE-PRESIDENT, ADVERTISING DIRECTOR

Rick Boyce is Vice President, Advertising Director, for HotWired, the online companion to *Wired* magazine that launched on the World Wide Web in October of 1994. Prior to joining HotWired to lead marketing and sales, Rick spent ten years on the agency side. Most recently he was Vice President, Associate Media Director, at Hal Riney & Partners in San Francisco, assigned to a host of accounts including Saturn, First Interstate Bank, and Alamo Rent-A-Car. Rick also ran the Media Futures Unit at Riney and led the agency's exploration of new media.

JONATHAN LOUIE, SENIOR DESIGNER

Jonathan Louie has served as the Design Director for the HotWired network of online content sites since July 1995. Louie is responsible for the multimedia ideas and graphical user interfaces that take form as visual/editorial content. He maintains and develops the visual workings of the network for diverse projects ranging from interface design of search engines to defining relationships with commercial sponsors, as well as the editorial illustrations. Previously Louie was a partner for nine years in the design firm 2D3D in Los Angeles. Since the early 1980s, he has worked in digital media and has pioneered design and print efforts using digital tools. His background is in corporate identity, entertainment, and information and publication design. He holds a design degree from California Institute of the Arts: "I always feel you do what you do and your work speaks for itself."

IBM

JEFF CROSS, DIRECTOR, CORPORATE COMMUNICATIONS

Jeff Cross has been with IBM for seven years, first in sales promotion and, most recently, in public relations. He has worked at the AS/400 Division and at corporate headquarters. His responsibilities have included public relations for IBM's sponsorship of the Olympics, employee communications, and oversight of the corporate home page team (www.ibm.com). Before joining IBM, Cross worked for seven years in journalism, the last four as an editor for two trade magazines: *Convention World* and *Insurance Conference Planner*. Cross received a B.A. economics from Bucknell University in 1982, and an M.B.A. from Western Connecticut State University in 1992.

CAROL MOORE, DIRECTOR, CORPORATE INTERNET PROGRAMS

Carol Moore is responsible for the IBM home page and for editorial, technical, marketing, and design policy for the more than 75 IBM organizations with content on the World Wide Web. She has also acted as senior consultant for IBM's official sponsorship of the Olympic Games on the Web.

At IBM, she has been a media spokesperson, speechwriter, and employee communications strategist. She has also managed communications for IBM's financing subsidiary. Before joining IBM in 1986, she was director of communications for AMF, Inc., a freelance writer and television anchor in Tokyo (where she lived for four years), and a television and print journalist in New York and Washington.

ED COSTELLO, WEBMASTER, IBM

Twenty-eight-year-old Ed Costello (epc@gemini.ibm.com; Costello@netcom.com) received a B.A. in English from Allegheny College in 1989. His minor was in Computer Science. He also earned an M.A. in Professional Writing from Carnegie Mellon University in 1991 (with concentrations in online documentation and the rhetoric of electronic media). Costello has worked with IBM since 1990. From 1990 to 1993, he served as an Information Developer in IBM's Myers Corners Laboratory, Poughkeepsie, New York, where he worked on documentation for MVS, RACF, TSO, and an internal programming language. From 1993 to 1994, he served as an Information Developer/Programmer. Since 1995, he has been the Webmaster, IBM Corporation, and technical manager, IBM Corporation Internet programs, at Armonk, New York. In this position, he helped use the IBM home page during the Lotus acquisition and has designed and implemented code to generate the IBM home page dynamically according to browser, language, and time zone.

USAID

JOSEPH GUERON, DIVISION CHIEF, INFORMATION RESOURCE MANAGEMENT

With 29 years of expertise in information resource management, Joseph Gueron possesses considerable experience in rapid development applications, modeling/simulation, information systems planning and groupware applications. His most recent experience has been in the areas of information technology (IT) and transfer and data communications, including the establishment of Internet services. He manages the CIS Division within the Information Resources Management Office. This division consists of three branches, whose functions include: project support services, Internet data services, end user applications, information center, business analysts' group, and, most recently, a user help desk and a missions support group dedicated to serve the IM/IT needs of posts overseas. Gueron expanded the range of consulting services to USAID projects that have an IT/IM component. He established a team of bilingual analysts that provide consultancy to host-country institutions on IT and information management issues. In fiscal year 1993–1994, 270 projects were supported, with an IT/IM value of $115 million; Overall, his team conducted 1,150 technical assists and 112 short-term field consultancies.

Gueron also established a rapid applications development team (SWAT) capable of designing, developing, and implementing PC-based information solutions for end users in less than three weeks. Simultaneously, he spearheaded the introduction of groupware software as a productivity tool to develop solutions in which sharing and routing of information are critical.

Various Internet services—like Gopher, FTP, Listserv, and two Web services—have been created to post procurement actions, program information, and public affairs notices, among others. Most recently, a user help desk has been created from scratch to serve about 8,000 PC users worldwide, dispersed in about 75 overseas posts and five buildings in AID/Washington.

Gueron's previous experience includes positions as Director of Data Administration and Network analyst at GTE-Telnet and Senior Programmer Analyst at the Urban Institute. Mr. Gueron received a B.S. in Mathematics/Physics from Tusculum College (1964), an M.S. in Mathematics from East Tennessee State University (1969), and an M.A. in Communications from the University of Maryland (1976).

JOAN M. MATEJCECK, ACTING DIRECTOR, OFFICE OF INFORMATION RESOURCES MANAGEMENT

Ms. Matejceck is a career information technologist with 18 years' experience in the federal sector. Prior to joining USAID in 1994, she managed a review group for the General Service Administration, evaluating the performance of federal agencies in the management of their information and technology programs. She has significant experience in large technology modernization programs in the federal government, having spent several years working in the Tax System Modernization program at the Internal Revenue Service and in the Comprehensive Health Care Systems program at the Department of Defense.

JIM RUSSO, PROJECT MANAGER FOR THE INTERNET, DATA SERVICES GROUP

Jim Russo has had more than 10 years experience developing enterprisewide information systems through the full development life cycle. He has worked in Czechoslovakia, Manila, and Egypt. He has hands-on experience with systems analysis, Oracle database development, Internet-related services, and technical management. In 1977, a B.A. from Rutgers University, in Business and, in 1986, he earned an M.B.A. from the University of Maryland in Management of Information Systems. Since November 1993, he has been Project Manager-Internet Data Services Group, for the USAID. As Project Manager-Intranet Corporate Web Project, he is responsible for planning, analysis, design, and implementation of USAID's Intranet project. The agency Intranet ties together 44 overseas missions across 24 time zones utilizing TCP/IP. The backend/server software includes Oracle DBMS, Lotus Notes, and Basis Plus indexed text, all with WWW front ends. The front-end/client is Netscape. As Project Manager-Internet Services, Russo was responsible for planning, analysis, design, and implementation of USAID's initial participation on the Internet. The agency home page received Point's "Top 5% of the Web Award" in February 1996.

Russo established an agency Internet file management system that includes a gopher (gopher.info.usaid.gov), World Wide Web home page (www.info.usaid.gov), and FTP server on a Sun Sparc 20 with a T1 connection to Suranet. He has worked with USAID's regional bureaus, information bureaus, Legislative and Public Affairs Bureau, and the Office of Procurement to select over 4,000 documents for Internet public access. The gopher and home page contain development-related information as well as agency business-related information (CBDs/RFPs). The Internet server receives over 25,000 outside connections per month and the agency Internet site is becoming the Internet hub for development-related information on the Net. Russo is a member of the project design team and steering committee for the Leland Initiative (LI). The LI is a $15 million project to provide full Internet protocol services to 20 African countries. Russo developed the project implementation plan and wrote technical specifications. For USAID/Manila, he conducted a technical feasibility study and wrote specifications for putting the mission on the Internet. Manila is the first USAID mission to have full Internet access (www.usaid-ph.gov). He has written *Intranet: Architecting and Building a Corporate Web*; *Introduction to the Internet*; *Network Implementation*, and *Management Strategic Plan for the Remote Management of MS Windows Workstations*.

US WEST

MARGARET (PEGGY) TUMEY, VICE PRESIDENT, FINANCIAL OPERATIONS

Ms. Tumey began her career with Pacific Northwest Bell in 1966 as an operator. She assumed her current position in 1994. (Pacific Northwest Bell merged with Mountain Bell and Northwestern Bell in 1984 to become US WEST.)

Ms. Tumey has held numerous key positions with US WEST in areas including treasury, revenue operations, federal relations, and auditing. Just prior to being named to her present position, she was chosen to head a billing process team charged with overhauling US WEST's massive billing operations to make them more customer-oriented and cost-effective. In her current position, Ms. Tumey directs US WEST Communications' accounting operations, federal regulatory compliance, financial process improvement efforts, and the integration of all business and technology systems related to customer billing. A native of Seattle, Ms. Tumey holds a B.S. degree from City University, Seattle.

SHERMAN WOO, DIRECTOR, INFORMATION TECHNOLOGIES

Sherman Woo's group of approximately 20 people is called the Information Tools and Technologies Group. Woo was born in Seattle, Washington, in 1945. With undergraduate and graduate work in English literature and philosophy, Woo was a baby boomer who performed in street theater in the 1960s, visited Vietnam, started working for the telephone company, raised a family, and reentered the 1960s through the World Wide Web. Woo has worked with US

WEST Information Technologies for 23 years, beginning with large mainframe financial systems, then microcomputing, a research project involving CD-ROM development, client/server computing with 4GLs and, finally Web technologies in a Global Village project that he devised. Woo's other interests include studies of complexity and chaos, poetry, cooking, tennis, and travel.

SUZANNE MULLISON, WEBMASTER, GLOBAL VILLAGE INTRANET

Suzanne Mullison is one of five original founding Intranet team members and has responsibility for the day-to-day site maintenance of the internal Web site. In this position, she links in new pages, ages off sites that have served their time in "new" categories, and answers user questions. She is currently working on the redesign of the content layout and graphic presentation, which will give the home page an updated and easy-to-use look and feel. On the marketing front, Ms. Mullison gives informational presentations to groups of employers who have yet to connect to the company's Intranet. She has also authored a helpful administrative web tool for US WEST's Denver area employees called the *Mile High Virtual Secretary*.

Ms. Mullison has been 26 years with US WEST, holding a variety of positions during that time. The Global Village has been her first technical position. She is currently working toward her B.A. in Business, which she expects to complete in the spring of 1997.

XEROX

CINDY CASSELMAN, MANAGER OF INTERACTIVE EMPLOYEE COMMUNICATIONS

Cynthia Casselman joined Xerox after 18 years as an independent consultant/producer to Fortune 500 corporations. During those two decades, Cindy received numerous awards for her work in corporate communications. She has worked in every possible medium from multimedia events to live television broadcasts. Currently, Cindy is devoting most of her time to the development of the internal Web site as a knowledge base and a community for Xerox employees. With a degree in Sociology from the University of Massachusetts, Amherst, she finds the virtual online world a fascinating place to work and learn.

MALCOLM KIRBY, MANAGER OF APPLIED COLLABORATIVE TECHNOLOGY

Malcolm Kirby is Manager of Applied Collaborative Technologies in the Global Process and Information Management Division of Xerox Corporation. His work is focused primarily on developing strategic positioning through the linkages between human cognition, knowledge, social behavior, and information systems. Kirby joined Xerox in 1982 and has held a variety of technical, managerial and strategy positions in information systems, including manager of the Xerox global corporate Internet and principal distributed computing strategy. He received his B.A. in History and Music from Trinity College and his M.A. in Communications from Temple University; he continues postgraduate study in cognitive science and psycholinguistics. In his spare time, he plays music with his children, experiments in his gardens, and does *tai chi* daily.

RICK BEACH, GENERAL MANAGER ADVANCED TECHNOLOGY BUSINESS SERVICES

Rick Beach is General Manager, Advanced Technology Business Services, in the Xerox Business Services Division of Xerox Corporation. He leads a small team in Palo Alto, California, the XBS Concorde Team, to create new business services from emerging technologies by training XBS people to use those new services to satisfy customers' unmet requirements. He joined Xerox in 1982 as a summer intern at Xerox PARC doing research on electronic publishing. He became manager of the Electronic Documents Lab at PARC in 1988 and Manager, Document Services Architecture in 1992. For his work in creating collaborative coalitions between research, marketing, development, sales, and lead customers, he was honored with the Xerox President's Achievement Award in 1992. Beach received his Ph.D. in Computer Science from the University of Waterloo. He cofounded the Wiley Journal of Electronic Publishing (Origination, Dissemination & Design) in 1988. He was the editor-in-chief of ACM

SIGGRAPH from 1986 to 1991. His hobbies are driving his 1988 Alfa Romeo Milano Verde and attending sports events at Stanford University.

MICHAEL JOSEPH RYAN, INTERNAL AND EXTERNAL WEB SITE MANAGER

Michael Ryan is a member of the technical staff of Xerox Business Services. He graduated with a B.S. from the University of California at Berkeley in 1986. He joined Xerox in 1989 to work on office automation systems, database applications. He worked to get his division, XSoft, on the Web in 1994 and then went on to Internet products in 1995. Ryan is Webmaster for both Xerox's internal and external Web sites.

SUN MICROSYSTEMS

JUDY LINDBERG, INTERNET PROGRAM MANAGER

Judy Lindberg started at Sun Microsystems in 1985. She has managed several engineering departments and has led cross-functional teams to create solutions for system level issues. Judy led Sun's Internet Web efforts from January 1994, when the deadline for the first external Sun home page was April 1994, in time for a major product launch. On schedule, Sun Microsystems had its home pages on the Internet with complete product line information. Next, she led the Web team on the 1994 World Cup Soccer event. This was the first robust, real-time, updated sports event on the Internet. (Sun had also supported the Lillehammer, Norway, server for the February 1994 Winter Olympic Games updates.) Internally, the use of the Internet to publish, distribute information, and streamline productivity has grown exponentially.

DEBRA MARTINSON WINTERS, INTRANET WEBMASTER

Debra Martinson Winters joined Sun in 1993, assuming the Webmaster role in January 1995. Debra has 18 years industry experience with a vast background as a programmer/analyst designing and implementing large scale mainframe business applications, and

project management including field automation/nomadics programs. She now Webmasters and manages the Web team that builds
and runs the infrastructure of Sun's Intranet, the internal Web site,
home page service and special Web projects, including the recent
redesign of the internal site.

JERRY NEECE, ENTERPRISE TRAINING PROGRAMS MANAGER, SUNUNIVERSITY, SUN MICROSYSTEMS, INC.

Jerry Neece is responsible for the curriculum of Sun's Field New
Hire Sales Training and is currently reengineering both the format
and delivery of this training to take advantage of emerging Internet
and video server technologies. Prior to assuming his current training responsibilities, Jerry was responsible for SMCC's Internet marketing and product strategies. One of the early proponents of the
use of the World Wide Web at Sun, Jerry cofounded the highly successful home page, www.sun.com, and is recognized as one of the
leading experts on uses of the WWW in corporations and in education to reengineer information dissemination processes and reduce
costs.

Prior to joining Sun in 1993, Jerry spent five years with Amdahl
where he was a Product Manager within the Processor Division and
a Product Planner in the Communications (4745) Division. During
his 23-year career, he has spent time at AT&T, Pacific Telephone, Xerox, and Informix in a variety of education, sales, marketing, and
management positions.

Jerry received his B.A. in Psychology and Sociology at the University of California, Santa Barbara, in 1970, and, after serving as
U.S. Army officer during the Vietnam War, received his M.B.A.
summa cum laude from Pepperdine University in 1976. For the past
six years, Jerry has been on the graduate business school faculty at
Santa Clara University, where he teaches classes in Electronic Marketing and High Tech Product Planning and Strategy.

INDEX

artwork, 115
Artzt, Ed, 38
Association of Internet Professionals, 8
Atlanta Summer Info, FEDEX Web site, 49
ATM (asynchronous transfer mode)
  technology, 197
AT&T Web site
  development, 201
  funding, 206
  internal communications, 149
  management, 204
  outside resources, 207
  strategic objectives, 203
automotive advertisers, HotWired Web
  site, 94

B

Balaskas, John, 36
banner ads, 84, 86, 97–98, 101
Barry, Rick, 152
BBS (Bulletin Board System) passwords,
  26
Beach, Rick, 158, 159–160, 163, 164, 224,
  256–257
Bean Counter tool, 25, 124
Bear, Stearns & Company, 36–37
Beardsley, John, 116
Ben & Jerry's Web site, 39
Bernoff, John, 42
Berzinsky, Irwin, 185
beverage advertisements, HotWired Web
  site, 94
Blanco, Al, 24–25, 248
Bloomberg Financial Services, 109
Booz-Allen & Hamilton Inc., 147
Boss, Al, 210
Boyce, Rick, 97–98, 103–104, 249
BPA International, 26
The Breakdown of Hierarchy:
  Communication in the Evolving
  Workplace, 51
Bristol-Myers Squibb site, 38
"Build a Web Site That Will Draw
  Reporters," 113
Business and Procurement, USAID Web
  site, 137
Business Finder, GE Web site, 69–70
business-to-business marketing, 37,
  41–42, 262

C

cable TV
  advertising, 80
  compared to ads on the Net, 82
  growth, 109
  marketing, 14
  television shopping, 36–37
Cadence Design Systems, 149
Canada NewsWire Ltd., 114
Canadian Corporate News, 113
Canadian media, Internet use, 114
Cantor, Eddie, 9
case studies
  FEDEX Web site, 50, 212–215
  GE Web site, 215–216
  IBM Web site, 216–219
  Sun Microsystems Web site, 225–227
  US WEST Web site, 222–224
  USAID Web site, 219–221
  Xerox Web site, 224
Casselman, Cynthia, 155, 158, 160, 161,
  162–163, 164, 255–256
Center for New Media, Columbia
  University, 112
Chevron Inc., 147, 148
Chiat, Jay, 41
CHIAT/Day Idea Factory Web Site, 41
CIC Research, "Net Traveler Survey,"
  21–22
"clickstream," 26
c|Net, 78
Coca-Cola Web site, 39
Cocktail, HotWired Web site, 93
Coen, Robert J., 77
Cognitive Communications Inc., 146
Colgate-Palmolive, 38
Collings, Abigail, 216
Columbia University, Center for New
  Media, 112
Commerce Business Daily (CBD), 133
CommerceNet survey, 21
commercial Web sites, 83
communications
  See organizational communications
Community of Practice site, National
  Semiconductor, 149
CompuServe, 84, 115
Computer Intelligence InfoCorp., "Home
  PC Study," 20
Condé Nast Traveller, 81, 85–86

EUGENE MARLOW, PH.D.

E ugene Marlow, Ph.D. (emabb@cunyvm.cuny.edu), has been involved with the strategic application of print and electronic
media for over 30 years.

Since 1979, he has consulted to organizations in the media, technology, health care, consumer products, and nonprofit sectors. He
has produced over 500 video, radio, multi-image, videodisc and teleconferencing presentations and has received dozens of awards for
videoprogramming excellence from a variety of national and international organizations.

Dr. Marlow has had extensive experience working with marketing, advertising, public relations, and organizational communications executives (including dozens of top-level executives) over the
course of his professional life. He has also worked with numerous
celebrities and politicians in his role as an electronic media producer.

Between 1972 and 1982, Dr. Marlow held executive positions with
Citibank, Prudential Insurance, and Union Carbide Corporation. At
Citibank, he helped evolve the pioneering application of video tech-

nology for employee communications. At Prudential Insurance, he planned and developed an internal media communications unit.

As Manager/Corporate Video Communications with Union Carbide Corporation, he expanded and integrated the company's embryonic worldwide videocommunications network and designed and implemented a $2 million media production facility, working with such companies as Sony, RCA, and Imero Fiorentino Associates. During his tenure, his department garnered an unprecedented 40 awards for videoprogramming excellence, including Department of the Year honors from the Information Film Producers Association.

Dr. Marlow is also a frequent guest speaker and seminar leader at organizational and professional conferences. In the last year he has given talks on electronic media for the international law firm of Morrison & Foerster, Baruch College, New York University, the International Quality and Productivity Center, Cowles Media, advertising agencies McCann-Erickson and Dentsu, and The National League of Cities.

His sixth book, *Electronic Public Relations*, was released by Wadsworth Publishing in January 1996. Of this book, John Beardsley, 1995 President of the Public Relations Society of America, said: "Dr. Marlow provides the best road map and guidebook I've seen for practitioners who know they have to travel in what has become a bewildering landscape."

He has also coauthored *The Breakdown of Hierarchy: Communication in the Evolving Workplace* for Butterworth-Heinemann (due March 1997). This book is an expansion of "The Electrovisual Manager," an article authored by Dr. Marlow and originally published in 1994 in Business Horizons (Indiana University Graduate School of Business), which surveys and analyzes the collective impact of electrovisual technologies—videotape, satellites, and computer networks—on organizational middle managers and the structure of American corporations.

He is the author of *Winners! Producing Effective Electronic Media* (Wadsworth, 1994), *Corporate Television Programming: Applications and Techniques* (Knowledge Industry Publications, 1992), *Shifting Time & Space: The Story of Videotape* (coauthor) (Praeger, 1991),

Managing Corporate Media (2nd Ed., Knowledge Industry Publications, 1989), and *Communications and the Corporation* (United Business Publications, 1978).

He has published more than 80 articles on television programming and video technologies in the United States and Europe.

Prior to his involvement in the electronic media field, Dr. Marlow was an award-winning Vietnam War historian and news editor for a mass merchandising trade journal.

Dr. Marlow teaches graduate and undergraduate courses in electronic journalism and business communications at Bernard M. Baruch College (City University of New York). He has also taught graduate courses in corporate communications at Fordham University (Lincoln Center campus).

Dr. Marlow earned a B.A. in English from Hunter College (City University of New York), an M.B.A. from Golden Gate College, and a Ph.D. in media studies from New York University.

He is a member of the New York New Media Association, the International Interactive Communications Society, and the International Association of Jazz Educators.